THE CLOSED CIRCLE

Columbia Studies in Terrorism and Irregular Warfare

COLUMBIA STUDIES IN TERRORISM AND IRREGULAR WARFARE
Bruce Hoffman, Series Editor

This series seeks to fill a conspicuous gap in the burgeoning literature on terrorism, guerrilla warfare, and insurgency. The series adheres to the highest standards of scholarship and discourse and publishes books that elucidate the strategy, operations, means, motivations, and effects posed by terrorist, guerrilla, and insurgent organizations and movements. It thereby provides a solid and increasingly expanding foundation of knowledge on these subjects for students, established scholars, and informed reading audiences alike.

For a complete list of titles, see page 277.

The Closed Circle

JOINING AND LEAVING THE MUSLIM BROTHERHOOD IN THE WEST

Lorenzo Vidino

Columbia University Press
New York

Columbia University Press
Publishers Since 1893
New York   Chichester, West Sussex
cup.columbia.edu

Library of Congress Cataloging-in-Publication Data
Names: Vidino, Lorenzo, author.
Title: The closed circle : joining and leaving the Muslim Brotherhood
in the West / Lorenzo Vidino.
Description: New York : Columbia University Press, [2020] | Includes bibliographical
references and index.
Identifiers: LCCN 2019034878 (print) | LCCN 2019034879 (ebook) | ISBN 9780231193665
(cloth) | ISBN 9780231193672 (paperback) | ISBN 9780231550444 (ebook)
Subjects: LCSH: Ikhwān al-Muslimūn—Western countries. | Ikhwān al-Muslimūn—
Membership. | Muslims—Western countries—Interviews. | Islamic fundamentalism—
Western countries. | Islam and politics—Western countries.
Classification: LCC BP10.I385 V53 2020 (print) | LCC BP10.I385 (ebook) |
DDC 297.6/5—dc23
LC record available at https://lccn.loc.gov/2019034878
LC ebook record available at https://lccn.loc.gov/2019034879

Columbia University Press books are printed on permanent and durable acid-free paper.
Printed in the United States of America

Cover image: View over Paris at Dawn, France © Mark Thomas/Design Pics/Bridgeman Images
Cover design: Chang Jae Lee

Contents

[v]

Preface and Acknowledgments

I first became interested in the Muslim Brotherhood in 2001, shortly after the tragic events of September 11. The ensuing investigation revealed various links between the attacks and a well-known mosque in my hometown of Milan, Italy. It was the same mosque that, in the early 1990s, had been the hub for hundreds of militants from all over the world who had gone to Bosnia to fight in the bloody conflict that had engulfed the Balkan country—tellingly the head of the Arab foreign fighters engaged in the conflict, Anwar Shabaan, was also the imam of the mosque in Milan.

What surprised me by digging into the Milan mosque was that it was financed not by a bunch of stereotypical gun-toting fanatics with bushy beards the media portrays Islamist terrorists to be—or at least did back then. Rather, behind it were a few high-profile Middle Eastern businessmen who also presided over a web of companies in various continents, controlled a bank incorporated in the fiscal paradise of the Bahamas, and had spent decades rubbing elbows with the elites of both the East and the West. They were Yussuf Nada, Ahmed Nasreddin, and Ghaleb Himmat, remarkably astute members of the Muslim Brotherhood in their countries of origin who had settled in the West in the previous decades to escape persecution and had played a crucial role in establishing the network of the Brotherhood in Europe and North America.

The U.S. government and the international community, which had long known about the mosque in Milan, acted swiftly—perhaps, actually, too swiftly. In October 2001 Nada, Nasreddin, and Himmat were designated as terrorist supporters and their ample assets frozen. The designations led to criminal investigations in various countries, which ultimately led to the acquittal of the men. As one prosecutor involved in the investigation once told me, "to perhaps have a chance at proving what this network was about, we should have locked in one room for at least a year a team of top prosecutors and investigators from the dozen or so countries—many of them offshore paradises—where the men had interests and forced everybody to share information in ways that are rare in international investigations. Maybe that way we would have solved the puzzle."

The Milan case introduced me and, to some degree, many authorities throughout the West to the challenges related to the Muslim Brotherhood. Global jihadism, with its multiple ramifications in the West, was a relatively new and unexplored phenomenon back then. Yet despite its complexities and secrets, it was—and still is—fairly linear. Jihadists have, broadly speaking, a Manichean worldview and engage in violence to defeat those whom they openly declare to be their enemies. While back then many were surprised—and to a degree, some still are today—that jihadist ideology attracted young men who often were well educated and lived comfortable lives in the West, its message and tactics were relatively easy to understand and analyze.

But the Brotherhood, that's different. Every aspect of it is complex, never black or white, never prone to simplistic explanations—starting with its ambiguous relationship to terrorism, which first drew me to it. The Milan cluster and those connected to it, for example, provided a glimpse into the sophistication and transnationality of the Brotherhood—banks in the Bahamas, shell companies in Liechtenstein, a poultry factory and a software company in the United States, real estate investments in Africa and the Middle East, high-profile contacts all over the world. While investigators certainly found this complexity frustrating, from a researcher's point of view it was fascinating.

Another aspect gripped me with even greater intensity. While the Brotherhood was founded in Egypt and its original ideology focused on reshaping the Muslim-majority societies of the Middle East, it was clear that it had long established a presence in the West. It soon also became evident that it had created organizations that, while not calling themselves "Muslim Brotherhood" and actually refuting charges of being linked to the movement, were closely linked to the movement and played a crucial role in the dynamics of Western Muslim communities. They controlled a large number of mosques and had become the de facto representatives (some would say gatekeepers) of said communities in the eyes of Western establishments. What were the implications of these developments that, albeit with some differences, had taken place in most Western countries?

Driven by these interests and concerns, I have spent the past nineteen years studying the Muslim Brotherhood in the West. In 2010 I published a book on it, which largely overlapped with my doctoral dissertation on the topic. In it I tried to describe how the Brotherhood arrived in the West (and to dispel the more conspiratorial theories about this passage), how it evolved, how it operates, and what its aims are. I also attempted to explain Western policy-making patterns toward the Western Brothers, highlighting how conflicting interests and overlapping factors have led all Western countries to struggle in finding consistency—not just among them but within each of them—in assessing and interacting with the movement.

The topic of the Brotherhood in the West gets strong attention from policy makers and the media at times yet has been severely overlooked by scholars (with some notable exceptions). As a senior British official explained to me, in an honest yet unflattering way, when I asked why the British government in 2014 had chosen to retain me to contribute to its official review on the Muslim Brotherhood, "if we want an expert on the Brotherhood in Egypt, there are at least forty; Brotherhood in Jordan, a dozen; Syria, a dozen; Brotherhood in the West: it's basically just you." It's a puzzling dynamic that I wish changed for the sake of a more informed debate on an important topic.

Over the years I repeatedly stumbled on individuals who had left Muslim Brotherhood networks in various countries. A few of them I met personally; others had written about their experiences in books or blogs. Their insider's perspective struck me as a unique way to deepen my knowledge of a proverbially secretive organization. I was also fascinated by the psychological processes that had led them to join and, even more, leave the Brotherhood.

I therefore decided to write a new book on the Brotherhood in the West that built on and expanded the accounts of the dozen or so former members of the movement who openly discussed their experience. It covers some of the same topics of the previous one (how the Brotherhood was established in the West, how it operates, what its aims are), but with substantial additional information coming from the knowledge of the individuals profiled and an additional decade of research. It also includes a chapter describing how the Muslim Brotherhood in the West acted during and after the Arab Spring and assessing the impact of the tumultuous geopolitical events of the past decade on Western Brotherhood milieus.

Obviously, this book would not have been possible without the help of the former members of the Brotherhood who generously decided to tell me their stories. For this reason, it is to them that my first acknowledgment goes. I am aware of how difficult it is to share very personal and, in many cases, painful memories with a stranger. I also appreciate them taking, in some cases, entire days to talk to me in person and then replying to my many follow-up questions. I know it is impossible to capture the endless complexities of their lives, actions, and thought processes, but I hope I have done justice to these individuals by telling their stories as accurately as possible.

I would also like to acknowledge the many people who have contributed in different ways to this book. In writing it I counted on a stellar team of coworkers who help me run the Program on Extremism at George Washington University. First and foremost is Seamus Hughes, who is not just a great friend but also a phenomenal partner, masterfully manning the fort at the program during my long absences. Alexander Meleagrou-Hitchens, Audrey Alexander, Bennett Clifford, and Mokhtar Awad have also helped in countless ways. Special thanks go to Roland Martial and Silvia Carenzi for their help researching the Brotherhood in France and Sweden, respectively.

Many scholars, researchers, journalists, investigators, and government officials in several countries have helped me in these years. To respect their privacy I do not want to list them, and I would surely forget some; they know who they are, and I take this opportunity to thank them all. I would be remiss if I did not personally acknowledge Bruce Hoffman, editor of the Columbia University Press series Columbia Studies in Terrorism and Irregular Warfare and a longtime mentor and friend, for his support of this project.

Finally, I would like to dedicate this book to Clarissa and Neal. Without their love, support, and encouragement (and companionship during the many travels related to it), this book would not have been possible.

Abbreviations

AKP	Adalet ve Kalkınma Partisi
AMC	American Muslim Council
AGESMI	Associazione Giovani e Studenti Musulmani in Italia (Association of Muslim Young and Students in Italy)
BIF	Benevolence International Foundation
CFCM	Conseil Français du Culte Musulman (French Council of the Muslim Faith)
CVE	countering violent extremism
ECFR	European Council for Fatwa and Research
EFOMW	European Forum of Muslim Women
EMF	Étudiants Musulmans de France (Muslim Students of France)
FEMYSO	Forum of European Muslim Youth and Student Organizations
FIOE	Federation of Islamic Organizations in Europe
FJP	Freedom and Justice Party
GCC	Gulf Cooperation Council
ICNA	Islamic Circle of North America
IESH	European Institute for Human Sciences
IFiS	Islamiska Förbundet i Sverige (Islamic Federation in Sweden)
IGD	Islamische Gemeinschaft Deutschland (Islamic Community of Germany)

IIFSO	International Islamic Federation of Student Organizations
IIIT	International Institute of Islamic Thought
IRPA	Islamisches Religion pädagogisches Akademie
IRW	Islamic Relief Worldwide
ISNA	Islamic Society of North America
IUMS	International Union for Muslim Scholars
JMF	Jeunes Musulmans de France (Young Muslims of France)
LFFM	Ligue Française de la Femme Musulmane (French League of the Muslim Woman)
MAB	Muslim Association of Britain
MAS	Muslim American Society
MAYA	Muslim Arab Youth Association
MCB	Muslim Council of Britain
MRR	Mouvement de la reforme et du renouveau (Movement for Reform and Renewal)
MSA	Muslim Student Association
MTI	Mouvement de la tendance islamique (Movement of the Islamic Trend)
MUR	Movement for Unicity and Reform
MWH	Muslim Welfare House
MWL	Muslim World League
MJD	Muslimische Jugend in Deutschland 9Muslim Youth in Germany)
NAIT	North American Islamic Trust
OIC	Organization of Islamic Cooperation
QC	Qatar Charity
SAP	Sveriges socialdemokratiska arbetareparti (Social Democrat Party)
SMR	Sveriges muslimska råd (Muslim Council of Sweden)
UCOII	Unione delle Comunità Islamiche d'Italia (Union of Islamic Communities of Italy)
UOIF	Union des Organisations Islamiques de France (Union of Islamic Organizations in France)
WAMY	World Assembly of Muslim Youth
WMS	World Media Service

THE CLOSED CIRCLE

CHAPTER I

What Is the Muslim Brotherhood in the West?

Let me explain to you one important fact about the Muslim Brotherhood. That's what I usually tell the media people in Egypt especially, and the people who claim to be ex-members, I tell them: you cannot understand, properly, the Muslim Brotherhood, and fully, unless you graduated and [got] promoted from 0 to 100, unless you become a member of Makhtab al Irshad [Guidance Office], global Makhtab al Irshad, and global Shura [Council], you cannot understand. Neither the CIA, nor the Pentagon, nor the [Department of] Homeland Security, nor any other group, the KGB, they will never [understand it], because it's a long story, Lorenzo. Long, long story. And the more you talk, the more you discover things.

—KAMAL HELBAWY, JUNE 2017

The Muslim Brotherhood is the oldest and the world's most influential Islamist movement. Since its foundation in 1928, it has played a crucial role in political, religious, and social developments in the Arab world and has deeply influenced Muslim communities beyond it, including in the West. The Brotherhood's view of Islam as a complete and all-embracing system, governing all aspects of private and public life, has shaped generations of Islamists worldwide, from those who seek to implement their vision through peaceful means to those who make acts of brutal violence their primary modus operandi.

Despite this enormous influence, few aspects of the organization are uncontested. Views of its inner workings, ideology, and aims differ widely among scholars, policy makers, and the general public, in the Muslim world as well as in the West. The group's proverbial secrecy is one of the main reasons for this confusion. As the Brotherhood was founded and operates mostly in countries where local regimes have enacted various forms of repression against it, the movement has understandably always seen confidentiality and dissimulation of many aspects of its structure and goals as a necessary tactic to survive. In substance, a clear-cut assessment of the Brotherhood is, as Kamal Helbawy puts it in the epigraph above, a fool's errand for anybody who does not belong to the intimate inner circle that has served in the Brotherhood's top leadership positions at the global level.[1] Moreover, a universal assessment of what the Brotherhood is and wants is further complicated by the fact that, to some degree, the organization's ideology and tactics have changed over time and vary from country to country.

Even the very name of the organization can be interpreted in various ways. Arguably the term is most commonly used to refer to the organization founded by Hassan al Banna in 1928 in Egypt. Al Banna conceived a complex organizational structure, a web of strict rules and internal bodies aimed at making the Brotherhood a modern and efficient machine capable of Islamizing Egyptian society and establishing an Islamic regime in the country. The Egyptian Muslim Brotherhood has gone through many phases since then, including several crackdowns on the part of various Egyptian regimes and, in the aftermath of the overthrow of President Hosni Mubarak in 2011, a brief moment at the helm of the Egyptian state. Still today, despite its deep crisis, the term "Muslim Brotherhood" is frequently used in reference to its Egyptian branch, the mother group from which all others originate.

But since the 1940s the Brotherhood's message has spread to virtually all Arab and many Muslim-majority countries. In each country, individuals embracing the group's worldview have established networks that mirror its structure and have adapted its tactics to local dynamics and political conditions. In Middle Eastern countries where it has traditionally been tolerated, like Jordan, it has outwardly operated as a social movement, devoted to education and charitable activities, and as a political party. In those where it has been persecuted, like Syria, it has remained an underground movement devoted to *dawa* (proselytizing) and, in some cases, to violence. It is common to refer to these networks in each country as Muslim Brotherhood "branches," even though the term should not imply overemphasis of the authority of the Egyptian mother group over them.

The term Muslim Brotherhood is often used with a third meaning, encompassing the totality of the national branches of the organization and all the entities worldwide that adhere to al Banna's ideology and methodology. All these actors work according to a common vision but with operational independence, free to pursue their goals as they deem appropriate. Like any movement that spans continents and has millions of members and sympathizers, what is often referred to as the global Muslim Brotherhood is hardly a monolithic block. Personal and ideological divisions are common. Senior scholars and activists often vie with one another over theological issues, political positions, access to financial resources, and leadership of the movement. Despite these inevitable differences, their deep belief in the inherent political nature of Islam and their adoption of al Banna's organization-focused methodology make them part of the informal transnational movement of the Muslim Brotherhood.

In a 2008 interview Mohamed Habib, then first deputy chairman of the Egyptian Muslim Brotherhood, confirmed this assessment of the organizations that locate themselves in the Brotherhood's galaxy: "There are entities that exist in many countries all over the world. These entities have the same ideology, principle and objectives but they work in different circumstances and different contexts. So, it is reasonable to have decentralisation in action so that every entity works according to its circumstances and according to the problems it is facing and in their framework."[2]

Despite this complete operational independence, the individuals and entities that belong to the so-called global Muslim Brotherhood perceive themselves as part of a larger family. Their ties go beyond a common origin and a shared ideological foundation and are shaped by a deep, global web of organizational, personal, and financial connections. Past attempts to formally coordinate and supervise them through a formal structure, the International Organization of the Muslim Brotherhood, led by the Egyptian branch, gained little traction.[3] But the term Muslim Brotherhood could be used to identify an informal, yet tight-knit, global network of individuals and entities that share not just an ideology but regular operational connections as well.

Finally, Muslim Brotherhood could also be used to identify a type of Islamist activism. "Ikhwanism" (from the Arabic word for brothers, *ikhwan*) is a commonly used term for a methodology of social-religious-political mobilization that, transcending formal and informal affiliations, is inspired by the Muslim Brotherhood. The adoption of its mindset by nonaffiliated groups has been seen positively by the "formal" Brotherhood, from its origins until today. Al Banna himself advocated for creating a global movement rather than a formally structured organization, as he saw the Brotherhood "as an idea and a creed, a system and a syllabus, which is why we are not bounded by a place or a group of people."[4] In 2005 Mohammed Akef, then *murshid* (supreme guide and leader) of the Egyptian branch of the Muslim Brotherhood, explained in an interview that "a person who is in the global arena and believes in the Muslim Brotherhood's path is considered part of us and we are part of him."[5] Other senior Brotherhood members have described the movement as a "common way of thinking" and "an international school of thought."[6]

The Muslim Brotherhood in the West

If the evolution of each national branch of the Muslim Brotherhood in the Middle East took particular turns based on each country's political culture and developments, the Brotherhood's history is particularly peculiar in the West, where it has had the unique characteristic of operating in non-Muslim-majority societies. The first active presence of Brothers in the West can be dated to the late 1950s and the early 1960s, when small, scattered groups of militants left various Middle Eastern countries to settle in cities throughout Europe and North America. A handful of these pioneers, like Said Ramadan and Yussuf Nada, were prominent members of the Egyptian Brotherhood fleeing the crackdown implemented by the regime of Gamal Abdel Nasser. In the following decades, Brotherhood members from other Middle Eastern countries similarly found refuge in the West from the repression of local regimes.

Yet the majority of Brotherhood-linked activists relocating to the West were students, members of the educated and urban middle classes of the Middle East who had already joined or had flirted with the idea of joining the Brotherhood in their home countries. Settling in the West to further their studies in local universities, these students continued their involvement in Islamic activities in their new environments. The combination of experienced militants and enthusiastic students bore immediate fruits, as Brotherhood activists formed some of the West's first Muslim organizations. Most Western cities at the time lacked Muslim places of worship, and the Brothers' mosques, generally little more than garages or small meeting rooms on university campuses, often were the first religious facilities for Western Muslims. The West's freedoms allowed the Brothers to openly conduct the activities for which they had often been persecuted in their home countries. With few funds but plenty of enthusiasm, they published magazines, organized lectures, and carried out all sorts of activities through which they could spread their ideology.

The arrival of the first Brothers in Europe and North America was hardly the first phase of a concerted and sinister plot of the Muslim Brotherhood to Islamize the West, as it is sometimes portrayed.[7] They initially represented a small, dispersed contingent of militants whose move reflected not a centralized plan but rather personal decisions that fortuitously brought some Brotherhood figures to spend years or the rest of their lives in the

West. Yet the small organizations they formed soon developed beyond their most optimistic expectations. The Brothers' student groupings evolved into organizations seeking to fulfill the religious needs of the West's rapidly growing Muslim populations, and their mosques—often structured as multipurpose community centers—attracted large numbers of worshippers. Following al Banna's complex organizational model, they established youth and women's branches, schools, and think tanks. The ample funds they received from wealthy public and private donors in the Arab Gulf allowed the Brothers to operate well beyond what their small numbers would have otherwise provided for.

By the late 1970s the Brothers' isolated clusters throughout the West increasingly began to interact with one another, thereby establishing formal and informal networks that spanned Europe and North America and reinforcing their position on both continents. Yet because most of the pioneers' hearts were still in their native countries, they viewed their sojourn in the West as only a temporary exile in a convenient sanctuary before returning home to continue their struggle. Nevertheless, some Brotherhood activists slowly started to perceive their situation differently. Redefining some centuries-old religious qualifications, they increasingly stated that the traditional distinction between *dar al Islam* (land of Islam) and *dar al harb* (land of war) did not reflect the current reality.[8] While the West could not be considered *dar al Islam*, because sharia was not enforced there, it could not be considered *dar al harb* either, because Muslims were allowed to practice Islam freely and were not persecuted. Brotherhood scholars like Faysal Mawlawi and Yusuf al Qaradawi decided, therefore, that it was possible for them to create a new legal category. They concluded that the West should be considered *dar al dawa* (land of preaching), a territory where Muslims live as a minority, are respected, and have the affirmative duty to spread their religion peacefully.[9]

The implications of this decision go far beyond the realm of theology. By redefining the nature of the Muslim presence in the West, the Brothers also changed their own role within it. While still supporting in words and deeds their counterparts' efforts to establish Islamic states in the Muslim world, they increasingly focused their attention on their new reality in the West. Having redrawn the West as *dar al dawa*, they intensified their efforts at spreading their interpretation of Islam throughout it. They established an ever-growing constellation of overlapping organizations devoted to tasks ranging from education to financial investments, political lobbying, and charity, thereby catering to the West's growing Muslim populations.

Moreover, in many countries the Western Brothers have positioned themselves at the forefront of the competition to be the main interlocutors of local establishments. Although circumstances vary from country to country, when Western governments or media attempt to reach out to the Muslim community, it is quite likely that many, if not all, of the organizations or individuals that are engaged belong, albeit with varying degrees of intensity, to the network of the Western Brothers. It is not uncommon to find exceptions to this situation, and things have changed in various countries over the past few years, but overall it is apparent that no other Islamic movement has the visibility, political influence, and access to Western elites that the Western Brothers have obtained over the past decades. In light of these facts, it is fair to portray the competition for the representation of Western Muslims as the relative victory of a well-organized minority over other, less organized minorities for the voice of a silent majority.

Three Categories of the Brotherhood in the West

One of the most challenging aspects related to the Muslim Brotherhood in the West is identifying which organizations and individuals can be linked to the movement. Governments and commentators have endlessly debated whether the organizations founded by the Brotherhood's pioneers and their offshoots—established decades ago and increasingly guided by a second generation of mostly Western-born leaders—can be described as Muslim Brotherhood entities. Complicating things, most Western-based, Brotherhood-linked activists, aware of the negative stigma that any possible link to the Muslim Brotherhood can create, have traditionally gone to great lengths to downplay or hide such ties.

Terminology can indeed be deceiving and, as in the Middle East, the term Muslim Brotherhood in the West can mean different things. While other categorizations are certainly possible, it can be argued that the term Muslim Brotherhood refers to three separate yet highly connected realities, which, in decreasing degrees of intensity, are the pure Brotherhood, Brotherhood spawns, and organizations influenced by the Brotherhood.

Pure Brotherhood are the nonpublic/secret networks established in the West by members of Middle Eastern branches of the Brotherhood. In all

Western countries the first generation of pioneers arriving from the Arab world set up structures that mirrored, albeit on a much smaller scale, those of the countries of origin. Establishing, de facto, a small Brotherhood branch in every Western country, they re-created the organization's traditional system of selective recruitment, formal induction, fee-paying membership, and the pyramidal structure that goes from the *usra*, the nuclear unit of a handful of activists that meet weekly at the local level, to an elected leadership supervising the activities in the country. The Western Brothers keep this structure strictly secret and vehemently deny it (or, in some cases, describe it as just a thing of the past) when critics bring it up. It still represents the cornerstone of the Brotherhood in the West.

Brotherhood spawns, on the other hand, are visible/public organizations established by individuals who belong to the "pure Brotherhood." As previously mentioned, over time Western Brothers established a wide web of entities devoted to a broad array of activities. None of these organizations publicly identifies as having links (if not, at times, in purely historical or ideological terms) with any structure of the Muslim Brotherhood. But, in reality, these organizations represent the other side of the coin to the pure Brothers—the public face of the secretive network, and the part that advances the group's agenda in society without giving away the secret structure.

Given the lack of formal affiliation and the conscious effort by the Western Brothers to downplay or deny their links to the Muslim Brotherhood, identifying an organization as a spawn is a challenge. Nevertheless, there are a number of indicators that, while not conclusive, help to assess whether a certain organization is a Brotherhood spawn. These include the history of the organization; its founders and main activists' links to the Brotherhood; its consistent adoption of Brotherhood texts and literature; substantial financial ties with other Brotherhood structures and funders; and formal or informal participation in transnational Brotherhood initiatives and organizations.

Finally, organizations influenced by the Brotherhood are those that, while adopting an ideology that is clearly influenced by that of the organization, have no clear operational ties to it. Traces of Brotherhood presence might be present, for example, in the composition of the board, the organization's sources of funding, or some ideological influences. But at the same time, organizations belonging to this third tier of the Western Brotherhood might have diverse memberships (including non-Islamists and even non-Muslims), might engage in progressive reinterpretations of classic Islamist thought, and might try to emancipate themselves from Brotherhood tutelage.

Inevitably, this tripartite classification cannot encapsulate all the degrees of complexity that surround organizations linked to the Brotherhood. As Brigitte Maréchal puts it, "What makes the Brotherhood so complex is that it consists of various types of superimposed structures, some of them evolving out of the local European situation, while others trace their history back to the organisation's country of origin."[10] The movement's secrecy makes most efforts aimed at understanding its and its spinoffs' inner workings challenging. By the same token, fluidity is another element that needs to be taken into consideration, as it is not uncommon for organizations and individuals to increase or decrease their levels of personal, structural, and ideological connectivity with the Brotherhood and therefore shift position in the tripartition.

Despite these important limitations, this classification aims to provide some nuance and order to a debate that often becomes polarized along two "extreme" and simplistic positions: the "there is no Muslim Brotherhood in the West save some isolated activist" approach and the "all organizations with some Brotherhood trace are part of the Muslim Brotherhood" line of thinking. The rest of the book aims to provide a more substantial amount of information to clarify these murky dynamics.

The Brotherhood's Ideology in the West

Since reinterpreting their role in the West in the late 1970s and early 1980s, Western Brotherhood networks have understood the need to adapt their rich intellectual heritage to their new environment. Over the past thirty years the Western Brothers have tried to find ways to contextualize the teachings of their ideological forefathers to their reality as a movement operating freely in non-Muslim societies. It soon became obvious to a movement as pragmatic as the Brotherhood that blindly applying to modern Europe and North America what al Banna had prescribed in Egypt in the 1930s made little sense. The ideas of al Banna and of other leading Islamist thinkers who came after him still provide invaluable guidance on several aspects of their faith and activism, starting with the immutable idea of Islam as a comprehensive way of life and an all-encompassing methodology.[11] Nevertheless, the ideas can be discussed, reinterpreted, adapted, challenged, and even dismissed as times, places, and circumstances change. The Brotherhood, in the West as elsewhere, is not a stagnant movement but rather makes flexibility and continuous evolution two of its core characteristics and strengths. Moreover, Western Brotherhood leaders often disagree with one another on how the movement should try to achieve its goals and, in some cases, even on what those goals should actually be.

Despite these complexities, it is possible to identify some goals that are common to all "members" of the Western Brotherhood. Foremost among them is the fostering of a strong, resilient, and assertive Islamic identity among Western Muslims. As individuals belonging to any religiously conservative movement, Islamists worldwide are concerned with maintaining the morality and piousness of their communities. Such defensive posture becomes even more important to Muslim minorities, as they incur the risk of being culturally absorbed by the host society. This point, along with other key principles of the Western Brotherhood's activism, has been cogently expressed by Yusuf al Qaradawi, the undisputed spiritual leader of the global and Western Brotherhood, in his landmark book *Priorities of the Islamic Movement in the Coming Phase* (1990). "It is the duty of the Islamic Movement," wrote Qaradawi, "not to leave these expatriates to be swept by the whirlpool of the materialistic trend that prevails in the West."[12]

Yet, unlike Salafism and most other Islamist trends that seek to strengthen the Islamic identity of Western Muslims, the Brothers do not advocate isolation from mainstream society. On the contrary, they urge Muslims to actively participate in it, but only insofar as such engagement is necessary to benefit the Islamist movement and change society in an Islamic fashion. According to Qaradawi, Muslims in the West should adopt "a conservatism without isolation, and an openness without melting."[13] Finding the balance between cultural impermeability and active sociopolitical interaction is not easy, and their borders are constantly redefined. But the Brothers see themselves as capable of defining how Muslims can be both loyal to their faith and active citizens of Western secular democracies.

The Brothers see this guiding role as an unprecedented opportunity for the movement, which, in the words of Qaradawi, can "play the role of the missing leadership of the Muslim nation with all its trends and groups."[14] While in Muslim-majority countries the Brotherhood can traditionally operate only in limited spaces, as it is kept in check by regimes that oppose it, Qaradawi realizes that no such obstacle prevents it from operating in the free and democratic West. Moreover, Western Muslims, whom Qaradawi describes as disoriented by the impact of life in non-Muslim societies and often lacking the most basic knowledge about Islam, represent an ideally receptive audience for the movement's message. Finally, no competing Islamic trend has the financial means and organization to compete with the Western Brothers. The combination of these factors leads Qaradawi to conclude that the West is a sort of Islamic tabula rasa, a virgin territory where the socioreligious structures and limits of the Muslim world do not exist and where the Brothers can implement their dawa freely, overcoming their competition with superior mobilization skills and funds.

A second goal common to all Western Brotherhood organizations is the designation as official or de facto representatives of the Muslim community of their country. Becoming the preferred—if not the exclusive—partners of Western governments and elites serves various purposes. Despite their unrelenting activism and ample resources, the Brothers have not been able to create a mass movement and attract the allegiance of large numbers of Western Muslims. While concepts, issues, and frames introduced by the Brothers have reached many of them, most Western Muslims either actively resist the Brothers' influence or simply ignore it. The Brothers understand that a preferential relationship with Western elites could provide them with the financial and political capital that would allow them to significantly expand their reach and influence inside the community.

By leveraging such a relationship, in fact, the Brothers aim to be entrusted by Western governments with administering all aspects of Muslim life in each country. They would ideally become those whom governments task with preparing the curricula and selecting the teachers for Islamic education in public schools, appointing imams in public institutions such as the military, the police, or prisons, and receiving subsidies to administer various social services. This position would also allow them to be the de facto official Muslim voice in public debates and in the media, overshadowing competing forces. The powers and legitimacy bestowed on them by Western governments would allow them to exert significantly increased influence over the Muslim community. Making a clever political calculation, the Western Brothers attempt to turn their leadership bid into a self-fulfilling prophecy, seeking to be recognized as representatives of the Muslim community in order to actually become it.

Finally, the position of representatives of Western Muslims would allow the Brothers to achieve their third main goal: influencing Western policy making on all Islamic-related issues, whether domestic or foreign policy related. As for the former, they aim to be the interlocutors that Western policy makers listen to when deciding issues that range from religion education in schools to counterterrorism, potential bans on face veils, and integration. Influencing foreign policy is equally, if not more, important to the Western Brothers. Once again, Qaradawi's writings perfectly encapsulate this vision. Understanding the crucial role that the policies of Western governments play in the struggle between Islamist movements and their rivals for the control of Muslim countries, he declares that "it is necessary for Islam in this age to have a presence in such societies that affect world politics" and that the presence of a strong and organized Islamist movement in the West is "required for defending the causes of the Muslim Nation and the Muslim Land against the antagonism and misinformation of anti-Islamic forces and trends."[15]

In other words, Qaradawi argues that the Western Brothers find themselves with the unprecedented opportunity to influence Western public opinion and policy makers on all geopolitical issues related to the Muslim world. And indeed, over the past thirty years the European Brothers have consistently tried to take advantage of their position of influence to advance Islamist causes. From private meetings with senior policy makers to mass street protests, editorials in major newspapers, and high-profile conferences, they have used all the material and intellectual resources they possess to advance the Islamist point of view on several issues, from Palestine to Afghanistan, and on the nature of the Islamist movement itself.

Assessing the Brotherhood in the West

Assessments of the Western Brothers closely resemble those of the global Islamist movement, with opinions split between optimists and pessimists. More specifically, optimists argue that the Western Brothers are no longer preoccupied with creating Islamic states in the Muslim world but rather are focused on social and political issues concerning Muslims in the West.[16] Their main goals are simply to defend the interests of Western Muslims and to diffuse Islamic values among them. The Western Brothers are a socially conservative force that, unlike other movements with which they are often mistakenly grouped, encourages the integration of Western Muslim communities and offers a model in which Muslims can live their faith fully and maintain a strong Islamic identity while becoming actively engaged citizens.[17] Moreover, the optimists argue, the Western Brothers provide young Muslims with positive affirmation, urging them to transfer their energy and frustration into the political process rather than into violence or extremism. Governments should harness the Western Brothers' grassroots activities and cooperate with them on common issues, such as unemployment, crime, drugs, and radicalization.

Pessimists see a much more sinister nature of the Western Brotherhood. Thanks to their resources and the naiveté of most Westerners, they argue, the Western Brothers are engaged in a slow but steady social engineering program, aimed at Islamizing Western Muslim populations and, ultimately, at competing with Western governments for their allegiance. The pessimists accuse the Brothers of being modern-day Trojan horses, engaged in a sort of stealth subversion designed to weaken Western society from within, patiently laying the foundations for its replacement with an Islamic order.[18] The fact that the Western Brothers do not use violence but participate with enthusiasm in the democratic process is seen simply as a cold calculation on their part. Realizing they are still a relatively weak force, the Brothers have opted for a different tactic: befriending the establishment.

According to pessimists, officials of Brotherhood-linked organizations have understood that infiltrating the system, rather than attacking it head-on, is the best way to obtain what they want; after all, in the West, at least for now, the harsh confrontations mounted by jihadist groups lead nowhere. By becoming the privileged partners of the Western establishment, they are taking advantage of the Western elites' desperate desire to establish a dialogue with any representatives of the Muslim community and put themselves forward as the voices of Western Muslims, subsequently using the power and legitimacy that comes from such interactions to strengthen their position inside the community. Pessimists also point to a constant discrepancy in the Western Brothers' discourse: moderate and expressing their adherence to democracy externally, radical and spewing hatred toward the West internally.

Opinions on the Brotherhood swing dramatically not just within the academic community but also within virtually every Western government. In substance, no Western country has adopted a cohesive assessment followed by all branches of its government. There is no centrally issued white paper or set of internal guidelines sent to all government officials detailing how Western Brotherhood organizations should be identified, assessed, and eventually engaged. This leads to huge inconsistencies in policies, not only from one country to another but also within each country, where positions diverge from ministry to ministry, and even from office to office of the same body.

Despite the difficulties experienced by all Western countries in doing so, determining what the Western Brothers' nature and aims are is hugely important, as it has significant implications on several policy levels. Domestically, it plays out on many domains related to religion, integration, and immigration. In education, should Western governments partner with Brotherhood organizations, which often control a larger and better organized cadre of teachers than other Muslim organizations, to teach Islam in public schools? Should they be allowed to run private schools? Should they be the partners of Western governments in training and selecting chaplains for the prison system, the military, the police, and other similar bodies? Should they receive public funding to conduct outreach, education, and integration activities with the Muslim communities and the recent large numbers of refugees who have arrived from Muslim-majority countries? Should they be made partners in a domestic counterterrorism and counterradicalization strategy?

The implications are plentiful also on the foreign policy side. In recent years several important Arab countries (Egypt, Saudi Arabia, United Arab Emirates) have designated the Muslim Brotherhood as a terrorist organization. In the case of the UAE, the government has also placed several Western Brotherhood organizations on its terrorism list. Should the West follow suit, as some lawmakers in the United States have suggested? And how should the West behave toward countries like Qatar and Turkey that fund the Western Brotherhood?

These issues are deeply intertwined, making them even more complicated. It is apparent that the first step in determining cogent policies is to understand how the Muslim Brotherhood, both in the East and in the West, operates, what it believes, and what it wants. In the hope of contributing to the debate, this book, using a novel approach, seeks to shed some light on the inner workings and the worldview of Western Brotherhood milieus through the unique perspective of a handful of its former members.

CHAPTER II

Joining and Leaving the Brotherhood

One should not suffer this pain throughout his life. It turns into a memory and becomes a learning experience. There isn't any bitterness [in me]. I've said before I was proud I belonged to the Brotherhood and proud I left it. Both benefited me greatly.

—THARWAT EL KHERBAWY, FORMER MEMBER
OF THE EGYPTIAN BRANCH OF THE MUSLIM BROTHERHOOD, 2012

Joining the Brotherhood

Joining the Brotherhood, whether in the East or in the West, is an extremely complex process. Even though the organization seeks to propagate its vision to the masses, those who wish to become a full-fledged member must undergo two extremely intensive and lengthy procedures: selection and cultivation.[1] Both stages enable the group to screen for only the best recruits, individuals with specific characteristics who possess the qualities and the determination to pass years of tests and scrutiny by the organization's leadership. It is this very process that makes those who pass feel they belong to an elite movement, a secretive band of brothers working in unison to achieve a divine mission.

The journey starts, in most cases, without the knowledge of the future member. Indeed, the Brotherhood takes the initiative when it comes to admitting new members, proactively looking for the unique individuals deemed to possess the right characteristics to become a Brother. One does not seek out and apply to the Brotherhood. As Khalil al Anani puts it, "Individuals do not join the Brotherhood but are chosen by it."[2]

The selection process, like most aspects of the organization's operation, has been meticulously studied and regulated, with committees established to oversee it. The Brotherhood divides the process into three stages. The first is the dissemination of the call (*nashr al dawa*). All Brotherhood members are required to act as models of kindness and piousness in order to inspire imitation in all Muslims. But that behavior also serves the purpose of attracting individuals who might possess the right characteristics for themselves to become Brothers.

Brothers working on recruitment then move to the next level, general connectivity (*arrabt al-'am*). A study group at a university, a unit working for a Brotherhood-leaning charity, volunteers at a mosque—these all constitute the perfect target groups for general connectivity: small, selected group of individuals that can be introduced to Islamist ideology and closely observed by an experienced Brother. In universities, the Brotherhood member Amr Magdi says, "Certain members of the Muslim Brotherhood are supposed to meet and befriend new students and engage them in very normal, nonpolitical activities—football, tutoring—stuff that appeals to everyone."[3] Carrie Wickham perfectly described this process in the setting of urban Cairo. "A group of my committed friends and I will think of getting two or three other guys from our neighborhoods more involved," a Brotherhood militant whom she interviewed told her. "So we invite them to play soccer, but of course it's not only soccer; we also talk to them about right and wrong. They see that we play fair, that we don't cheat, that we set a good example, and gradually, gently, over time, we try to show them the right path."[4] Environments frequented by the Brotherhood are particularly fertile hunting grounds, but recruiters are always on the prowl for individuals who seem to possess the traits of a potential Brother, constantly vetting neighbors, relatives, colleagues, and people they meet in social contacts.

Regular interactions enable the trained eye of the Brotherhood recruiter to find individuals with the right characteristics: piousness and a strong sense of Muslim identity are paramount. "This is what makes us different from political parties," explains Khaled Hamza, a former editor of the Brotherhood's English-language website. "We are an ideological grassroots group, and we use our faith to pick members."[5] But religiosity is not enough, and a prospective Brotherhood member needs to be diligent, enterprising, honest, and sharp. Being well-educated and knowledgeable about religion or politics are not viewed as especially desirable. To the contrary, the organization often looks for very young recruits, in some cases preadolescents, whose worldview can be more easily influenced. "It is better to come with an empty glass," observes one Brotherhood member interviewed by Egyptian scholar Hazem Kandil. "You learn faster."

Things are different for those who come from "Brotherhood families." Young men—or, more often, boys—whose fathers are Brotherhood members are more or less expected to join the group, and their parents guide the process of their entry into it. Individuals who have a close relative in the Brotherhood also have, de facto, a preferential pathway into the group, whether by being introduced by the relative or by deliberately making themselves attractive candidates.

Once a potential recruit is identified, the Brotherhood recruiter zeroes in on him, in the phase known as the individual call (*al dawa al fardiya*). The recruiter tries to glean as much information as possible about the recruit's views, attitudes, and private life. He also strengthens his relationship with the younger man, often becoming a trusted mentor. And he starts a gradual introduction of the Brotherhood's ideology by recommending books written by some of the group's scholars, always gauging how receptive the target is.

After extensive screening that lasts, on average, about three years, the target deemed Brotherhood material is invited to join the group.[6] In most cases, it is also at that time that the recruiter first reveals his role as a Brotherhood recruiter—something that is generally kept secret until it is necessary to reveal it. The recruit who accepts the offer is invited to Brotherhood gatherings and to meet other Brothers—all activities that serve the purpose not just of further introducing him to the group but also of further scrutinizing him.

Upon accepting the offer, the new recruit has to take exams; if he passes them, he is asked to swear the oath of allegiance (*baya*) to the general guide (*murshid al'am*), the group's supreme leader. This complex and lengthy selection process has two goals: it ensures sure that the Brotherhood properly picks its new members and it makes infiltration by government agents more difficult. What comes next serves the same purposes, as selection to entry-level membership is just the beginning of the long and intricate process that ends with full membership.

The Brotherhood has a very complex structure, with fixed levels of membership through which every new member must pass. These have changed over time, and there are now five: *muhib* (sympathizer), *mu'ayyid* (supporter), *muntasib* (associate), *muntazim* (regular or registered), and *'amil* (active member).[7] As he progresses from one level to the next—perhaps taking a few years to complete each—the new recruit is introduced to increasingly intimate and complex aspects of the Brotherhood's ideology and inner workings. More demanding tasks are also required of him, and tests, of both his knowledge and his commitment, are frequent. Each step up is conditioned on a positive evaluation from the complex web of individuals and committees that, in typical Brotherhood style, oversee and meticulously record the process. After at least five years as a *muntazim* and a positive evaluation, the aspiring member undergoes special religious and psychological tests; upon passing them, he finally becomes an *'amil*, a full Brotherhood member. Only then can he participate in all the group's activities, including voting and running in its internal elections. Members, starting at the level of *muntasib*, also pay a membership fee, known as *ishtiraq*, which is calculated based on the member's salary.

This grueling incubation process, aside from weeding out infiltrators and elements unfit to become Brothers, enables an "exceptionally discreet group" like the Brotherhood to open itself to new members, and to do so only incrementally.[8] Moreover, it aims at gradually introducing recruits to the other Brothers and deeper into the group's message. To do so, the Brotherhood relies heavily on the process of *tarbiya* (education, sometimes referred to as cultivation or even indoctrination), which al Banna termed the "rope that binds Brothers together." One of the defining internal features of the Brotherhood, tarbiya is the process through which the group shapes its new recruits, teaching them not just ideology and interpretation of Islam but also how to behave at home, at work, and in their interpersonal relations.[9] The tarbiya curriculum, an extensive list of readings selected by the group's tarbiya committee, covers all aspects of the Brotherhood's ideology, and as the members slowly make their way to full membership, they dive deeper into it.

If the tarbiya outlines the theory, practice makes it perfect. New Brotherhood members are inserted in the lower level of the group's multilayered hierarchy, thereby integrating their studies with constant socialization with experienced members. All Brotherhood members, irrespective of their level of seniority, are part of an usra, the group's nuclear unit.[10] The usra is generally composed of four to five Brothers (although some are slightly larger) who live in the same area. It meets at least once a week to carry out tarbiya (an obligation that applies not to new members alone) and to discuss all matters, from personal to religious, political to organizational. Tellingly called "family" (the literal meaning of usra in Arabic), this is the group's core unit, the one with which each Brother interacts most frequently. A Brother tends to form his closest bonds with members of his usra (even though, to avoid cliquishness, usra members are regularly reshuffled). He prays with them, eats with them, and often has business or familial relations with them.

Every usra is headed by a naqib (captain), an experienced Brother who oversees all aspects of its functioning. Even though meetings take place in an intimate and informal setting (often at his house), the naqib sets the agenda for the meetings and maintains detailed records on them and on the usra members' behavior, particularly that of the junior and still-to-be-vetted members. At the end of the meeting the naqib assigns tasks and gives instructions to each member.

The Brotherhood employs the "intensive process of socialization" that stems from learning the tarbiya and participating in the usra to increase identification of all members—not just new ones—with the group and, consequently, the group's internal cohesiveness.[11] "You read Brotherhood literature, written by Brothers on Brothers. You pray in Brotherhood mosques, built and run by Brothers," explains a member to Kandil. "You marry a Sister nurtured in a family according to Brotherhood guidelines. Even on recreational trips, you meet Brothers, ride buses owned by Brothers, to stay at a place administered by Brothers."[12] A Brother's relation to another Brother is different, more complete and trusting, than the one he has with a non-Brother, including family members. Being a Brother is a way of life and encompasses every single activity. His life is a web of usra meetings, committee work, collective prayer, political activism, business ties, friendship ties, family ties—all alongside other Brothers. This tight-knit community is further bound by the sense of divine mission that its members believe they have, creating almost a parallel society characterized by immense cohesion. "The Brother lives, gets educated, makes friends, gets married, finds a job, gets politically engaged in a fully Muslim Brotherhood-based environment," writes Hossam Tammam. "The group's attempt to build its own society made it emerge as if it were a religious sect."[13]

Leaving the Brotherhood

Various elements tightly bind a Brother to the group. The rigorous vetting and long cultivation he undergoes to join the group give him a sense of pride in belonging to an elite. Once he is a member, most of his personal ties and activities are connected to the Brotherhood, so that his entire life revolves around the group. Moreover, the Brotherhood strongly emphasizes the concept of obedience to the group's leadership. Internal dissent is at the least frowned on, and a Brother is taught from his initiation that criticism of the group and its leaders is harmful to the group.

In parallel, the Brotherhood's ideology stresses the importance of internal harmony and collective action. Constantly under attack from external forces, the group can carry out its divine mandate only if it remains cohesive. Working for the Brotherhood is equated to working for Islam, meaning that defending the Brotherhood is defending Islam. Going against the group, undermining it even by merely questioning its leaders, is framed by Brotherhood leadership as an unacceptable religious doubt. The Brotherhood has to be a close-knit body in order to be successful, and its members have to be blindly devoted to the organization if they want Islam to succeed. "Without the movement, there can be no return to Islamic rule," Kandil notes, also highlighting that "in time, however, means and ends become conflated."[14]

One might imagine that leaving a group that puts so much importance on cohesiveness and internal unity is no ordinary decision. Resigning from it means abandoning the divine mission of establishing Islam. It means betraying the trust placed on the member by an organization that perceives itself as fulfilling a divine mandate—an organization that had invested in him and accepted him. It also means turning one's life upside down. A member "lives and breathes" the Brotherhood only as long as he is inside it. Once out, he also is removed from all the personal and social activities that are so integral to it. By the time the process of full induction (which can take from five to eight years) is completed, "the Muslim Brother's social life revolves almost entirely around the organization, and leaving the organization would thus entail excommunication from his closest friends."[15] In the harsh warning issued by Ahmed al Bialy, a senior Brother who served as governor of the Gharbiya governorate during the regime of Mohammed Morsi, to those thinking of leaving the group, "Whoever deserts the group will find nothing but estrangement. His own soul will denounce him, and his family and friends will no longer recognize him."[16]

While scholars, as we have seen, have long examined the process of joining and the inner workings of the Brotherhood, few have investigated departure from the group. Given this absence, many analytical tools, providing a valuable theoretical framework, can be borrowed from the extensive body of literature on disengagement more generally. Obviously, each movement or organization, like every personal story, has unique features. Nonetheless, a number of patterns in the process of disengagement are common to all organizations that require a high degree of involvement by their members. Over the past few years, for example, several studies have attempted to analyze how individuals abandon jihadist groups.[17] Scholars worldwide have also long studied various aspects of how individuals disengage from cults, new religious movements, evangelical churches, criminal gangs, and a wide range of other movements to which followers are intensely committed. The academic approaches toward these phenomena draw on various disciplines, including political science, anthropology, and social psychology.[18]

Most of the literature describes disengagement as a process, characterized by the complex and highly individualized interplay of push and pull factors.[19] While the former are "adverse organizational characteristics that [lead] someone to reconsider their continued involvement in the group," the latter are "features outside of the group the individual finds attractive."[20] Scholars often use rational choice theories to analyze the process, postulating that whether individuals decide to disengage will depend on their rational and thorough examination of the costs and benefits of participation versus the costs and benefits of disengaging.[21] Some studies have even attempted to capture the process in almost mathematical terms, unduly reducing the complexity of the human mind in a cold formula.[22]

Scholars also tend to agree that the process of disengagement is not linear and that each person's trajectory is different. In some cases, disengagement can take place overnight; in others, at the end of a long development. In some cases, a trigger event can kick-start the process, while in others such a trigger might accelerate a process that was already under way. Disengagement can also vary significantly depending on how structured, militant, and secretive the organization being left is. The position inside the organization of the one leaving also affects the process, as dynamics for a high-ranking member and for a mere hanger-on are likely to differ. Moreover, disengagement can occur as a quiet separation, as a public and dramatic rupture, or in some fashion in between.

Just as disengagement follows no single course, so too reasons for leaving vary from case to case. Scholars of movements to which followers are intensely committed find that their motivations for leaving tend to fall into two macro categories: disenchantment with the group itself or with its ideology.[23] Not uncommonly, an individual has motives from both categories, and, as is usually the case, the distinctions between them are not as clear-cut in life as in an academic treatise. Personal reasons unrelated to any dissatisfaction with the group or its ideology may also play a role.

Disenchantment with the Group's Leadership and Inner Workings

Seemingly mundane reasons relating to how the group is managed are often among the most common sources of frustration that can ultimately lead to disengagement from movements to which followers are intensely committed. The most frequent among them are concerns about transparency (often related to management of funds), loss of faith in the leadership's ability and effectiveness, manipulative and hypocritical practices, and lack of internal democracy and meritocracy.

While all these issues at times feature in accounts of disenchanted former Brothers, the last of them appears to be particularly common. Over the past twenty years members of the Egyptian branch of the Brotherhood have engaged in heated debate over internal democracy and transparency. Activists have challenged leadership for undertaking internal elections in secret, with results that puzzled many. Similarly, even the group's bylaws were long inaccessible to members (internal pressure forced the leadership to publish them in 2010).[24] The defense for not having transparency is that secrecy is necessary to avoid surveillance and infiltration by the regime, but some have argued that it is instead a way for leaders to retain control and manipulate the group's direction. Whatever the truth of the matter, several Brothers have left the group because they perceive that it lacks internal democracy.

In addition, some Brothers bemoan a culture of blind obedience that eschews any sort of independent thinking and disagreement with the leadership. "You don't have a say in the Brotherhood," complains Mohammed Abbas, a young Brother who led protests against Hosni Mubarak in Tahrir Square and left the organization soon afterward. "It's not a democracy."[25] Tharwat El Kherbawy, a former member who has since written extensively about the group in very critical terms, has harsher words: "Anyone who thinks cannot be a part of the Brotherhood because it is a military group; it has a military way of thinking. You do not have to think, for it is done for you. You only have to implement. The Brotherhood only grants high ranks to those who can implement; executive personalities who implement but do not think. Has the Brotherhood got any famous writers, poets, scientists? It is proof enough that they are unable to produce any because they do not allow creative thinking."[26]

Once again, the Brotherhood's leadership justifies this strong emphasis on internal discipline by pointing to the need to maintain cohesiveness in the face of ruthless regimes.[27] But some, particularly young members, are left feeling undervalued and become extremely frustrated with the group. This response was particularly strong in Egypt in the post–Mubarak days, when many felt that the new political environment no longer required and justified constant secrecy, undemocratic internal practices, and the stifling of internal dissent.

The democratic deficit appears to play out largely along a generational divide. Younger members accuse the leadership, often age fifty and above, of running the organization without accepting any input from the cadres. The younger generations also accuse elders of being an out-of-touch clique whose tactics are ineffective. Further exacerbating the frustration of many younger Brothers is that the levers of internal power appear to be firmly held by a small number of extended "Brotherhood families."

Marriage within the Brotherhood is a common practice encouraged by the group. Young Brothers seeking to marry are asked to choose members of the Sisterhood or daughters or sisters of other Brothers. It is a custom that strengthens the group's cohesiveness and naturally creates one of the core units envisioned in al Banna's program of gradual Islamization—the Islamic family. Over time, though, the powerful Brothers whose families intermarry, together with the sons of those marriages, have created what some disgruntled members refer to as "Brotherhood cartels."[28] Critics within the organization argue that this consolidation of influence has "transformed the organization into a patrimonial and clientelistic machine," rife with nepotism.[29]

Another common source of grievance among the Brotherhood's members is the choice of tactics adopted by the leadership. Over the past twenty years, all organizations belonging to the Brotherhood family throughout the world have experienced tensions between those members who believe that the group should be deeply involved in politics and those who maintain that such political participation is a deviation and a distraction from the organization's traditional aim of grassroots Islamization through dawa. The dynamics of this internal debate vary from country to country, also depending on what the local political environment allows them to do. But in all countries where the Brotherhood operates, a "traditionalist" wing more devoted to al Banna's education-based approach and somewhat wary of delving into political processes opposes a wing that sees political participation as the most effective way to advance the group's agenda.

This debate has been particularly heated in Egypt, in the years both before and after the fall of the Mubarak regime. Various Egyptian Brotherhood members, of all ranks, had major clashes with the organization's leadership, accusing it of relinquishing dawa to engage in politics. Though defections caused by such accusations also took place from the 1990s onward, they increased after the fall of the Mubarak regime, as after the revolution the Brotherhood's leadership decided to fully engage in Egypt's political process and various senior leaders, including members of the group's governing bodies, decided to leave the organization. While the main reason cited was the perceived deviation from al Banna's teachings, they often named the organization's internal secretiveness as an additional motivating factor.

Abul Ila Al Madi, a former member of the Brotherhood who left it in 1996 to start the Wasat Party, lays out these dynamics clearly: "The Brotherhood has two trends, one of which is reformist and open-minded (similar to us) and another that is more rigid and unfortunately represents the controlling majority. We distinguish between missionary (da'wa) and political activities, because mixing the two is extremely dangerous, threatening both the nation and religious groups themselves. We are calling for the separation of the two missions—which is what makes us a civil party—while the Muslim Brotherhood combines the two." Bemoaning the lack of transparency, Al Madi adds that within the Brotherhood "there are members known to the public who have no decision-making powers, and others not known to the public who do, another symptom of the mingling of political and religious missions."[30]

A similar criticism comes from Ibrahim al Zafarani, a member of the group for forty-five years who also served on the Shura Council; he resigned in 2011 "for several reasons, the most important being the lack of separation between advocacy work and politics." "In its origins," he adds, "the MB [Muslim Brotherhood] is an advocacy grouping that strengthens values in individuals then leaves them to face their lives, whether in public work or in joining a political party. Excess involvement in politics was at the expense of advocacy work within the group and allowed the Salafi advocacy to control the religious scene in the mosques."[31] The next chapter will further outline these tensions.

Disenchantment with the Group's Ideology

Disenchantment with the group's ideology is one of the most common reasons for disengagement by members of all sorts of movements that require intense commitment. It also motivates the departure of Brotherhood members, although there are no hard data giving even a vague sense of the percentage of former Brothers who have left because of disillusionment with the organization's credo. Such ideological disillusionment can take two very different forms: disillusionment with the kind of Islamism adopted by the Brotherhood or, more broadly, disillusionment with Islamism itself.

The first occurs when individuals who were part of the Brotherhood's infrastructure at some point find the vision and the approach adopted by the group unsatisfactory and are moved to join a competing Islamist movement or organization. The Brotherhood is just one of the many entities within the Islamist galaxy. It has its own vision of the perfect Islamic society and a very specific approach to achieving that goal. Though it wields an important influence over all Islamist movements, anyone interested in being engaged in Islamist activism has many choices. Most Brotherhood members, having undergone a selection and cultivation process that no other Islamist organization requires, tend to be loyal to the group, but some do become dissatisfied and switch their allegiance to other forms of Islamism.

Of those who embrace other forms of Islamism, many apparently are driven by frustration with the group's patient and gradualist approach. With some variations from country to country, the Brotherhood pursues a relentless project of slowly Islamizing society. But what tangible results can it show for its efforts? The Brotherhood's leadership, seeking to divert attention from this discrepancy between expectations and outcomes, frames success in different terms, as something achieved in generations, not years. But it is not uncommon for Brotherhood activists, whether or not their criticism will lead them to leave the organization, to doubt the group's effectiveness and question whether its approach based on grassroots activism, education, and participation in politics can yield concrete results.

The first years of the Arab Spring, when Brotherhood movements came to rule in Egypt and Tunisia and gained broader influence throughout the Arab world, obviously fueled great enthusiasm within the movement, a demonstration that decades of patient work and suffering did eventually bear fruit. Yet the dramatic turns of events that, in the following months, dethroned the Brotherhood in both countries and led to widespread resentment against it throughout the region have caused many Brotherhood activists to have reservations about the group's methods. Their fall from power, whether blamed on the loss of popular support or, in the case of Egypt, on the machinations of the military, the "deep state," and other actors, was a major blow to even the most confident of Brothers.

This frustration might lead those members who decide to leave it in various, even in some cases opposing, directions. One of them is represented by more orthodox and less compromising Islamist forces. In particular, over the past few years, the Brotherhood has suffered significantly from the competition of various strains of the Salafist movement. Some Brotherhood members, particularly among the younger generations, have been attracted by the more direct approach of the Salafists and left one movement for the other.

Some frustrated Brothers embrace the most radical of the many Salafist subcurrents, jihadism. Scholars and policy makers have endlessly debated the relationship between the Brotherhood and jihadism. Positions vary significantly: On one end of the spectrum it is argued that the two ideological currents have little to nothing in common and that the Brothers actually act as a firewall, "preventing otherwise susceptible Muslims from descending down the path of radicalization."[32] Others argue the exact opposite, postulating that the Brothers and jihadis are simply two sides of the same coin, fellow travelers guided by the same worldview who simply occasionally differ in the choice of tactics. This line of thinking sees the Brothers not as firewalls but as conveyor belts, providing a narrative and a fertile environment that naturally lead toward violent radicalization.

The relationship between the Brotherhood and jihadist movements is extremely complex, varying over time and context, and deserves a depth of analysis that is beyond the scope of this book. It is nonetheless fair to state that the two have common roots, and most scholars, no matter what position they take on the relationship, do see in the writings of Brotherhood thought leader Sayyid Qutb the starting point of the Salafi-jihadi movement. Since then, the points of both convergence and divergence are many. To some degree the end goal is the same, as both strive to establish an Islamic society, yet it is fair to say that the Islamic state envisioned by Brothers "would look very different from a Salafi-jihadi Islamic state."[33] A key difference is in tactics, as the Brothers have chosen ballots over bullets, while jihadist groups argue that participation in the political process is heretical. At the same time, though, it would be a mistake to think that the Brothers have fully abandoned jihad as a strategy to achieve their goals, as examples of their involvement in violent actions, even in recent years, abound.

These differences and similarities translate into a complex relationship. It is fair to argue that the two movements are in constant competition between themselves for attracting the most conservative segments of the Muslim population and that the two regularly attack each other with vitriolic diatribes. Yet at the same time there are many circumstances in which Brotherhood and jihadist groups cooperate, thereby defying any unidimensional analysis.

While a separation between the Brotherhood and the jihadist world is evident, and any analysis that lumps them together is grossly simplistic, it is equally clear that more than occasional moments of overlap do exist. It is therefore not surprising that the migration of individual Brotherhood members toward the jihadist movement, while not a mass phenomenon, is not episodic either. Various studies have shown that a substantial number of individuals who belonged to the jihadist movement had previously been involved with the Brotherhood.[34] Generally this passage happens because the individual is frustrated with the Brothers' overly gradual approach and thinks that the jihadists' more direct approach is more likely to bear fruit.

It is noteworthy that many of the most prominent leaders of the contemporary jihadist movement appear to have moved through that very trajectory. Abdullah Azzam, the Palestinian cleric who was instrumental in mobilizing jihadists to fight in Afghanistan against the Soviet Union, had joined the Muslim Brotherhood in Palestine in the 1950s.[35] His disciple Osama bin Laden had gravitated in the Brotherhood's orbit in Saudi Arabia before deeming the group ineffective and taking a more action-heavy direction. According to his own writings seized by U.S. forces during their 2011 raid on his safe house in Abbottabad, bin Laden was also unimpressed by the group's lack of focus on religion. "From a religious [or theological] aspect," he wrote, "I was committed within the Muslim Brotherhood. Their curriculum was limited. . . . Once a week, the meetings. The number of pages was limited. The extent of influence by them was not much from a religious aspect."[36]

Similarly, bin Laden's successor at the helm of al Qaeda, Ayman al Zawahiri, had been a member of the Brotherhood in Egypt before leading the Islamic Jihad organization. While one should not draw overly general conclusions from it, it is remarkable that the three most important figures in al Qaeda's early history were all former members of the Brotherhood. And it is equally noteworthy that also Abu Bakr al Baghdadi, the current leader of the Islamic State (ISIS, Daesh) was reportedly a member of the Brotherhood in Iraqi before finding the Brothers "people of words, not action" and leaving them for more militant outfits.[37]

Zawahiri's case is particularly interesting, as the current al Qaeda chief has repeatedly lashed out at the Brotherhood, highlighting once again the complex relationship between jihadists and Brothers. In 1989 he penned a book, *The Bitter Harvest*, that is a quintessential anti-Brotherhood screed. Zawahiri accuses the Brotherhood of treachery and heresy for having abandoned the duty to fight jihad and having entered in compromises with the region's regimes, participating in elections and integrating into institutions. "The Brethren," writes Zawahiri, "fan the enthusiasm of young Muslims in order to recruit their services, but thereafter put this enthusiasm into deep freeze. And instead of devoting themselves to jihad aimed at the tyrants, they hold political assemblies and participate in elections."[38]

With these words Zawahiri perfectly encapsulates the frustrations that have led many Brothers to leave the organization and pursue the jihadi route. These dynamics have played out once again in the wake of the downfall of the Brotherhood-led government in Egypt, leading the jihadists to renew their criticism of the Brothers' politics-based approach and some members of the Brotherhood, particularly among the youth, to join various jihadist groups.[39]

But disenchantment with the Brothers' ideology can lead in many directions. If some leave the group for more militant ideas and outfits, others embark on the opposite journey. It is not uncommon for Brotherhood members to develop a commitment to pluralism, democracy, and human rights and come to the conclusion that the Brotherhood's ideology, or at least part of it, clashes with these principles.

Over the past twenty years, the cases of Brotherhood members who have left the organization and have tried to find their own, more liberal way of Islamic activism abound. Many individuals who were Brotherhood members or active in Brotherhood-leaning organizations have sought to move away from the organization's ideological rigidity, recontextualizing some of its ideas and frames to better suit a modern and often multireligious society. It is difficult to lump the heterogeneity of trajectories of former Brothers who have moved in a more liberal direction in one category, but post-Islamism is a term that, despite many flaws, is at times used to do so. The level of ideological and organizational connectivity that these post-Islamists have with the Brotherhood is of course debatable, and different from case to case.

Different is, on the other hand, the situation of those former Brotherhood members who leave not only the organization but Islamism altogether, reneging on all aspects of the ideology. There have been cases, in fact, of individuals who made a complete break with any interpretation of Islam that had a political or activist inclination, and in some extreme cases even leaving Islam itself.

Life After the Brotherhood

Leaving any political or religious movement to which one feels highly committed is almost always difficult, with far-reaching psychological and personal consequences.[40] The emotions involved in the decision-making process are usually intense and conflicting. Individuals often weigh whatever misgivings they have about the group and their involvement in it against the many personal, social, status, and financial challenges that might come with leaving it. This calculation is not cold and mathematical but rather is fraught with emotion. The decision to leave, whether made after lengthy self-examination or in the heat of the moment, is often traumatic. "It was a difficult night. I could not sleep all night, neither [could] my wife," recalls Ibrahim al Zafarani. "For two weeks, we received thousands of calls from Brothers and Sisters inside and outside Egypt. They begged me to change my mind. These phone calls used to kill us emotionally on a daily basis."[41]

Many former members of the Brotherhood and of other high-commitment movements cite being honest with oneself as key to this process. Admitting to oneself first, and then to others, that years or an entire life have been devoted to an organization or a cause in which one no longer believes is a daunting task. Understandably, the higher the commitment to the organization and the price paid because of it, the more challenging a dispassionate self-examination. "Those members who were jailed for the group live in denial and find justifications for all the group's actions," perceptively notes Haytham Abou Khalil, an Egyptian Brother who left the organization after the Arab Spring. "It is hard for them to believe that they made sacrifices for a fallible entity."[42]

Once the difficult decision to leave is made, communicating it to the organization's leadership and to fellow Brothers is the next, equally challenging step. The Brotherhood does not take kindly to disengagement. From its perspective, a member who leaves undermines the group's unity and may reveal its internal secrets. He has betrayed his brothers and has reneged on the sacred pledge he made. Moreover, if, as we have seen, working for the Brotherhood is equated to working for Islam, leaving the group is often framed as leaving the faith—the worst conceivable action for any pious Muslim. "You are renouncing faith, not an ideology," a member of the Egyptian Brotherhood explained to Kandil; "you are abandoning God, not Hassan al-Banna."[43]

The consequences of leaving the Brotherhood are wide-ranging. In some instances, former members have accused the organization of reacting violently, even of attempting to assassinate them. The Brotherhood has always denied these claims, which, to be clear, are rare.[44] Significantly more common is the hefty social toll exacted against Brothers who depart. "When a Brother leaves the group, he is uprooting himself from a milieu with which he has organic, emotional and fateful ties," says Khaled Dawoud, an Egyptian Brotherhood leader married to two Muslim Sisters and the father of eight children, all of whom are Brotherhood members. Mohamed al Qassas echoes his observation: "Resigning from the Muslim Brotherhood is a very tough decision, because the group is more of a society that engulfs your social, familial relations, as well as intellectual and political activities."[45]

Ostracism and marginalization are standard responses to former Brothers. Dawoud describes the shunning: "After you leave the group, you get a special treatment from some Brothers. Your friends can boycott you. They may not even say hello if they bump into you in the street. Your wife's friends, who are usually from the Muslim Brotherhood, may boycott her as well."[46] Rumors about former Brothers are frequently spread. "The Brotherhood assassinated me morally," bemoans Dawoud.[47] Abdel Gelil al-Sharnouby, the former editor of the Egyptian Brotherhood's website Ikhwan Online, recounts his experience: "They tried to turn my family against me. They went to my home town and spread rumors about me, saying that I've become an atheist and that I drink alcohol. They told my wife that I frequent prostitutes."[48]

The Experience of Former Brothers

Given the secretive nature of the Muslim Brotherhood, it is very difficult for outsiders to obtain extensive details on the patterns described thus far. Some scholarly works and journalistic reports have provided useful glimpses into the processes of joining and leaving the group in Egypt and other Arab countries, even though many aspects are still quite obscure. Most of what is known comes from the memoirs of former members. In Egypt, for example, Tharwat El Kherbawy, Sameh Fayez, and a few others have published well-known exposés of the group in books that outline their reasons for leaving.[49] These works constitute invaluable sources for those seeking to understand the process of joining the Brotherhood and the organization's inner workings, on the one hand, and the process of leaving it, on the other. In efforts to analyze a ferociously private organization like the Brotherhood, direct testimonies of former members are vital, even though the risk is always present that their recollections might be tainted by their negative feelings toward the group.

The challenge is even greater when it comes to the Brotherhood in the West. The dynamics of selection, cultivation, and socialization described above are found in Egypt and, more generally, the Arab world. What about the Brotherhood in the West? Does it select, cultivate, and socialize its members in the same way? Is there an usra system? Is there a tarbiya curriculum? And, when it comes to leaving the organization, do we see in the West some of the same patterns observed in the Arab world? Essentially, are the dynamics of the East replicated in the West?

These questions are not easy to answer. First, the secrecy that shrouds the Brotherhood is somewhat greater in the West. Organizations belonging to the Brotherhood family in the Arab world have, understandably, gone to great lengths to hide various aspects of their inner workings and their membership. But they have never denied their own existence—a denial that, as we have seen, is common among the Western Brotherhood. Individuals and networks that disavow any affiliation to the Brotherhood are unlikely to be keen to provide details on the Brotherhood's structure or modus operandi.

Moreover, knowledge of the Western Brotherhood is scant. Scholarly works on the subject are limited, and none of them focuses in any detail on the dynamics of joining or leaving the Brotherhood, concentrating their analysis instead on the group's history and ideology and governmental approaches toward them.[50] Interesting information on these aspects comes from a handful of books written by former members of the Brotherhood in the West, even though all of them focus on the personal account of the author and do not attempt to offer a broader analysis.[51] Various nonscholarly and journalistic works similarly provide useful insights without drawing a systematic analysis.

This book seeks to partially fill that gap by leveraging the testimonies of former members. Each of the following seven chapters is based on an in-depth interview with an individual who either is a former member of the Brotherhood in Europe or North America or, in two cases, has extensive and intimate knowledge of Western Brotherhood networks (Swedish and American, respectively) from the inside. The seven individuals profiled occupied various ranks in their organizations, from top leaders to hangers-on. They operated in different countries and at different times, and obviously they had different reasons for joining and leaving. All, however, left spontaneously. Though some spent some of their years as members of the Brotherhood outside of the West, all lived at least a substantial amount of time there while active in Western Brotherhood networks. And all are identified by name.

I conducted the interviews with these seven individuals over eighteen months (although my dealings with some of them extend back for years, in some cases predating their decision to leave the Brotherhood) and in five countries. Each was interviewed for at least half a day; some interviews stretched over several days. These conversations were supplemented with research and interviews with related subjects in order to both verify and contextualize the information provided by those who disengaged. An additional dozen former members of various Western Brotherhood organizations and individuals with close connections to that milieu were interviewed for this book in seven countries. Some agreed to be quoted by name, some only anonymously. All provided important insights into joining and leaving the Brotherhood.

Each chapter is similarly structured, patterned on the three cycles of militancy: becoming, being, and leaving.[52] The first part focuses on how each individual joined the Brotherhood, with particular attention both to the recruitment methods employed by the organization and to the psychological impulses that drove the individual to join. The second section describes life inside the organization: the role the individual played, the activities he engaged in, and the organizations and people he interacted with. The third section covers disengagement: the reasons that led each individual to leave the organization, how he did so, and what the aftermath was.

There are several pitfalls inherent to a scholarly analysis based predominantly on interviews with former members of an organization.[53] Anyone would find it difficult to recall events and psychological processes that took place years, if not decades, earlier, but for individuals who disengage from high-commitment movements there is the additional risk of bias—their recollections and views may be partial, distorted, or indeed deliberately fabricated. And the interviewer may introduce more problems by asking leading questions or by misinterpreting the answers; the ethical and practical concerns associated with interviews are widely recognized. I am well aware of these issues, and I have tried to address them in several ways. I made substantial efforts to verify several claims that on their face appeared possibly untrue, defamatory, or both, omitting a few that I could not confirm.

Nevertheless, a microsociological analysis based on the testimonies of former members of the Brotherhood or its larger milieu offers unique value. Their recollections about how and why they joined, what they did while members, and why and how they left constitute unparalleled sources of information about the inner workings, modus operandi, and ideology of a highly mysterious organization. They also provide useful glimpses into the psychological processes that lead some of its members to join and then disengage from the organization. Moreover, each chapter, taken on its own, tells the story of a fascinating life, the personal trajectory of an individual who went through his own complex evolution and, in some cases, played a key role in important political events.

CHAPTER III

Kamal Helbawy

Joining the Brotherhood

Charismatic, indefatigable, and deeply committed to the organization for more than 60 years, Kamal Helbawy belongs to a handful of individuals who have shaped the course of the Muslim Brotherhood in the West.[1] Helbawy was born in 1939 in Kafr el Batanoon, a small village in Egypt's Delta area, in the Menoufia governorate. Having proven himself in elementary school to be particularly gifted, his parents decided to enroll him in a fast-track school that would have allowed him to reach university at a younger age than the norm. While various schools offered such a program, his parents choose one run by the Muslim Brotherhood. Even though they did not belong to the organization, the Helbawys thought that a Brotherhood school, while also providing a solid education in various subjects, better reflected the conservative Islamic values of their rural community. In 1951, at age 12, Kamal Helbawy enrolled in secondary school in the town of Shibin El Kom (incidentally, the same school that the Egyptian president Hosni Mubarak had attended a few years earlier).

"For three years," reminisces Helbawy with a smile, "I did not know that I was a member [of the Muslim Brotherhood]." In recounting his lifelong experience in the Brotherhood, in fact, Helbawy starts from the observation period that most future members of the group—particularly those not born into Brotherhood families—undergo and that was described in the previous chapter. "You are in an elementary course for two or three years. In that elementary course, you don't need to pay any money, you don't need to attend night prayers, or you are not responsible, you are more free [sic]." According to Helbawy, senior Brotherhood members, some of whom were the very teachers who taught regular subjects such as Arabic or mathematics, observed their students' intellects, personalities, dependability, and devoutness. When they spotted individuals possessing these characteristics they involved them with increasing frequency in activities (classes on Islam, social outings) organized by the group—without ever mentioning that the Brotherhood was involved.

Individuals who are in the preliminary stages of joining the Brotherhood, recounts Helbawy, are continuously tested. "They test your honesty, they test your courage, they test your understanding, they test your behavior, they test your character." Many tests entail performing seemingly pointless acts just to gauge the candidate's obedience and dependability. "For example, they tell you, 'At 1 o'clock [in the morning], we have a very important meeting. At such a place. At the railway station.' And then you show up, and then your supervisor, we call him *naqib*, as you know, he says to you 'I am happy to see you, go back home.' So some people may say 'Why did you bring us?' But this was a test."

Helbawy also explains that this policy of testing extends to individuals who have already formally joined the organization in their youth. Thus, he said, aspiring members of the Secret Apparatus, the secret branch of the Brotherhood devoted to security and paramilitary operations, undergo a stricter and constant scrutiny. For example, they might be asked to carry a heavy bag from one place to the other, perhaps without using any means of transportation on the way, and with instructions not to open it. The bag might contain simply stones or iron bars of no value, but the task serves to test their commitment.

According to Helbawy, these dynamics first tested and then shaped individual members' behaviors; but they also provided the group with internal discipline, one of the Brotherhood's crucial characteristics. Helbawy recounts how this phenomenon became apparent to him during the protests against the monarchy that took place throughout Egypt in the early 1950s: "I noticed big differences between the demonstrations led by the Muslim Brotherhood brothers and those led by other political parties." The former, in fact, were well structured, with senior members cordoning off the Brotherhood group marching in the street. "Nobody can get in and nobody can get out unless there is a necessity." In contrast, in his view, demonstrations organized by forces other than the Brotherhood lacked that order and internal discipline, and its participants would frequently commit acts of vandalism or theft.

This discipline at demonstrations, points out Helbawy, was also displayed by the Brotherhood in the tense days of the 2011 Egyptian revolution, when street protest engulfed Cairo. The Brothers, seeking to avoid provoking a backlash from what they assessed to be a stable regime, were at first reluctant to participate in street protests. But as the days went by and the idea of toppling the regime no longer seemed far-fetched, the Brothers decided to descend into the streets. And, thanks to their organizational skills, they became leaders of the demonstrations, managing the encampments, delivering food, and running security—all actions that enabled them to gain the trust of the initially diffident fellow protesters whose backgrounds were not Islamist.

Life Inside the Brotherhood

Helbawy recalls his early days in the Brotherhood fondly. In stark contrast to the teachings of the group's current leadership, as we will see, he talks about the tenets of his first teachers in the Brotherhood as perfectly in line with Islamic values and capable of making anybody who follows them an exemplary person.

> I became a member because they never taught us something against, as I said to you, the moral values. Main, religious moral values. Be polite, respect your fathers and parents, respect your teachers, your elderly. Memorize your lessons properly. Try to become the first in your class. Compete with people nicely. Clean yourself, keep your books clean. Help others in the street if they need help. If you see a man, a blind man or woman, help them to cross the road. They encourage you to do charity, even with a penny, and sometimes with students, you don't have much money, very, very few, but they encouraged you, they cultivated love of charity in yourself. That is why I joined.

After three years "under observation," Helbawy officially joined the Brotherhood, becoming a full-fledged, dues-paying member. He continued his studies, progressing to university, where he obtained degrees in literature (from Cairo University, 1960) and business administration and simultaneous translation (from the American University in Cairo, 1971). By the early 1960s he was working for the Brotherhood's Central Training Organization, the unit devoted to training new members and spreading the organization's credo.

It was at that time that his troubles with the Egyptian authorities began. The 1960s were one of the darkest times for the Brotherhood, a decade characterized by the regime's brutal repression of the group. Helbawy found himself under heavy surveillance and routinely interrogated, although, unlike many of his Brothers, he was fortunate never to serve time in prison.

When Gamal Abdel Nasser died in 1970, the travel ban to which Helbawy had been subjected was lifted and he decided to leave Egypt. It was the beginning of decades of whirlwind traveling around the globe to spread the Brotherhood's approach to education and dawa—Helbawy's life-long passion. He first traveled to Nigeria, where together with Sheikh Ahmed Lemu and other local clerics he established the Islamic Education Trust in Sokoto, a city in the country's Northwest.

According to Helbawy, the success of his experience in Nigeria led "some Brothers" who had moved to Saudi Arabia to contact him. In the 1970s the Gulf country had become one of the main refuges for Egyptian Brothers (and some from other countries as well) seeking to escape persecution in their home country. They found hospitality in a country that shared a similarly conservative interpretation of Islam and had recently gained immense wealth through oil. Further cementing the relationship between Brothers and the Saudi monarchy was their common animosity toward the secular Egyptian regime, the former's sworn internal enemy and the latter's geopolitical foe.

Some Brothers engaged in lucrative business activities, enriching themselves and, consequently, the Brotherhood. Others were tasked by the Saudis with running the many organizations they set up to translate the country's newfound wealth into geopolitical influence by spreading its brand of Islam. Among the Egyptian Brothers who called Helbawy to Saudi Arabia was Tawfiq al Shawi, a member of the Brotherhood's founding committee whom Helbawy calls "one of the great senior Brothers." According to Helbawy, al Shawi had convinced King Faysal of Saudi Arabia that Saudi-funded but largely Brotherhood-run and -staffed organizations were the best vehicles to spread their ultraconservative interpretation of Islam worldwide.

The brainchildren of this cooperation between Brothers and the Saudi monarchy were organizations such as the Muslim World League (MWL, founded in 1962) and the World Assembly of Muslim Youth (WAMY, founded ten years later). In 1972 Helbawy moved to Jeddah and was appointed WAMY's executive director, overseeing many of its projects in the West and in other parts of the world. "I was the first executive director and we had to spread globally by establishing camps for youth and introducing Islam to them, providing them with books and activities, and to take care of Muslim youth and student associations. This gave me the chance to work globally."[2]

It was during these years that Helbawy, as a senior officer of an organization with an immense budget whose mandate was to support Muslim organizations spreading an interpretation of Islam compatible with the Saudis', began to travel throughout the West. As he puts it, WAMY was conceived after Tawfiq al Shawi had convinced King Faysal that "that there are now in the West societies, Muslim societies, in universities and communities, and this will have great effect and impact on the future, but they need help and assistance." Helbawy implemented this vision, as he organized conferences throughout Europe and North America and brought together the first pioneers of the Brotherhood in the West. And while Helbawy, by his own admission, had never been very involved in the financial aspects of the organization, other parts of WAMY (and the MWL) provided financial support for various Muslim but mostly Brotherhood-controlled or Brotherhood-leaning organizations in the West. In the words of the Pew Research Center, "Between the 1970s and 1990s, the European activities of the Muslim Brotherhood, the Muslim World League and the World Assembly of Muslim Youth became so intertwined that it was often difficult to tell them apart."[3]

To describe these dynamics, Helbawy fondly recounts his close connections to Turkish Islamism, which started with a visit by Necmettin Erbakan to Saudi Arabia in 1974. The godfather of Turkish Islamism, Erbakan founded various Islamist parties that were routinely shut down by Turkish authorities, and in June 1997 he was deposed by the Turkish military from the position of prime minister. The current ruling party in Turkey, the Justice and Development Party (Adalet ve Kalkınma Partisi, AKP), was founded in 2001 by veterans of Erbakan's various political parties who strategically opted for a less confrontational approach toward the secular Turkish establishment, and many of AKP's current leaders were once disciples of Erbakan. Erbakan was also the founder of Millî Görüş, the most prominent Turkish Islamist organization in Europe, with hundreds of thousands of followers throughout the continent. Erbakan's parties and the Brotherhood in the Middle East—and, by the same token, Millî Görüş and the European networks of the Brotherhood—have always been fellow travelers, independent and with a different local focus (Erbakan and Millî Görüş added a distinctive Turkish nationalist flavor to boilerplate Islamism) but tied together by fundamental ideological affinities.

During his Saudi visit, recounts Helbawy, Erbakan was received by top Saudi leaders, including the minister of education and the president of King Abdulaziz University, as well as the heads of WAMY. In his meetings Erbakan brought up the issue of Northern Cyprus, which that year the Turkish government had annexed through military intervention, and expressed his concerns that Muslims in Cyprus were thoroughly secularized ("There was no lady with a hijab in Cyprus, not one," recalls Helbawy). WAMY leaders then decided to establish a dawa center and host a large conference in Northern Cyprus in order to correct this situation.

Helbawy began traveling to Turkey along with Mohammed Mahdi Akef, at the time senior advisor to WAMY and later general guide of the Egyptian Brotherhood, to work on these projects. While Erbakan was his main contact in the country, he also interacted with some of Erbakan's most devoted disciples, who included the current president of Turkey, Recep Tayyip Erdoğan (whom Helbawy describes as "at the time, a student for the movement"). This work came to fruition in 1977, when WAMY organized its first camp and conference in Northern Cyprus. Helbawy and Akef met personally with Rauf Denktaş, the founding president of the Turkish Republic of Northern Cyprus, and obtained from him a favorable lease ("Ninety-nine years, the first ten years free of charge, after that $2,000") for eight villas near Kyrenia.

The camp near Kyrenia was, in Helbawy's words, "well attended"—one of the countless examples of well-funded events that over the past fifty years have brought together seasoned and budding Islamist activists from all over the world and have helped build the Brotherhood's transnational network. According to Helbawy, attendees were a who's who of 1970s Islamist activism, including Yusuf Nada, the Western Brotherhood's chief financier, and his lifetime business partner Ghaleb Himmat; Jamal Barzinji, Ahmed Totonji, and Hisham al Talib, three Iraqi Kurds who played leading roles in establishing various Brotherhood-linked organizations in the United

States; and prominent Turkish Islamists like Temel Karamollaoğlu.[4] In describing the success of the event near Kyrenia, Helbawy stresses that "our means in [the] World Assembly of Muslim Youth were not traditional means like sheikhs going to give lectures or money or so [on], but how to train young men." These young men were the future leaders of the Brotherhood's transnational network, well-trained individuals who could count on extensive financial resources and high-level contacts worldwide.

Helbawy's time in Saudi Arabia came to an end in 1988, when the Brotherhood dispatched him to Pakistan and Afghanistan to be its liaison to the Afghan forces battling the Soviet occupation. Though it has little direct relevance to the history of the Brotherhood in the West, Helbawy's time in the Afghanistan/Pakistan region is nonetheless filled with significant anecdotes that he recounts with particular pleasure. One of them has to do with how Abdullah Azzam—the man recognized by many as the founder of contemporary jihadism by virtue of the role he played in mobilizing thousands of Muslims worldwide to travel to Afghanistan and, more broadly, in crafting the concept of volunteering in jihadist causes worldwide—became involved in the Afghan conflict.

The Brotherhood's first envoy to Afghanistan, according to Helbawy, was Kamal al Sananiri, a prominent Egyptian Brotherhood leader who was married to Sayyid Qutb's sister Aminah. Sananiri represents a legendary figure in Islamist circles. Tellingly, his early role in liaising with the Afghan mujaheddin has been acknowledged also by Ayman al Zawahiri, the current leader of al Qaeda and himself a veteran of the Afghan conflict. "We were preceded to Peshawar by Kamal al Sananiri," writes Zawahiri in his book *Knights Under the Prophet's Banner*, "may he rest in peace. We could see that he had left his mark wherever we went. He had played a pioneer role in establishing the hospital where we worked and whenever we met with mujahideen leaders, they would speak of his assistance to them and his efforts to unite them. Although I never met him, his actions and contributions demonstrated his generosity and beneficial services in the cause of God."[5] By the time Zawahiri had arrived in Afghanistan, Sananiri had been arrested in Egypt in the crackdown that followed the assassination of Egyptian president Anwar Sadat and reportedly died in prison.

During the first months of the Afghan conflict, Sananiri reportedly traveled to the Arab Gulf to mobilize support for the cause. While visiting Jeddah he met Azzam, who had just obtained a post at Jeddah's King Abdul Aziz University after having been expelled from Jordan for his radical rhetoric. Azzam already had a reputation as a firebrand and skilled orator. Yet, according to Helbawy, at the time he met Sananiri, Azzam had not yet grasped the mobilizing potential of the Afghan conflict. When Sananiri visited Helbawy at his office at WAMY, the two went to see Azzam, as the campus of King Abdul Aziz University was only a few meters from WAMY's offices. Helbawy recounted that Azzam told Sananiri: "I am ousted from Jordan, and this is the only place [I can stay]; I came to work in the university as a professor." But it was Sananiri who told him, "It is better to go to Afghanistan," setting in motion Azzam's interest in the Afghan jihad and thus a chain of events whose consequences are still strongly reverberating today.

According to Helbawy, King Abdul Aziz University granted leave to Azzam, allowing him to work at King Faisal University in Islamabad and divide his time between the Pakistani capital and Peshawar, the Pakistani city on the border with Afghanistan that served as a base for the Arab mujaheddin. By 1988 Helbawy himself had relocated between Peshawar and Islamabad, where he worked as an advisor to the Institute of Policy Studies—an institute founded by Khurshid Ahmed, who was a prominent leader of Jamaat-e-Islami, the Brotherhood's sister movement in the Asian subcontinent. While Helbawy claims his Afghanistan-related activities remained purely political and humanitarian, he was intimately connected with the Arab mujaheddin who lived in Peshawar. He remained close to Azzam and argues that at the closing of the Afghan conflict, Azzam was in the crosshairs of those who sought to turn the Arab factions in Afghanistan into an organization that would continue the jihad worldwide—what would later become al Qaeda. Following one of the most plausible theories regarding the November 1989 assassination of Azzam, Helbawy is convinced that he "was treated by some of the violent groups as a kufr, not a Muslim, until they killed him."

Even during his time in Saudi Arabia and Afghanistan/Pakistan, Helbawy used to travel frequently to the West, attending conferences, giving seminars, and participating in meetings of the growing numbers of Western Brothers. In 1994, sensing that the U.S. government had put pressure on the Pakistani government to stem Arab Islamist networks on Pakistani soil and aware that the Mubarak regime was prone to incarcerating Islamists returning from the Afghan conflict, Helbawy found that the safest place he could land was London—a city he had frequented often in previous decades.

As soon as he settled in the British capital, Helbawy began lecturing at local universities and established various businesses, including a nursing home in Wembley, the area of North London where he still lives today. Most important, he immediately gained a prominent role in the thriving local Islamist scene. In 1995 he opened the Muslim Brotherhood Global Information Centre, the organization's first official office in the West. Helbawy says that the idea of launching a center that was openly affiliated with the Brotherhood was criticized by various Brotherhood activists in the West, who argued that the organization should operate more secretively and indirectly.

It is a point of contention that has for years pitted Helbawy against the majority of Brothers and that, eventually, was a major factor in his desire to leave the organization. "We are not selling opium or drugs, we are propagating dawa," emphatically argues Helbawy, who has long been critical of what he believes to be the Brotherhood's excessive secrecy and deception when presenting itself to the West.[6] "And I can't be ashamed of my selection [sic] or my dawa program," he adds. "If it is followed right, it is a source of happiness, not sadness." To Helbawy's chagrin, the Muslim Brotherhood Global Information Centre was renamed after he left its helm in 1997.

Helbawy also played a crucial role in laying the groundwork for two of Britain's most influential Muslim organizations. In May 1997 he was one of the founding members of the Muslim Council of Britain (MCB), the umbrella organization seeking to represent British Muslims. Although MCB was heterogeneous in its membership, its leadership was from the outset dominated by Islamists of the Jamaat-e-Islami persuasion. This Islamist bent has often been the source of tensions with the British establishment, which initially saw MCB as the de facto official and sole interlocutor within the Muslim community.

More openly Islamist is the other organization Helbawy cofounded in the same year, the Muslim Association of Britain (MAB); he became its first president.[7] Intended to unite various ethnic Arab activists based in Britain, MAB is a quintessential Western Brotherhood organization in its origins, ideology, connections, and methodology. Aside from Helbawy, MAB's leadership includes experienced political activists from various Middle Eastern countries, among them the Palestinian Mohammed Sawalha; Anas al Tikriti, the son of the leader of the Iraqi branch of the Brotherhood; and Azzam Tamimi, the former director of the parliamentary office of the Islamic Action Front, Jordan's Brotherhood offshoot. A founding member of MCB, MAB is also a key member of the Federation of Islamic Organizations in Europe (FIOE), the Western Brothers' Brussels-based pan-European umbrella organization.

Despite having been in the United Kingdom as a permanent resident for just a couple of years, Helbawy found himself at the center of the local Muslim and Islamist scene. This position was due in part to his stature and charisma, in part to the fact that he had been traveling throughout the West for some twenty-five years. While technically a relative late addition to the Western Brotherhood, Helbawy had known the scene well and had actually played a key role in developing it through his activities with WAMY. His description of how that scene was formed and how it still operates therefore carries particular weight.

Helbawy confirms that the Brotherhood "never intended to come to the West so early; the aim was to concentrate on the Arab countries, but when the problem occurred with Nasser, in 1954, some students fled to the West." He adds, "Some other Brothers came to study [in the West] from different countries like Iraq, like Jordan, like Syria." In Helbawy's account, student organizations were the first embryo of Brotherhood presence in the West. "They came to study," he explains, but "they did not forget their dawa. They got acquainted in the university campuses, and they began to form the Muslim societies, Muslim student societies. I remember when I used to come to lecture in England, in 1975, 1976, and I went to America [in] 1977 for the first time in Indianapolis University." Helbawy's recollection of a visit to a college campus in Indiana (albeit Indianapolis University, which did not exist) is not surprising. The Muslim Student Association, the organization created by longtime associates of Helbawy's including Jamal Barzinji, Hisham al Talib, and Ahmed Totonji, had its inception on various campuses in the Midwest, and it was in Indianapolis that the Islamic Society of North America (ISNA) was established by some of the very same founders of MSA.

In describing the passage from MSA to ISNA in the United States, Helbawy captures a dynamic that was replicated, albeit in different time frames, in all Western countries as some of the first Western Brothers decided or were forced to stay in the West: they turned their original nuclei of student organizations into all-purpose entities that today still represent some of the most active and visible Muslim organizations in the West. At that time, the Islamic revivalism that has swept through the Arab and

Muslim world over the past forty years was in its infancy, and most Muslims living in the West were largely secular in their outlook. But among those embracing a more conservative interpretation of Islam, remembers Helbawy, "the most flourishing groups were the Muslim Brotherhood's." As he recalls, "Before Salafis came, and the jihadists came, and violent groups came, it was the Muslim Brotherhood." By turning their student organizations into organizations with larger aims, as in the transformation from MSA to ISNA, the Brothers demonstrated their understanding that their presence in the West was permanent and needed new forms.

Among the pioneers Helbawy remembers Said Ramadan, Hassan al Banna's son-in-law and personal secretary, who was among the first Brothers to establish a base in Europe (first in Cologne and then in Geneva). He also acknowledges the crucial role played by Yussuf Nada, one of the Brotherhood's main financiers in the West. The importance of Ramadan and Nada in creating the first kernel of the Brotherhood in the West by establishing some of its first Brotherhood organizations and linking them to Arab Gulf money cannot be overstated.[8]

But Helbawy is most intimately familiar with Anglo-Saxon countries, throughout which he used to travel frequently in the heyday of the Western Brotherhood. In North America he cites as leaders of the "earlier generation" the three Kurds already mentioned above (al Talib, Barzinji, and Totonji); the late Ahmed el Kadi, who in 2004 became one of the few Brotherhood leaders in the West to agree to an interview with a newspaper (the *Chicago Tribune*) and to publicly disclose his role in and some of the inner workings of the organizations in America;[9] Mahmoud Abu Saoud, a prominent economist who was instrumental in developing the modern concept of Islamic banking and—demonstrating the key role played by marriage in the Brotherhood's structure—was el Kadi's son-in-law; the University of Halifax professor and ISNA cofounder Jamal Badawi; and Sayed Hassan Desouqi, who moved to the United States in 1964 to work at Lockheed Martin and taught aviation engineering in various American universities while also setting up the movement in the country.

In the United Kingdom the names Helbawy cites as pioneers of the first generation are Zaghloul el Naggar, a renowned Egyptian scholar who has written countless treatises combining his passion for geology and natural sciences with his faith in Islam;[10] the former Iraqi Muslim Brotherhood leader (and father of MAB cofounder Anas al Tikriti) Usama al Tikriti; and Ahmed al Rawi, an Iraqi who is the longtime director of the

Europe Trust, one of the European Brotherhood's most important financial structures.

Discussing how the Brotherhood established itself in the West naturally leads to the problematic issue, already examined in the previous chapter, of what the Brotherhood in the West actually is. In tackling this complex question, Helbawy adopts a tripartite framework, based on different degrees of connectivity to the Brotherhood, that is similar to my own. Helbawy agrees that the "pure Brothers"—the highly skilled and devoted individuals who are sworn members of the organization (whether they have publicly disclosed their affiliation or not)—represent a relatively small group at the heart of the much larger machine that is the Brotherhood in the West broadly conceived.

In describing the inner workings of this core, Helbawy paints a picture of a formal structure that resembles, albeit on a smaller scale, how the Brotherhood works in Egypt or other Middle Eastern countries. "The first unit or block is the usra," he explains, "a group of five to ten people, either living in a neighborhood or working in the same mission, orientation: engineers, doctors. So they meet every week, or every other week, and are trained properly to understand Islam properly. That is one." Exactly as in Egypt, also in the West "ten usras come together under one leadership and they have certain programs. . . . And then you have the executive local unit that takes administration of that area, and then you have the, you can say, the local *shura* of this region."

Obviously, because the number of Brothers in Western countries is relatively small, this structure is not always perfectly replicated, and the region of competence of the *shu'ba* or the local *shura* might be the entire country. Helbawy, who was a key clog in the U.K. Brotherhood system for decades, estimates that the number of individuals in Britain who are "active Ikhwan"—that is, sworn members who are inserted in the usra system—is somewhere between six hundred and one thousand. In many other Western countries the number is significantly lower. That small number, according to Helbawy, does not preclude their effectiveness: "Since they are well organized, and they are obedient to their leaders, they can implement a lot. Do this, you are assured that it will be done. Do that, no need for much thought, it will be done. And this is what I meant about active members."

Part of this discipline is also implemented at the financial level. Every active member, according to Helbawy, "has to pay some of his income, maybe sometimes 3 percent, 7 percent, 10 percent to the organization."[11]

"In times of crisis, like Palestine, for example, or Somalia, or Syria, we pay one day of our salaries or income to help certain issues—this is in addition to the [original amount]." Helbawy adds that it is not unusual for wealthy Brotherhood members to make large one-off donations to the organization and that many also give some of their possessions to the organization after they die. As noted above, external sources of funding have been crucial to the Brotherhood's success. But given that most Brotherhood members, including some who do not devote the entirety of their time to activism, are successful professionals or businessman—a natural consequence of their being highly educated and belonging to the upper middle class—this form of internal taxation provides the organization's coffers with ample resources.

Essentially, the core Western Brothers have created a secretive structure that mirrors the one adopted in Middle Eastern countries in all aspects. At the same time, according to Helbawy, they have created a large web of heterogeneous organizations that, while fully controlled by Brothers, have a tangential connection to that core structure—what some have termed "Brotherhood spawns." Helbawy brings up the Muslim Welfare House (MWH), an organization he helped establish in 1970 in London in a corner building in front of the Finsbury Park underground station.[12] MWH, according to Helbawy, "maybe was the first organization established by Brothers in the U.K.," and "it was established with two intentions."

The first was to "receive Muslims coming from abroad for any reason and help them." Beginning in its heyday, the Brotherhood, a transnational organization par excellence, has created an efficient hospitality network for its members. Brothers traveling to a foreign country or another city can rely on the aid of the organization's local members, who can host them in their homes and help them with all their needs during their visit. This system naturally increases the organization's transnational connections and the members' feeling of belonging to a genuine band of brothers. It was only to be expected that in London, historically one of the global hubs for the Brotherhood, the Brothers would establish a purpose-built hostel to receive visiting members.

The second goal of an organization like MWH—illustrating the organization's mind-set as clearly as does the first—is for "those who are living in the West, not to Westernize their lives. . . . They can eat halal foods, they can marry Muslim women, or even Christian women, but to keep Muslim; to meet once a week or once every month to gather in one place to pray together. So that's why we established the Muslim Welfare House at that time." MWH was, essentially, one of the first organizations created by the Brothers that protects from contact with Western society that would dilute the Muslim identity of its members and, more broadly, the larger Muslim community.

MWH was thus one of the first examples of Brotherhood "para-mosque."[13] Rather than being a simple place of worship, Brothers intend their mosques as the center of the community's life, a forum for social, religious, educational, and political engagement. Even though such a range of activities is not exclusive to Islamic centers controlled by Western Brothers, it reflects their vision of religion as a comprehensive system encompassing all aspects of life. According to an internal memorandum penned by Mohammed Akram, a self-avowed member of the American wing of the Brotherhood, Islamic centers should become a place for "study, family, battalion [sic], course, seminar, visit, sport, school, social club, women gathering, kindergarten, the office of domestic political resolution and the center for distributing our newspapers, magazines, books."[14] Located in every major American city, the Islamic center is meant to become, according to Akram, "the axis of our Movement"—"the base for our rise," necessary to "educate us, prepare us and supply our battalions in addition to being the 'niche' of our prayers." All the activities of the paramosque, from football games to field trips, from lectures to initiatives to clean up local parks and neighborhoods, are designed to forge a sense of community and to advance the movement's message.

The difference between pure Brotherhood structures and Brotherhood spawns is at times blurry, as Helbawy admits. Secrecy, one of the Brotherhood's main features, makes categorization complicated. As Helbawy puts it, "There are different types of [Brotherhood] organizations in the West; there are organizations purely for Ikhwan, and maybe no one will know about the name, or know about the existence." Even more complex is the identification of a Brotherhood link in organizations belonging to what has been identified as the third category: organizations influenced by the Brotherhood. In many cases, as other chapters will show, making that identification is difficult even for people who have been deeply involved in those very organizations for years.

"There are other organizations," explains Helbawy, "especially in the field of welfare and relief organizations, that are run by [the] Muslim Brotherhood . . . and can involve Muslim Brothers and non–Muslim Brothers."

As example, Helbawy points to Islamic Relief Worldwide (IRW). Founded in 1984 in Birmingham, IRW has become a global aid giant with, according to its website, "over 100 offices in 40 countries worldwide."[15] Somewhat epitomizing the complexity of ascertaining the true nature of this kind of organization, on the one hand IRW has partnership agreements with entities like the UNHCR, the World Food Program, and the European Commission's Humanitarian Aid and Civil Protection Department; on the other hand, in 2014 it was included in a list of terrorist organizations by the United Arab Emirates and banned by the governments of Israel and Bangladesh from operating in their territories.

"[IRW's] leadership," explains Helbawy, "are Brotherhood, but the people who contact [donors] for donations are not necessarily even Muslims; they can be Christians, and Jews, and whatever." Essentially, Helbawy argues that organizations like IRW are funded and run at the senior leadership level by Brotherhood members. In the case of IRW the clear links between the charitable organization and the Brotherhood include one of IRW's cofounders, Essam el Haddad, a senior Egyptian Brotherhood official who served as President Mohamed Morsi's assistant for foreign relations and international cooperation.[16] But, argues Helbawy, most of the people who work for IRW, even in senior positions, are not members of the Brotherhood and in most cases have no idea of—and would even strongly and sincerely deny—IRW's links to the Brotherhood.[17] Their relatively small numbers, according to Helbawy, do not diminish the Brothers' domination of these organizations, as they will always maintain sway by controlling the board and using other tactics. At the same time, the presence—often in very visible positions—of individuals who clearly are not Muslim Brotherhood members is advantageous to the Brotherhood, as it makes the accusation that these organizations are "Muslim Brotherhood" a difficult one to sustain.

Leaving the Brotherhood

Throughout the second half of the 1990s and the following decade, Helbawy was one of the most visible and influential faces of Britain's Muslim and Islamist scenes. Faithful to the view he has often publicly expressed that people older than sixty-five should not hold executive positions, in 1998 he resigned from the Brotherhood's Guidance Office (Makhtab al Irshad).[18]

While still deeply involved in the dynamics of the Egyptian branch of the organization—despite having been in exile from the country for years—he focused most of his seemingly endless energy on a number of other projects. In 2004, in the wake of the U.S. invasion of Iraq and concerned about the sectarian tensions that immediately followed it, he headed the Forum for Islamic Unity, an organization seeking to promote Shia–Sunni understanding. In 2006, at the height of the so-called War on Terror and in the wake of the July 2005 attacks in London, he started the Centre for the Study of Terrorism in order to "try to prove that terrorism has no home and no specific culture."[19] He continued to lecture throughout Britain and worldwide, appear on TV, pen articles, mentor budding activists, and act as a central node in the Brotherhood's transnational network, a larger-than-life figure who was appreciated and listened to within the Islamist movement and beyond.

As was true of most Brotherhood activists in the West, Helbawy's life changed completely with the advent of the so-called Arab Spring in 2011. His native Egypt was swept by particularly intense revolutionary winds, and on February 11 the regime of Hosni Mubarak, who had ruled the country with an iron fist for almost thirty years and was seen as providing the quintessential example of stable Arab government, was toppled. On April 5, after twenty-three years in exile, Helbawy returned to Egypt; he received a hero's welcome at Cairo's airport from family members and senior Brotherhood leaders, including Mohammed Akef, his old friend and the organization's former murshid.

Upon returning to the country, Helbawy immediately immersed himself in the political frenzy that was engulfing post-Mubarak Egypt. He reconnected with fellow Brotherhood senior leaders, lectured to younger ones, and became a staple in the country's newspapers and television debates. Yet this initial enthusiasm was quickly tempered by various decisions taken by the Brotherhood's leadership with which Helbawy disagreed. "They were flip-flopping in their position and aspiring for power in a way that did not differ much from [Hosni Mubarak's] National Democratic Party," Helbawy has stated in an interview. In particular, the Brotherhood abandoned its initial pledge to field candidates for only one-third of the seats in Parliament. Helbawy was direct in his criticism: "I think if you break your promises, you can't be trusted and you will never succeed."[20]

Helbawy was also disturbed that the Brotherhood's leadership began to ostracize members, including very senior ones, who raised objections to some of their decisions. The harsh treatment the group reserved for Abdel Moneim al Futuh, a widely respected Brotherhood leader who had been in the group's inner circle since the 1970s but had loudly criticized some of the group's positions in the post-Mubarak phase, was especially concerning to Helbawy. While he acknowledges that internal discipline is a crucial characteristic of the Brotherhood, historically the organization has allowed its members to hold a plurality of views. He felt that publicly humiliating and spreading rumors about its dissenting members were actions that did not meet the true ethical standards of the Brotherhood.

Disappointed by these and other decisions by the Brotherhood's current leadership, Helbawy began firming up his decision to leave the organization to which he had devoted his life. On March 31, 2012, the night the Brotherhood decided to walk back on another political promise it had made—of not running a candidate for the presidency—Helbawy took the dramatic step of formally and publicly announcing his resignation from the group. "Despite my deep sadness," he told a reporter for an Egyptian newspaper, "my conscience is clear that I am not participating in this nonsense."[21]

Much has been said and written in and outside Egypt about his decision, both because of Helbawy's high profile and because the announcement of his resignation was so public. Predictably, theories as to what motivated him abound, particularly in Islamist milieus. Some hinge on preposterous conspiracies, but a seemingly plausible theory is that upon returning to Egypt, Helbawy expected to receive a prominent position within the Brotherhood or in the political institutions the Brotherhood came to control in the first months of the post-Mubarak era. The leadership of the Brotherhood, composed mostly of individuals who were some twenty years his junior and had had only limited interactions with him while he was in exile, saw him as an elder to respect but also as somebody who was not part of the inner circle and who had been away from Egypt for too long. Feeling unjustly sidelined, on this account, Helbawy left the organization in anger.[22]

Though only Helbawy can know his true motives, this conjecture seems improbable. In the years before the Egyptian Revolution Helbawy had voluntarily abandoned various executive roles, including that of member of the Guidance Bureau, arguing that individuals over sixty-five should not serve in such positions. And there are no concrete indications that Helbawy sought executive positions while he was in Egypt, whether while still in the Brotherhood or later, when, as we will see, his opposition to the

Brotherhood made him popular with the regime of General Abdel Fatah al Sisi.

What this theory does surely capture is a generation gap that divided Helbawy from the Brotherhood leadership he found when he returned to Egypt. While individuals such as the former murshid Mohammed Akef and his successor, Mohammed Badie, were individuals of Helbawy's generation who had personal connections to him, most decision makers inside the group had joined in the 1970s, after the purges initiated by Nasser and during the time when the Brotherhood was regrouping under Anwar Sadat. Helbawy did not have strong ties to this younger generation, and he even had strong antipathies toward one of the most influential among them— the prominent businessman Khairat al Shater, the Brotherhood's first presidential candidate.[23]

Helbawy admits to this gap but frames it more in ideological than in personal terms. "For one year after I came back," he explains, "I stayed in the Muslim Brotherhood, but I noticed some deviation from the curricula and from the way we were brought up to be members."[24] He argues that the Brotherhood's leadership in the post-Mubarak era focused almost entirely on gaining political power and relinquished what he believes to be the group's core activity: dawa. In doing so, according to Helbawy, the Brotherhood has deviated from al Banna's teachings. "His real teachings could have actually led the Brotherhood to have a leading role in the new world order through intellectual propositions, fighting for justice and against oppression, and educating the youth," he argues.[25] Instead, the group's leadership has focused solely on seizing power, forgetting its original approach of reforming society from the bottom up.

Helbawy remains a steadfast defender of the Brotherhood's ideology. He believes that if correctly implemented, al Banna's vision would lead to just and prosperous Muslim societies and communities. But, according to Helbawy, "the leadership deviated from the route of Hassan al Banna and his curriculum; they are more Qutbist in their way of looking at society."[26] In this sentence Helbawy encapsulates the philosophical tension that has affected the Brotherhood over the past fifty years. One line of thinking has emphasized dawa and education, believing in a patient effort to Islamize society. But another has been more in line with the teachings of Sayyid Qutb, the Brotherhood leader executed by the Egyptian regime in 1966. In treatises written during his prison years, Qutb argued that the Brotherhood, blocked by the regime from spreading its dawa, should have prioritized other tactics, including violence, to achieve its goal of creating an Islamic society. Qutb's argument has been embraced by various Islamist groups that opted to use violence as the main tactic to reach their goals. But it has also influenced large cross sections of the Brotherhood, leading them not to follow the jihadist route but to prefer politics and a top-down approach toward Islamization to al Banna's dawa-centric approach.

Helbawy argues that this latter group—what he terms the "Qutbist wing of the Brotherhood"—has gained power within the organization over the past fifteen years. Many of the members of this wing joined the organization in the 1970s and therefore belong to the generation that is now controlling the group. Moreover, many of them belonged to the Secret Apparatus, the section of the Brotherhood devoted to military and counterintelligence operations.

Given its mission, publicly available details on the Secret Apparatus are scant, and some Brotherhood members even deny its very existence. But Helbawy indulges in a brief history of the circle and its impact on today's Brotherhood. "In 1940," he explains, "Hassan al Banna began to think of the Private Apparatus, that's called 'secret' now." He adds, "The Private Apparatus had three missions to perform. One of them was to follow the colonialists and counter them and their activities and Westernization." Created at a time when Egypt was still a monarchy under a British protectorate, the Brotherhood's apparatus engaged in various covert operations— including the assassination of key figures—against the British presence and its local supporters.

"The second aim," continues Helbawy, "is to prepare for [the] Palestine issue, and Zionists." This aim was a natural by-product of the colonial era. As tensions simmered in British Palestine and the Zionist movement was making rapid steps toward the creation of the state of Israel, the Brotherhood in neighboring Egypt saw the Palestinian cause as its own and readied itself to aid in a military confrontation—which occurred in 1948. "The third aim," concludes Helbawy, "is to protect, they call [it], the back of [the] dawa, to protect the dawa from the back." Essentially, according to Helbawy, the Secret Apparatus was tasked from its inception with the protection of the rest of the Brotherhood. Proselytism and education, the group's main activities, could function only if a muscular defense intercepted threats against them by all means possible.

But some of the members of the Secret Apparatus, Helbawy argues, "began to think in the way that Osama bin Laden was thinking, and they began to think in the way that the jihadists were thinking: they have power, they have arms, they are responsible for a big aim." "But their interpretation of Islam, the fiqh [interpretation of Islamic law]," he continues, "was not correct. Because they began to say, 'The king is unjust, the British are not good, but the Egyptians who are dealing with the British are not good also, and they need to be killed.' So that jihad was wrong, because they began to kill some people whom they believed are attached to colonialists, and they love colonialists more than Egypt, so that is why you can have some crimes."

Helbawy stresses that the role of the Secret Apparatus was originally intended to be, and for the first decades of the Brotherhood's history it remained, strictly ancillary to dawa. The Secret Apparatus's tendency to use violence and resort to tactics other than dawa was kept in check, and the "dawa current" retained control of the organization. But in his view that began to change after the turn of the century, as many of the upcoming leaders of the group belonged to the Secret Apparatus (which he interchangeably refers to as "the Qutbist current"). Helbawy argues that the Qutbist current began to control the organization after Mohammed Akef became murshid in 2004.[27]

The vicissitudes of Akef's tenure as murshid are well known to Helbawy, given his close personal relationship with Akef. Helbawy claims that in 2009 Akef had spoken to him about his intention to leave the position of murshid before completing his mandate—an event unprecedented in the Brotherhood's history—because he could no longer bear to stay in an organization that effectively had been taken over by the Qutbist current. Helbawy recalls telling his longtime friend that he should stay on, arguing that he was one of the most respected Brothers and one the few who could "bring all the Muslim Brothers together." The two men also discussed potential replacements, substitutes, and Helbawy reportedly suggested the Hamas leader Ismail Haniyeh, "because Palestine is a cause that can bring all Muslims together; not [the] Muslim Brotherhood alone but all people, Arabs and Muslims and some people from the West." In the end Akef completed his term and was replaced by Mohammed Badie in January 2010.[28]

Helbawy's view of the Egyptian Brotherhood's current leadership is dire. He believes, agreeing with various scholars, that the "Qutbist current" has gained dominance of the organization's Guidance Bureau, which in recent years has acquired significantly more power than the Shura Council.[29] This, in turn, has created major changes in the way the Brotherhood as a whole interprets its mandate and priorities. "They [the Qutbist wing] will not live their dawa mission and they will bring more catastrophe than ever on themselves and the society," he warns. "I left [the Brotherhood] because I couldn't bear to deal with this group."

One of Helbawy's biggest criticisms directed at the Brotherhood's current leadership is its obsession with a culture of excessive secrecy—arguably a legacy of their experience in the Secret Apparatus. That mind-set, he asserts, also plagues the Brotherhood in the West. Many Brotherhood members in Europe and North America deny belonging to or having even indirect affiliations with the organization. And it is not unusual for individuals or organizations with clear links to the Brotherhood to engage in aggressive legal disputes with anybody who alleges such links. Helbawy finds this behavior immoral and foolish: "I never went incognito, in Egypt or abroad. 'Are you a Muslim Brother?' 'Yes, I am a Muslim Brother.' But I am a Muslim Brotherhood [sic] who understood Islam properly, on the hands of great scholars, and they were proud of their affiliation to the Muslim Brotherhood, they never participated in something that makes them unhappy or guilty."

Helbawy argues that the reluctance of members of the Brotherhood in the West to be publicly linked with the organization is a legacy from the Middle East, where affiliation with the group was often severely punished. He finds it understandable that some of the group's pioneers in the West would harbor those same fears. But after decades in the West, Helbawy insists, that mind-set should have been shed:

> They believe it is safer for them, unfortunately. That's why I was telling the brothers, when I started the Muslim Association of Britain in 1997, I was telling them, "Are we fighting dictatorship in the West?" They say, "No." "Are we asking for freedom in the West?" They say, "No." So why still [do] we have that mentality and intellect? We have one aim, that is to, first of all to please God by spreading the word of Islam and correcting the misintroduced [sic] image of Islam and the prophet. That's all. Training our youngsters to be like that. But be good citizens in the West, not to be good thinkers for the East, I used to tell them that, but unfortunately. . . .

If Helbawy's departure from the Brotherhood shocked many, so did his support for the abrupt end of the Brotherhood government of Mohamed

Morsi and the presidency of Abdel Fattah al Sisi. In interviews, Helbawy has also used strong words to describe what happened in Rabaa al Adaweya, the Cairo square occupied in August 2013 by Morsi's supporters and cleared by the Egyptian military with deadly force:

> The leaders of the Muslim Brotherhood allied with [Egyptian terrorist organizations] Al-Jamaa Al-Islamiya, Al-Jihad, and other Salafis in Rabaa Al-Adaweya, made an alliance "to support legitimacy" and used violence. They did not accept the will of the people who went out on 30 June, who were asking for early presidential elections. . . . It was clear that the Islamists insisted to stay and blocked the roads and were preparing for a battle, and had some arms inside [the sit-in]. So the army and police had no other way. I do not agree with killing, but I once said: if wise people see a train, they will not stand in front of it. They will move. But they stood in front of the train.[30]

After the dramatic events of Rabaa, the Sisi government appointed Helbawy to be deputy chairman of the Constituent Assembly tasked with amending the constitution that the Brotherhood-dominated parliament had approved in 2012.[31] He engaged in various political initiatives aimed at bringing together prominent Egyptian figures from both Islamist and non-Islamist backgrounds. He also continued to travel around the world, giving lectures to audiences of various political stripes. Beginning in the spring of 2017, health concerns have led him to spend more time in London, where he still maintains a house.

For Helbawy, as for most members who do so, leaving the Brotherhood was not an inconsequential decision. It is debatable whether his high status and very public statements made it easier or instead made it more complex. In the early days after his resignation Helbawy claims to have received several death threats, although none that Egyptian authorities deemed specific. He was also heckled by Brotherhood supporters at various public engagements.

But for somebody like Helbawy, whose entire life was steeped in the Brotherhood, his departure also had many personal implications. His wife and many of his closest relatives are still very active members of the organization. Helbawy is reluctant to speak about family dynamics, saying simply that "my family respected my views and I respected their attitude."

Moreover, most of his social ties were inside the organization. "It is very distressing," he observes, "when you are friends with someone and next day you find that they are either talking to you in a bad way or will not respect the humanity or different views or ideas or come to discuss or want to listen."

As a senior Brother devoted to education, Helbawy had a worldwide network of students, younger Brothers who saw him as a teacher and a mentor. Their reactions to his decision varied significantly. Predictably, some stopped talking to him. "I participated in establishing Muslim Brotherhood in many countries from zero," he remarks, saddened. "So when you find that your students who you taught for ten to twenty years they are not happy with your attitude because you left the organization . . . but if the organization is diverting from the main course should I go with them? No." Others took the opposite position and left the organization as well. Most still talk to him but have privately debated his decision. Many, he claims, have expressed agreement with his criticism of the Brotherhood's current leadership but have told him he should not have left the organization, encouraging him instead to fight it from the inside.

Similar dynamics were manifest in Brotherhood circles in the West. Upon his return to London, Helbawy found that most British-based Egyptian Brothers refused to talk to him. Azzam Tamimi, a cofounder of the Muslim Association of Britain as well as a longtime prominent member of the London Islamist scene, is also "reluctant to talk" to him ("He has a temper," quips Helbawy). Many other Islamist leaders from other Middle Eastern countries, on the other hand, do interact with him. An indefatigable debater, he privately and publicly engages with them over the need to return to the basics of the Brotherhood's credo, urging them not to repeat the mistake made by the Egyptian Brotherhood in abandoning dawa for politics and power.

Despite his dramatic resignation from the group, Helbawy remains a firm believer in the goodness of the Brotherhood's message. "I can never detach myself completely from the Muslim Brotherhood, even if I wanted to. Even when I criticize [them] publicly, I'm hoping it helps reform them," he has declared. Helbawy has had grave doubts about the leadership of the group, which he accuses of having strayed from the organization's ideological and methodological roots. But he is still committed to the Islamist project outlined by al Banna. "I agree with having a nation based on Islam," he has stated, "but insofar as it respects Islam's basic values of respecting equality and human rights, providing basic necessities to your communities, and preserving the society's dignity."

Helbawy's case is unique. Even though many of his militant actions occurred outside of the West and his decision to leave the Brotherhood has mostly to do with dynamics related to Egypt, he is arguably the highest-ranking Brotherhood leader who has spent substantial time in the West to have left the organization. His resignation has also reverberated throughout the Western Brotherhood because of his role in establishing many Western Brotherhood organizations and his personal connections to many of the activists who are running them. And many Western Brothers have debated the issues that led him to resign, part of the collective and individual soul searching that has taken place since the Arab Spring.

CHAPTER IV

Ahmed Akkari

Joining the Brotherhood

Ahmed Akkari was born in Lebanon in 1978, the son of a cultured family from Tripoli's upper middle class.[1] The civil war that entangled Lebanon in the 1980s led the Akkaris to leave the country and ask for political asylum in Denmark in 1985. After a few happy years in the Scandinavian country, the Akkaris decided to return to Lebanon, thinking that the end of the war would lead to the return of the good life that had characterized the "Switzerland of the Middle East," as Lebanon was sometimes called in the 1970s. Faced with the harsh reality of continuous civil strife, Syrian occupation, and economic malaise, the Akkaris returned to Denmark after just one year, settling in a small town in Jutland, in the country's bucolic North.

Ahmed does not remember being particularly affected by splitting his childhood between two very different countries; to the contrary, he juggled the cultures well. His parents were largely secular, and he grew up without much of a connection to his faith. But when he was fourteen, a family friend began taking him to a mosque in Aalborg, the largest town in the vicinity. Ahmed found the environment at the Masjid Al-Furqaan in Aalborg's Danmarksgade appealing. "Everybody was nice and smiling," he recalls. "Nobody talked to me about politics, but just about God, the meaning of life and salvation."

Enthusiastic and intellectually gifted, Ahmed attracted the attention of Abdul Karim Amin, a Kurdish Iraqi who was a regular attendee of the mosque; he had just received asylum in Denmark and, according to Ahmed, "was affiliated to the Brotherhood." Abdul Karim began spending substantial amounts of time with Ahmed, slowly introducing him to an increasingly more activist interpretation of Islam. "It was no longer just about salvation," says Ahmed. "It was about the importance of Islam as a mission, not just as a personal belief." Riveted, Ahmed became absorbed in the Islamic literature Abdul Karim was supplying to him.

Ahmed attended Danish public high school with profit. Abdul Karim encouraged Ahmed to do well in school since, as Ahmed explains, "he thought education was important for the sake of building an Islamic society." Yet during those formative years his "identity changed gradually." He had many friends, both Muslim and Christian, but he increasingly identified with conservative Muslim values, something that also put him at odds with his family. "I was a seeking young man," Ahmed notes. That quest for knowledge and identity led Ahmed to engage with activists from various Islamist organizations that revolved around the Danmarksgade mosque. For some time, he explored the world of the Tabligh, which he described as a group of "nice people but simplistic."[2] He also connected with Salafists adhering to various strands of the movement, from those embracing the Saudi current to those with jihadist leanings. The latter reportedly tried to recruit Ahmed, who refused because of his discomfort with violence.

Ahmed's intellectual nature, along with Abdul Karim's influence, guided his quest in the direction of the Muslim Brotherhood. "He was my guru," he says of Abdul Karim, "and he guided me through the jungle of Islamist groups." Abdul Karim taught Ahmed that most other Islamist groups meant well and had been influenced by the Brotherhood but relied on incorrect and ineffective approaches. "Abdul Karim told me that dawa is peaceful," he recounts, "and that we should keep out of confrontation; jihad was right only in some cases, like Palestine, but not everywhere; the right approach is a gradualist and patient one that takes into consideration the circumstances of the place." He adds, "I loved this about the Brotherhood: it's intellectual, it's complex, it's sophisticated. But its heart is in the mission."

By 1998 Ahmed had started to regularly attend an "open circle," a study group that read "very general Islamic texts and pamphlets, with small doses of Brotherhood literature." The bookish Ahmed dove in headfirst,

devouring the texts of Mohammed Said Ramadan Al-Bouti, Faysal Mawlawi, Said Hawwa, Sayyid and his brother Mohammed Qutb, Yusuf al
Qaradawi, and various Islamist scholars from the Arab Gulf. The open
circle was not "openly Brotherhood," but it became increasingly clear to
Ahmed that the Brothers had a major intellectual influence on it and that
some people in Ahmed's orbit were Brothers. Yet the open circle, insists
Ahmed, "is not indoctrination, it's very free, you discuss democratically,
[it is] much more religion than politics, it focuses on the idea of changing
your lifestyle to mold it around what you are learning, Islam."

As his involvement in the open circle led by Abdul Karim increased,
Ahmed understood that his mentor was progressively and continuously
testing him. These small challenges were intended to test his intellect but,
even more, his obedience and loyalty. "It's about building strong, endur-
ing personalities," he explains. Ahmed also had the constant feeling of being
under evaluation, though he was never told he was. But that pressure stim-
ulated him: "It was exciting, I love competition, I wanted to pass his
exams, I want to impress Abdul Karim." After years of diligent behavior,
Ahmed was promoted from the open circles to more selective "closed circles,"
a privilege bestowed on only the best students of Abdul Karim and other
selected individuals in Denmark. In the closed circle, explains Ahmed, the
literature is more focused on Brotherhood-related authors; yet the pedagogic
approach is not "indoctrination, read, and repeat, but more indirect," with
the naqib leading an open conversation. The closed circle introduced Ahmed
to a concept that has crucial importance for the Brotherhood: silence.
"Abdul Karim told me not to speak to other people about the circles and
that it was important to protect the unit," he explains. "I started to understand that there is danger in what we did and found that extremely exciting.
I also kept it secret from my family because I learned [from senior Brothers]
that most Muslims don't understand the call [the Brotherhood's mission]."

Even though he had only some inklings of it, Ahmed was getting closer
to the inner circles of the Muslim Brotherhood's milieu in Denmark. One
night Abdul Karim told Ahmed he was taking him to an Arab cultural
evening in Aarhus, Denmark's second-largest city. Held at a local community center, the event included prayers, speeches, and a communal meal.
Ahmed understood that many of the roughly twenty attendees to the
invitation-only event were Brothers, even though he was smart enough
not to ask many questions. "But I felt the honor of being there, the sense
of exclusiveness," he explains, "like a Rotary club, if you will. I was very

excited." That evening Ahmed met, among others, two key players of the Danish Brotherhood milieu: Abu Bashar (Mohamad Al Khaled Samha), the Syrian-born imam of the Islamic Society in Denmark (Islamisk Trossamfund) in the city of Odense, and Mohammad Fouad al Barazi, a fellow Syrian based in Copenhagen. Both men would eventually play a key role in Ahmed's time inside the Brotherhood.

That evening in Aarhus was only a foray into the Brothers' world, but Ahmed's actual induction came soon thereafter, in 2002. Ahmed recounts that it took place in Barazi's Copenhagen home, as at the time the Syrian was the head of Denmark's "closed movement," as Ahmed calls the secret structure of the Brotherhood. Ahmed describes the moment as not particularly formal, even though his excitement at finally joining a group he had studied and heard so much about was uncontainable.

Life Inside the Brotherhood

While it made official his membership in the Brotherhood, the baya did not represent a major change for Ahmed. "I was already in a closed circle," he notes. "I already had access to Barazi, Abu Bashar, and other local Brotherhood leaders; it was just a natural progression." At the same time, being inducted enabled Ahmed to progressively discover more information on the Brotherhood's inner workings. He realized, for example, that there were some one hundred Brotherhood members in Denmark. Some were fairly well known as such in Muslim circles and beyond, but others— the "unsuspectables"—were not. "The movement always wanted to have people who were unknown," he explains, "who can run it if all gets exposed, people who stay behind the scenes." He also realized that some inducted Brothers who no longer involved themselves in the group's activities but had not formally left the group had their membership frozen.

The structure of the Brotherhood in Denmark became clearer to him as well. According to Ahmed, a murshid, elected by members at the national level, supervises the group's functioning in the whole country. Senior members oversee the various areas in which the organization has divided the country—Ahmed, for example, became active in the Aarhus region, as he attended university there. And a naqib is put in charge of individual usras, to which all Brothers are assigned. "The usra meets weekly, secretly, without even family members knowing what's going on" explains Ahmed, "and the usras in the same region come together once a month, and there is a meeting for the whole country once a year." The movement's women, most of them wives and daughters of the members, are involved in various supporting activities and have their own usras.

Life inside the Brotherhood allowed Ahmed to spend time focusing on what attracted him to the group in the first place: its complex ideology. Ahmed claims that the tarbiya curriculum for all Brothers had been set by Barazi, who was the regional murshid of the Danish Brotherhood milieu at the time, based on that of the Egyptian branch but with slight variations— "We don't have to follow it as closely as they do in the Arab world." He dug deeper into texts written by some of the main thinkers of the global Brotherhood movement and other Islamists, a number of whom he had already discovered while attending the open circle and some of whom were new to him: the former murshid Mustapha Mashour, the American Brotherhood thinker Taha Awlani, the Saudi clerics behind the Sahwa movement, the Lebanese cleric Fathi Yakan, the Kurdish cleric Ali al Qaradaghi, the Egyptian scholar Said Sabiq, and many others. He also translated one of Mawlawi's books and various letters by al Banna from Arabic into Danish.

These intellectual endeavors led him to immerse himself in the big questions discussed within the highest echelons of the global Muslim Brotherhood movement at the time: Is the Muslim world still in a state of *jahiliya*, or pre-Islamic ignorance, as Qutb wrote? Is democracy compatible with Islam? What should the role of the Brotherhood in the West be? Ahmed was also fascinated by debates on whether the Brotherhood should be a more open, popular movement, as Fathi Yakan advocated, or should remain highly selective and focus on recruiting a limited number of people with key qualities, as others thought.

Through reading the books, moreover, Ahmed immersed himself in the nuances of principles he saw applied in the day-to-day work of the Brotherhood milieu. He was particularly fascinated by the flexibility employed by Qaradawi in fiqh (jurisprudence), which Ahmed contrasted with the rigidity of the Salafists. According to Ahmed, "It allows you to work within the system, be flexible, work in society, and then, at the end, the truth will prevail; you are bringing about change, just with a different tactic, a more flexible approach."

While ideas were important, money, Ahmed came to soon understand, was an equally crucial part of life inside the Brotherhood. Every member, he says, had to pay a fee corresponding to 2.5 percent of his income—a percentage similar to what is customary to give as zakat, the almsgiving mandatory in Islam. The system is relatively flexible, and Brothers, argues Ahmed, are allowed to pay less or asked to pay more, depending on their financial circumstances. There is also an informal system of internal financial solidarity, particularly among members of the same usra, through which Brothers in need are helped. But he points out that the Brothers have many other funding sources, ranging from donations raised in mosques to private businesses, from funding they manage to receive from various governmental agencies for some of their endeavors to the financial support they receive from foreign countries. "There is no independent control of these flows; it's all about trust," he states. And he adds that he frequently "carried bags full of cash," without asking questions about origin and destination.

Ahmed realized that specialization was one of the Brotherhood's key features. "There are those who do dawa," he says, "those who know how to deal with politicians, and those who work money." While he never concerned himself much with the financial aspects of the organization, he is aware that others, who often occupied less visible positions, did. A case in point is the now dissolved Islamic Bank International of Denmark, which was set up in the early 1980s in Copenhagen by key Brotherhood figures as one of Europe's first banks regulated by the principles of Islamic banking. Its board included key Brotherhood activists such as Gamal Attia, the Luxembourg-based financier and Yussuf Nada's close friend; Hassan Abuelela, the late head of the Islamic Center of Stuttgart and a board member of the Islamic Society of Germany; Mahmoud Abu Saud, the U.S.-based godfather of Islamic banking (about whom more later); and various high-ranking government officials from several Arab Gulf states.[3]

Ahmed slowly came to understand the dynamics of the Brothers' transnational networks. Regarding several aspects of the Brotherhood, says Ahmed, "nobody tells you how it works—you find out in bits and pieces; only the leadership has the full picture, only the top discusses the big secrets." According to his understanding, the global movement of the Brotherhood works informally, as the Egyptian branch no longer has the same control over the others that it did before the leadership of the Egyptian murshid Umar al Tilmisani (1972–1986). During those years the Egyptian Brotherhood, struggling for its own survival because of the pressure put on it by the Egyptian regime, allowed the other branches to operate more freely, independently choosing their tactics and priorities, but "still kept together by the structure that binds them across countries."

"When it comes to Europe," argues Ahmed, "the Brotherhood has indicated the main guidelines, the general course of action in books, in seminars, and in meetings with European Brothers; but they do not control things in detail." Moreover, according to Ahmed, the branch in each region (a division that can but does not always correspond to a country) has its own structure, which replicates that of the mother group but can somewhat differ from it. The Scandinavian region, for example, was reportedly divided in two: one containing Sweden, Norway, and Finland and overseen by the Swedish Brotherhood milieu, and the other encompassing Denmark. "I had to obey the leadership of the Brotherhood in Denmark," explains Ahmed, "and only the leaders of the Danish Brotherhood milieu interacted with their peers in Sweden."

Despite these clear geographical and hierarchical divisions, he maintains, the Brothers are a transnational family, an informal milieu built on personal, organizational, financial, and ideological connections. "You travel around the world," says Ahmed, "and there is the same spirit. When you knock on the door there is common trust, help." Being an inducted Brother enables one individual to be able to count on a support network wherever he travels by simply demonstrating his membership. "Let's say I want to go fund-raise in Qatar for some project," explains Ahmed, "and one of the big leaders of my local branch supports me: he writes a letter of recommendation or makes a phone call, vouches for me, and then I go to the Gulf and have my fund-raising meetings based on that. That's how it's done." According to Ahmed, this informal network, rooted in a sense of common purpose and long-standing personal interactions, extends beyond the Arab-based Brotherhood to apply as well to its two sister movements: the South Asian Jamaat-e-Islami and the Turkish Islamist movement founded by Erbakan, which sees in Millî Görüş its main Western representative.

Ahmed's activities inside the Brotherhood were diverse, from the mandatory participation in the usra to traveling to conferences ("where I met the big stars of the Brotherhood"). But his main job, which he undertook with enormous passion and devotion, was dawa. "I didn't like the administrative part of it [of being a Brotherhood member]," he explains, "but more the message and 'the ideals.'" A skilled orator with ample knowledge of Islamic texts and an outgoing personality, Ahmed was perfect for traveling around Denmark to give speeches to Muslim communities. "There is open dawa and closed dawa: open dawa is about Islam and closed dawa is when you influence people with a Brotherhood mind-set," he says, adding, "I focused mostly on open dawa." In substance, Ahmed would deliver speeches to small and large congregations in mosques, public events, and private gatherings, introducing the audiences to a conservative interpretation of Islam but with only "a sprinkling, nothing too overt" of Brotherhood ideology.

That does not mean, Ahmed makes clear, that "the concept of recruitment [for the Brotherhood] was lost on me." "Open dawa," speaking to groups of Muslims, served the dual purpose of further introducing them to a conservative and politically aware form of Islam and, at the same time, identifying potential new members. But he admits to being better at the former ("I was a big speaker") than the latter. He recalls a fellow Danish Brother, a Tunisian named Asad, as being much better at recruiting new talent: "He studied people, always proceeded quietly, knew when to push and when not." The two figures complemented each other: while Ahmed was "the bridge between the first and the second generation," because of his perfect fluency in Danish and his upbringing in the country, Asad was better at zeroing in on and cultivating the best potential recruits attracted by Ahmed's rhetoric and charisma.

Ahmed's incessant dawa activities often brought him in contact with other Islamist groups active in Denmark. While loyal to the Brotherhood, he always appreciated various aspects of other Islamist tendencies and did not look at them with the same suspicion or sense of superiority exhibited by many of his fellow Brothers. "I preached or came in contact with many different places not associated with the Muslim Brotherhood," he explains. "This is something not many can understand. Especially in Denmark, people think it's not easy to be in contact with various groups from across the Islamist spectrum; but I did go between the Salafists, the Sufis, the traditionalists, and others, including short dialogues with some of the jihadi persons attending mosques."

He frequently interacted with Millî Görüş milieus and with the Somali variation of the Brotherhood and became close to various Danish Salafist leaders. Most prominent among them were the late Ahmed Abu Laban, a Palestinian who had settled in Copenhagen in 1983 after being expelled from both Egypt and Kuwait for his involvement in the Muslim Brotherhood and who later embraced the Sururi school of thought,[4] and Raed

Hlayhel, a Lebanese graduate of the University of Medina who had become an imam in Aarhus's most conservative mosque. Ahmed remembers his frustration at hearing the negative comments about other Islamists from Abdul Karim and the other Brotherhood elders, who would at best see individuals like Abu Laban and Hlayhel as fellow travelers with whom to occasionally partner. "In my mind they were all doing a good thing," explains Ahmed. "It was just frustrating how they [the Brothers] were competing with and shutting down the others."

Aside from this vexation, Ahmed was enthusiastically engaged in the activities of the Danish Brotherhood milieu, in which he quickly reached a mid-tier level, throughout the first years of the twenty-first century. He readily admits that his drive was motivated by what in hindsight feels to him like a naïve belief in the pure ideological nature of the Brothers, devoid of personal interests and jealousies. Yet this image of perfect Muslims, "marching together in unison for the advancement of the *ummah* and al Banna's vision" without any interest in achieving power and money for themselves individually, was shattered by several episodes that shocked Ahmed and eventually led him to leave the group.

The first took place in 2004, when a personal feud erupted between Mohammad al Barazi, then head of the Brotherhood and in whose house Ahmed had sworn baya, and the late Jehad al Farra (also known as Abu Abdel-Alim), a respected orthopedic surgeon of Syrian decent and a high-ranking member of the Danish Brotherhood.[5] Ahmed reports that the dispute arose as the Danish Brothers had managed to raise a substantial amount of funds to support a new umbrella organization they had created "to show Danish society they represent all Muslims." As this new, ambitious project was coming to fruition, claims Ahmed, the members of the Danish Brotherhood milieu were scheduled to hold their internal elections—technically elections for the "public organization," but in reality, according to Ahmed, for the Brotherhood's secret structure. Barazi, "not wanting to lose power, changed the elections' rules so that he could keep his position"—a move that upset Farra, who thought he would have won the elections by a large margin.

In response to Barazi's decision, Farra began resorting to the help of various Brothers in Denmark and throughout Europe, trying to "wrestle the leadership from Barazi." When his efforts did not come to fruition, Farra started his own organization, the Danish Islamic Council (Dansk Islamisk Råd), creating a schism within the Danish Brotherhood milieu. Most Danish Brothers reportedly sided with him, while Barazi found himself, according to Ahmed, "isolated" but technically still in charge of the Danish Brothers' main organization. To diffuse this *fitna*, the term often used to indicate strife within the Muslim community, the Danish Brotherhood decided, as Ahmed puts it, "to solve it Brotherly": that is, through an intra-Brotherhood dispute resolution process.

At first the process was informal and entailed simply a visit by senior figures of the Brotherhood from other countries, including Kamal Helbawy, who set up meetings with all relevant parties to try to bring them to an agreement.[6] Once that failed, according to Ahmed, Farra requested that a formal Brotherhood panel adjudicated the matter. To summon that panel, asserts Ahmed, Farra wrote a letter to the Federation of Islamic Organizations in Europe leadership. FIOE is the Brussels-based umbrella organization created by the Brotherhood milieus of individual European countries. The fact that FIOE was involved in sorting out internal Brotherhood members in an individual country is a claim that, if confirmed, would represent solid evidence of the organization's links to the Brotherhood, something FIOE leaders have often denied.[7]

According to Ahmed, FIOE created a three-member panel, headed by Mawlawi, that heard evidence from the parties and various witnesses and eventually made a judgment in favor of Farra. "They didn't say that [Farra's] Danish Islamic Council represented the Brotherhood. They simply stated that his organization is the one that belongs to FIOE in Denmark; but people in the milieu understand what that means." In substance, according to Ahmed, FIOE's decision to view the Danish Islamic Council as its official affiliate in Denmark made clear that Farra's organization represented the Brotherhood in the country. "From that day," he adds, "we all kept away from Barazi."

According to Ahmed, the Barazi–Farra feud led some in the Danish Brotherhood milieu to leave the organization. "It shocked me," he explains, "because I had learned [that] you should never seek power." He remained actively involved in the organization, but doubts about its true nature—or at least that of many of its members—began to form in his mind. The growth of Ahmed's negative perception of the Brotherhood was accelerated by an infamous incident that took place two years later and gave him instant global notoriety: the Danish cartoons controversy of 2006.

What months later would become the most significant foreign policy crisis in Danish history since World War II began in September 2005, when Jutland's main newspaper, *Jyllands-Posten*, published twelve cartoons depicting the prophet Muhammad. *Jyllands-Posten*'s culture editor, Flemming Rose, explained that the idea of running such cartoons came to him "in response to several incidents of self-censorship in Europe caused by widening fears and feelings of intimidation in dealing with issues related to Islam."[8] In the aftermath of the assassination of Theo van Gogh, ritually butchered in central Amsterdam by a jihadist militant who had been offended by the Dutch filmmaker's anti-Islam movie *Submission*, Rose was disturbed by several episodes in which European artists and publishers refused to display art or perform plays that could expose them to similar threats. Having learned that a Danish author writing a book on Mohammed was having problems finding illustrators, Rose contacted forty illustrators and asked them to draw cartoons on the subject, curious to see what their responses would be. Only twelve cartoonists responded. Most of the cartoons were harmless, but a few were offensive, and two depicted the Prophet negatively: one drew him with a bomb-shaped turban and another drew him as an assassin.

Their publication triggered a chain of events—in which Ahmed was one of the main catalysts—that rocked Denmark. The day that the cartoons were published, Ahmed recalls receiving phone calls from various Islamist leaders in Aarhus, the city where he lived at the time and where the headquarters of *Jyllands-Posten* are located. That very night he met with one of his closest mentors in the Brotherhood and with Raed Hlayhel, the imam of the local Salafist mosque, who seemed hell-bent on "doing something" against the newspaper. Their first action was making rounds of calls to invite Denmark's Islamist and conservative leaders to an emergency meeting, which they set in Copenhagen on October 3.

"Raed [Hlayhel] started calling Salafist organizations," recounts Ahmed, "and I called leaders of Pakistani, Turkish, and Somali organizations, the people I knew through my dawa activities." Sixteen leaders attended the meeting, which was hosted by Abu Laban, and they produced an eleven-point action plan intended to obtain an apology from *Jyllands-Posten*. To Ahmed's surprise, the one Danish Islamist milieu that responded lukewarmly to the call was his own, the Brotherhood. "Abu Bashar came as a freelancer," Ahmed says. "Barazi and Farra sent letters of support but did not attend."

For weeks, Ahmed's attempt to mobilize the leadership of the Danish Brotherhood against what he perceived as an unacceptable offense against Islam fell on deaf ears. Meanwhile, the other Islamist leaders took various actions to try to rally Danish Muslims and make their voices heard but to no avail, as *Jyllands-Posten* refused to budge and apologize. With their efforts going nowhere, the group contacted the ambassadors to Denmark of various Muslim countries to seek their assistance in convincing the Danish government to force *Jyllands-Posten* to apologize. Eleven of the diplomats, led by Egypt's ambassador Mona Omar Attia, sought a meeting with the Danish prime minister, Anders Fogh Rasmussen, to discuss the issue. Rasmussen refused. "This is a matter of principle. I won't meet with them because it is so crystal clear what principles Danish democracy is built upon that there is no reason to do so," the prime minister declared. "As prime minister, I have no power whatsoever to limit the press—nor do I want such a power."[9]

The refusal by *Jyllands-Posten* and the Danish government to apologize or even engage in a conversation with the group led by Abu Laban has been the subject of much debate in Denmark. Some have argued that it was a strategic mistake, as a much broader controversy could have been avoided by simply negotiating with them and issuing an apology. But while the newspaper was determined not to cave in on the right to freedom of expression and satire—the very reason the cartoons had been published in the first place—the Danish government was motivated to take a hardline stance in large part by its refusal to acknowledge a group of self-appointed leaders with well-known extremist tendencies as the legitimate representatives of the Danish Muslim community. And, according to Ahmed, it was this very point that infuriated the men. "It became a matter of principle," he explains. "You don't want to acknowledge my role as leader of the Muslim community? Then I'll keep going."

By the end of November Abu Laban's group decided that the only way forward was, in his words, to "internationalize this issue so that the Danish government would realize that the cartoons were not only insulting to Muslims in Denmark but also to Muslims worldwide."[10] According to Ahmed, Hlayhel began calling on his international connections in the Salafist movement, starting with celebrities like the Saudi scholar Salman al Awda. Various ambassadors to Denmark from Muslim countries mobilized their governments. As a result, the Organization of Islamic Cooperation (OIC) held an extraordinary session on December 7–8 to condemn the publication of the cartoons, which led to extensive coverage of the issue throughout the Muslim world. Yet Danish Brotherhood leaders stayed on the sidelines while Abu Laban's group took these actions. Ahmed, who had recently moved to Copenhagen and was teaching at a school linked to the organization, was the liaison between the two, serving as Abu Laban's group media spokesperson and keeping the Brothers informed about relevant developments. But to Ahmed's frustration, the elder Brothers refused to play any active role.

Abu Laban's "internationalization strategy" included sending delegations of Danish Muslims to the Middle East to mobilize support for their cause. The first delegation, which included Abu Bashar and the Danish leader of Millî Görüş, traveled to Egypt. It was during this trip that, infamously, the delegation showed its audience a booklet purportedly containing the cartoons that included additional and significantly more offensive images of the prophet Mohammed that had never appeared in *Jyllands-Posten*—an action that, whether taken because of sloppiness, as the Muslim leaders claimed, or with an intent to deceive, as many Danes believed, caused an uproar in Denmark.

Aside from the booklet controversy, the trip to Egypt was important because it triggered the interest of the Mubarak regime. In early December Egypt was holding parliamentary elections; according to Ahmed, the regime, feeling electoral pressure from the Muslim Brotherhood, tried to outdo the group on its own turf by "portraying itself as defenders of the honor of the Prophet and of Muslims." In what he views as an opportunistic move dictated purely by domestic politics, the Egyptian government began an aggressive messaging campaign against the cartoons in order to present itself as pious and chip away conservative support of the Brotherhood.

It was at that point, Ahmed argues, that both the global Muslim Brotherhood network and its Danish milieu decided to get actively involved. Sensing that the controversy was escalating and assessing that staying out of it would have caused them to cede ground to competing Muslim and Islamist leaders both within and outside of Denmark, they began to participate in the anticartoon activities. "Farra," explains Ahmed, "who had barely come to our [Abu Laban's group's] meetings, all of a sudden showed up all the time." In hindsight, Ahmed today describes this attitude as "typical Brotherhood modus operandi: stay behind, see where it goes." It is an approach that he compares to that of the leadership of the Egyptian Brotherhood in the early days of the Arab Spring, when the appeals of the young Brothers to join the antiregime protests in Tahrir Square were not heeded by the more risk-averse and calculating elder generation. Only when it became apparent that the anti-Mubarak protests were likely to achieve their goal of overthrowing the regime did the Brotherhood leadership sanction the group's involvement in them.[11]

But to Ahmed's surprise, the Brothers' involvement in the cartoon crisis was not just belated but (in his view) halfhearted if not outright begrudging. When a second delegation of Danish Muslims left for Lebanon and Syria, Farra reportedly put Ahmed, who this time was part of the group, in touch with Mawlawi, the head of the Lebanese Brotherhood. The late Mawlawi was "the way to get to Qaradawi and to mobilize the entire global network of the Brotherhood," explains Ahmed. Through his interactions with Mawlawi and other Brotherhood leaders in both the Middle East and Denmark, it became clear to Ahmed that the group's leadership "was not 'let's get angry about the Prophet' but rather 'what can we gain from this situation?'"

In effect, Ahmed felt that the leadership of the global Muslim Brotherhood had initially made a calculation that they would have benefited more by not raising a major fuss about the cartoons, as they were engaged in various conversations with Western interlocutors and felt the need to display an image of moderation: their priority was, as Ahmed puts it, on "not disturbing the political waters in Europe for the movement." Yet once it became clear that various actors in the Muslim world, from Salafists to secularists, had seized on the crisis, the Brothers felt outflanked and realized they could no longer "sit it out."

Under pressure, by late January the Brotherhood finally came out with an aggressive campaign against Denmark. Most famously, Qaradawi and the International Union for Muslim Scholars (IUMS), the Brotherhood-dominated jurisprudential body he presides over, called for a worldwide "Day of Anger." A statement from IUMS read: "Let us make Friday, February 3, a day for worldwide Muslim protests over the insulting campaigns against Allah and His Prophet Muhammad (PBUH), all messengers and religious sanctities. Let all Muslim scholars and preachers in all mosques make their sermons focus on the issue."[12]

Many Muslims throughout the world heeded the call. During the first days of February, hundreds of protests took place in many Muslim-majority countries and in the West. Many of them, often organized by local regimes or opposition movements and intertwined with larger political issues, turned violent—it is estimated that some two hundred people died worldwide.[13] Danish embassies (and, in some cases, those of other Western countries) were attacked in a number of countries. Al Qaeda and other jihadist groups began issuing threats against Denmark. The fact that the placid Scandinavian country was suddenly at the center of a global political storm due to cartoons published six months earlier by a privately owned newspaper is a testament to the instrumentalization and mobilization powers of various actors in the Middle East, certainly including the Muslim Brotherhood.

The Day of Anger was followed in March by a large conference held in Bahrain, where some of the most prominent religious leaders of the Muslim world discussed the next steps in the controversy and, more broadly, the issue of blasphemy and insults toward Islam. Ahmed, like the other leaders who had sparked the controversy in Denmark, attended the event. "It was held in a luxurious hotel, Gulf-style," he reminisces, "and all the big leaders of the Islamic movement were there: Qaradawi, Mawlawi, [Sudanese Brotherhood leader] Issam al Bashir, [prominent Saudi Salafist scholar] Aid al Qarni, all the others."

Ahmed should have felt proud to see what he had achieved. A campaign that started with a conversation between him and a handful of local Muslim leaders in a small apartment in Aarhus had triggered a worldwide campaign, and he was now rubbing elbows with the "stars of the Islamic movement," the people whose books and sermons he had devoured and translated for years. Yet his feelings were the opposite. "I saw Mawlawi sitting on a golden chair and I approached him," he recalls. "He asked me, in a sarcastic tone: 'Are you satisfied now?' It was clear that he was annoyed."

Ahmed argues that it became evident to him that the leaders of the global Muslim Brotherhood had only reluctantly embraced the cartoon-related outrage, which they deemed to be, in Brotherhood parlance, an "untimely action." "Untimely actions," explains Ahmed, "are those that the Brothers argue the jihadists often fall prey to because of their constant haste but that are ultimately counterproductive." Mobilizing against the cartoons was a necessary action for the Brothers, as they could not afford to be outflanked, but it was untimely. "But there was no genuine outrage, nothing of the rage I genuinely felt at seeing the Prophet made fun of," according to Ahmed. "It was just political calculation."

"It was there," continues Ahmed, "that something started crashing inside me." He says, "In Bahrain, I saw politicians in clerics' clothing, a lot of backstabbing, of grandstanding, personal jealousies. My picture of Islamic unity collapsed. All in that superfancy hotel and speaking about poor people. Lots of hypocrisy. I'm relatively naïve and a believer in the cause, and there I saw people who really liked to be powerful and politicians. It also exposed me to the Machiavellian political thinking of the Brotherhood." This experience led Ahmed to ask himself questions about his own role: "Am I part of a political organization hidden in religious clothes? Am I steering Muslims in the wrong direction?"

Disturbed by these questions, he returned to Denmark. As he pondered his past actions and future with the Brotherhood, he saw that his contract with the Brotherhood-affiliated school in Copenhagen in which he was teaching had been rescinded. Jobless, he took his severance pay and decided to spend some time in his native Lebanon to reflect. "I kept in contact with some Brothers in Lebanon," he recounts, "but I was jaded; I no longer had much interest in being part of the movement."

Leaving the Brotherhood

The slow process of introspection and of detachment from the Brotherhood culminated in 2010, when Ahmed formally disengaged from the organization. "I resigned by letter, which I hand-delivered to a leader of the movement in the north [of Lebanon] and to a man I respected a lot, sheikh Mawlawi," says Ahmed. Ahmed had met Mawlawi on other occasions, including in Bahrain, where he was taken aback by his "Are you satisfied now?" comment. Despite that incident, which had revealed to Ahmed the Brotherhood's "Machiavellian politics," he admired (and still today admires) the late Mawlawi both as a scholar and as a man. "I told him about my frustrations," explains Ahmed, "and he responded in a good way. He was a good man."

It is noteworthy that Ahmed resigned from the Brotherhood in Lebanon. Even though he was of Lebanese descent, he had grown up and joined the Brotherhood in Denmark. His entire experience within the Brotherhood—his baya, his usra, his dawa—had taken place exclusively in Denmark, with no connection to Lebanon. Yet when he wanted to "have my name deleted from the system," Ahmed, finding himself temporarily living in Lebanon, could do so there, suggesting a high level of interconnectivity between branches of the Brotherhood worldwide. While it might be true that each branch operates with considerable independence, the ability of an individual to leave the organization that he has joined in one country by communicating his resignation to the branch of another country indicates how the movement operates as one on many issues. And that seems to apply not just on the ideological but also on the operational level, down to the bureaucratic nitty-gritty, such as holding a register of individual memberships.

Ahmed felt liberated upon resigning from the group, but the period that followed was one of intense personal turmoil. While some Brothers tried to persuade him to rejoin the group, even suggesting he could hold more senior positions inside it, others went after him, maligning and ostracizing him. It is no coincidence that Ahmed and his wife divorced during that time. Part of his existential crisis involved a deep rethinking of his religious commitment. At first, leaving the Brotherhood did not affect his piety, and he remained a committed and practicing Muslim. But gradually that changed as well. "I began reading about philosophy, seeing Islam in a different way," he explains, "less dogmatic, more humanistic, putting things in a different perspective." He slowly became less observant and vividly remembers the moment he decided to break from orthodoxy: one day in Tripoli, Lebanon, he ordered a milkshake in the middle of the day during Friday prayer. He calls that moment "my quiet revolution."

In deep need of time to reflect about his life, Ahmed made another dramatic decision. Holding a master's degree in education, he applied for and obtained a teaching position in Narsaq, a town of 1,500 people in the southern part of Greenland. Reachable only by boats zigzagging around icebergs year-round and surrounded by the unforgiving yet beautiful arctic landscape, Narsaq is the definition of remote. Ahmed found it the perfect place to be at that juncture of his life. He took up various education-related projects with the local municipality and quickly became beloved by the small and hospitable local community. "Here you quickly become part of the local," he explains, "being appreciated. I also feel a sense of duty and giving back some good."

The ample downtime granted to him by life in quiet Narsaq (and, later, Qaqortoq, the slightly larger Greenlandic town to which he moved in 2015) enabled Ahmed to dedicate himself to his lifelong passion: devouring books. While from his teen years onward he had read almost exclusively books on Islam written by Islamists, he now read works by liberal Muslim authors, ancient Greek and Western philosophers, contemporary politicians, and, "in a gesture of utmost rebellion," Marvel comics.

These readings led him to dovetail his own experience with broader issues related to Islam, politics, personal leadership, immigration in the

West, and the future of democratic societies. "I began reflecting about how I got into Islamism," he explains, "and about how people are influenced by charismatic people, take up the orders, and then perhaps never look back. Al Banna's words, life, and tragic death made a huge impact on me, and he seemed fatherly and wholeheartedly dedicated to his cause." "I like clever leaders," continues Ahmed, "who use it [their charisma and ideas] for the benefit of others. These leaders may have of the best of intentions, like the Communist forefathers Marx or Engels had a vision of changing oppression, but I became aware to look for the structure and the ideology they left behind."

The idea of charismatic leaders swaying naïve followers is one that recurs frequently in Ahmed's mind, as he sees himself as having been duped by the Brothers when he was a well-meaning adolescent intending to work for his religion:

> Most Muslims have no idea what's going on [the activities or even the existence of the Brotherhood] and only see Allah and the mosques as the way to Mohammed's grace. And here come the Brothers, a small number [of people] trying to ride the saddle of representation of Muslims. I hate that very much, and today I understand the hidden mechanism of power (simply the elite Machiavellianism as in any other society) the Brotherhood leaders are working to achieve. So much more reason for disgust, using God to obtain power for themselves. Underneath all that there is the deception of the many Muslims who really believe in a better state under the Islamic rule—exactly like Stalinism twisted communism and Nazism twisted nationalism. The Brothers do not depend on numbers but on resourceful members and on thought. As proved by my experience during the cartoon crisis, they (we at that time) used the Muslim masses.

Ahmed has come to see the Brothers, in their quest for power, as using religion to manipulate fellow Muslims. "I tell you so, because it is what I felt at the time, and what I was pursuing," he says, emphatically. "It gives such an enormous strength and determination, that no prison or deprivation can shake." That "lust for power" is both collective and individual. As a group, the Brotherhood seeks power for itself, and is willing to employ all tools and bend all rules, including interpreting Islamic law in extremely flexible ways, to obtain it. But, Ahmed argues, the same also applies to individual Brothers. In his view, most senior Brothers have outsized personal ambitions and thirst for power, not necessarily wishing for money but seeking to be showered with respect and able to lead large cadres at will. He decries the cult of personality that exists within the movement, as senior figures are revered as virtually untouchable and infallible.

In their quest for power, Ahmed argues, the Brothers have been extremely clever at theorizing and then implementing a series of principles on the ground. While some are common to all branches worldwide, others apply specifically to the West and the particular condition of being a minority in non-Muslim-majority societies. Foremost among them are the principles of gradualism and patience. The Brothers, Ahmed claims, perceive themselves as the forefathers of all Islamist movements and look down on the others as "naïve hotheads." They perceive themselves as pursuing a goal that is similar to that of other Islamists but seek to avoid confrontation while doing so, and in some cases pursue cooperation with others while aiming to "steer clear of their aggressive ways because they will make them run into trouble."

Ahmed maintains that the Brothers have long understood, particularly after having suffered crushing repression in Egypt and Syria, that violence is a tool to be used only when necessary and that the approach used by jihadist groups is "understandable, but naïve and ultimately losing." It is an argument that he sees reiterated throughout Brotherhood's literature.[14] Indeed, among the many sources confirming this position, particularly important because of their authoritativeness and completeness of analysis, are the writings of Yusuf al Qaradawi. His 1987 book, translated into English by the International Institute of Islamic Thought (IIIT) as *Islamic Awakening Between Rejection and Extremism*, has often been touted as a seminal text that proves the Brotherhood's moderation.[15] Indeed, extensive sections of the book are devoted to the condemnation of religious extremism and violence, phenomena that, according to Qaradawi, plague some of today's Muslim youth. Qaradawi criticizes young Muslims for being too liberal with the practice of *takfir* (declaring fellow Muslims to be unbelievers) and for their excessive dogmatism, arguing that moderation, tolerance, and flexibility are crucial features for good Muslims to possess.

Yet in other sections, Qaradawi has softer words for the "extremist youth," arguing that they have "good intentions and sincerity" toward Allah. The blame for their violent actions has to be found elsewhere. "What we actually need," states the cleric, "is the unflinching courage to admit that our youth have been forced to what we call 'religious extremism' through our own misdeeds." According to Qaradawi, the "misdeed" that leads young Muslims to violence is the older generation's inability to establish an Islamic state. Those who use violence have good souls, and they are aiming for the right goals. Their only mistake, caused by their youth, is that of being too impatient and choosing the wrong tactics. Had the older generation established an Islamic state, no such problem would exist. And while the movement has its faults, the blame for such failures ultimately lies with a foreign conspiracy. "The problem can basically be attributed to the imposition on Muslim societies of secularism—an alien trend which is at odds with all that is Islamic," argues Qaradawi. He states that "contemporary crusaders" have infiltrated the Muslim world to spread Marxism and secularism in order to prevent the spread of Islamic ideals and keep Muslims subjugated. "Muslim youth are also aware that all of these negative attitudes towards Islamic causes—locally and internationally—are initiated by foreign forces, and carried out by some Muslim rulers who act as mere puppets manipulated by Zionist, Christian, or atheist powers."[16]

While in *Islamic Awakening* Qaradawi provides a veiled justification for violence, in his book *Priorities of the Islamic Movement in the Coming Phase* (2000) he is more explicit about the purely tactical nature of his rejection of violence against the West and secular Muslim rulers.[17] Here Qaradawi criticizes Sayyid Qutb and other jihadist theorists who seek to violently confront those who oppose the creation of an Islamic state and, more generally, the Islamic movement. But Qaradawi's criticism is based on the argument not that the Qutbist approach is un-Islamic but rather that it is ineffective. "How can we talk of launching offensives to subject the whole world to our Message," he asks, "when the only weapons we can muster are those given us by them [those against whom we want to launch our offensive jihad] and when the only arms we can carry are those they agree to sell us?"[18]

Qaradawi rejects violent confrontation not because it is wrong, immoral, or contrary to his interpretation of Islamic texts but simply because at present it will not get the movement anywhere. Indeed, it is a moral duty in places where Muslims are under direct attack, according to Qaradawi's interpretation of events, such as in Palestine, Kashmir, and Iraq. Here his endorsement of jihad is open and constant, urging fellow Muslims all over the world to aid their coreligionists. In other places, such as nations with secular Muslim rulers, jihad is ineffective and gives to powerful foreign forces an excuse to intervene. The Islamic movement, argues Qaradawi, should be more strategic and forgo the use of violence against secular Muslims rulers and the West until its strength matches that of its enemies.

The principles of gradualism, patience, and self-restraint apply not just to violence but to every course of action. "The Brothers don't say: 'Now we change Denmark!,'" explains Ahmed. "Rather, they work on small goals: building a school, making a connection with a political party, getting the right law passed. You strengthen the Islamic identity, build your movement, infiltrate the system, and do all things that give you influence: that eventually brings change. But all in due course, with time and patience."

Another feature of the Western Brothers' brand of activism that Ahmed finds particularly important is their skill at leveraging external resources to compensate for the limited human capital available to them. In all Western countries, the local Brotherhood milieu has outsized ambitions but can count on only a small number of inducted members (in Denmark, as noted above, around one hundred by Ahmed's count). "But the Brothers are great free riders," he says, "very capable of using people who are simply motivated by religious fervor, exploiting them to achieve their own goals." In agreement with other former members, Ahmed argues that the Brothers have a remarkable ability to find all sorts of fellow travelers who help them pursue their goals, thereby enabling them to operate on a much larger scale than their small membership numbers would otherwise permit.

The flexible nature of the Brotherhood is epitomized, according to Ahmed, by its ability to redefine Muslims', Islam's, and its own presence in the non-Muslim-majority countries of the West. "The Brothers," he claims, "see the West as a special dawa region, unlike the oriental, with its own conditions and challenges, and thus, the adaptation is necessary." Yet, Ahmed argues, this flexibility in approach and in interpretation of sharia, which many observers praise as a sign of moderation, simply indicates pragmatism and levelheadedness in the pursuit of goals that are hardly moderate. He sees the long-term relationship with the West as the quintessential example of this dynamic. "Within Brotherhood circles," he explains, "the hadith that forecasts the fall of Rome, claiming that the city will fall at the shouts of *Allahu akbar*, is quoted all the time; but what is also said [in the hadith] is that Rome will fall from within, without spilling one drop of blood. The lesson we [Brothers] used to take from it is that that's the vision, that the West will fall from within, will be tipped the democratic way, when Muslims will be strong enough, big enough, then people will understand that Islam is the truth and Rome will be Islamic." Ahmed argues that the Brothers constantly use and interpret in terms of civilizational clash readings from various Islamic texts (for example, the Quran's sura al Rum) that speak about Rome and Christianity, using them to reinforce their us-versus-them narrative.

While the Brothers use this "civilizational interpretation" of selected Islamic texts as a general framework to support their belief that they will ultimately conquer the West—an objective that they believe will be achieved because it has been promised by God—they also elaborate more mundane analyses on how that goal will be achieved. Violence, argues Ahmed, is never discussed as a tactic. Rather, the "conquest" the Brothers foresee entails a combination of various factors: a gradual infiltration of Western political establishments; a steady surge of the Muslim population, which the Brothers envision adopting their interpretation of Islam; and a progressive loss of faith of European population in the effectiveness of their current forms of governments and societal models.

Ahmed argues that the Brothers believe that this process might take centuries but will eventually succeed. And indeed there is ample evidence of the concept of "conquest" of the West by Islam in Brotherhood literature and in statements from its leaders. In 2004, for example, the then Egyptian Brotherhood murshid Mohammed Akef declared his "complete faith that Islam will invade Europe and America, because Islam has logic and a mission." He added, "Europeans and the Americans will come into the bosom of Islam out of conviction."[19] Qaradawi has repeatedly expressed the same view. In a 1995 speech at a conference in Toledo, Ohio, he stated: "We will conquer Europe, we will conquer America, not through the sword but through dawa."[20] And in a fatwa posted on *Islamonline.net* in 2002 he reiterated the claim. "Islam will return to Europe as a conqueror and victor, after being expelled from it twice," Qaradawi asserted. "I maintain that the conquest this time will not be by the sword but by preaching and ideology."[21]

These are hardly one-off comments, taken out of context. To the contrary, one can find extensive treatises, albeit many of them dating back some twenty or thirty years, written by prominent Brothers in the East and the West that outline methods, challenges, and the final outcome of this process.[22] Many Brothers and some of those who hold a positive opinion of them argue that these positions are not representative of the current thinking among Western Brothers. In doing so they rely on the many statements in which Western Brothers have expressed their desire to live harmoniously with people of other faiths and have limited their aims to maintaining the Islamic identity of Western Muslims. Pessimists argue that, to the contrary, they reveal the genuine long-term aims of the movement.[23]

Understanding that such discourses can make many Westerners uncomfortable and that loudly enunciating their long-term hopes would lead to the unnecessary scrutiny and confrontations they seek to avoid, the Western Brothers work on implementing their short- and midterm goals. "If the ideal Islamic society remains an objective that most members recognize can never be implemented in Europe," writes Brigitte Maréchal, "others still feel confident that their efforts will bear fruit: they are betting on the demographic rate of increase of the number of Muslims, and on the re-spiritualization of Islam in Europe, in hoping that their ambitions will be realized in a more or less distant future."[24] Members of a quintessentially pragmatic movement, the Western Brothers see no point in attracting undesired attention by publicly expressing a vision whose attainment, even in the most optimistic of views, lies far in the future. But in the Western Brothers' internal discourse the idea that Islam will become dominant, not through an arcane conspiracy or violence but rather with time and patient work that entails dawa and cozying up to Western elites, is a constant.

Ahmed claims that the Brothers perceive the real Achilles' heel of the West—the weakness that will eventually lead to its downfall—to be its "materialistic nature, its willingness to negotiate on everything, including its foundational values, based on interest." He notes that, as usual, the Brothers use religious references to demonstrate this point. They often refer, for example, to the claim that Muslim armies managed to conquer Christian Constantinople in 1453 by bribing some guards who left the city's gates unlocked for them. "To us [Brothers]," says Ahmed, "it was a sign that we can bend the will of the West by offering some of them short-term enticements." Ahmed argues that discussions about the ways in which Western leaders or entire societies can be bought off or tricked in order to achieve tactical victories that are stepping-stones toward achieving the movement's long-term goal of peaceful conquest occupy a substantial amount of the Brothers' time.

"We understood that the West is short-sighted," Ahmed elaborates, "and that it basically wants three things from us: money, votes, and not being Bin Laden." He argues that the Brothers believe that Western policy makers and elites are willing to turn a blind eye toward and even support the Brother-hood's activities in the West as long as the group provides them with finan-cial or electoral advantages and does not engage in violence ("not being Bin Laden") or, even better, makes gestures aimed at preventing jihadist violence. It is a quid pro quo that provides mutual advantages in the short term but that, argues Ahmed, the Brothers embrace with aims whose gen-erational time frame is completely lost on their Western partners.

According to Ahmed, electoral incentives are the main weapons the Western Brothers use to attract Western policy makers to enter into part-nerships with them. "The Brothers love to show politicians that they speak in front of five hundred men in a mosque," he says, "and those are five hundred votes which are in turn multiplied for all their family members; politicians know that and the outreach is constant." Similarly, the Brothers' proximity to various wealthy governments or investors in various Muslim-majority countries represents a major attraction for Western governments, policy makers, journalists, academic institutions, and other actors, who are willing to work with the Brothers in order to receive financial benefits from their sponsors.

Third in Ahmed's list of arrows in the Brothers' quiver to attract West-ern partners is the movement's ability to exploit the West's fear of jihadist terrorism and portray itself as the antidote to violent radicalization. "I hate how they [the Brothers] managed to convince authorities, including intel-ligence agencies, to use them to control jihadists," says Ahmed. "By doing so you empower a very resourceful group, and once you empower them it's difficult to take that power back."

Ahmed's description suggests that the Brothers seek to benefit from what in social movement theory is known as "positive radical flank effect"—the improvement in bargaining position enjoyed by more moderate wings of a political movement when a more radical fringe emerges.[25] In the case of Islamism, the positive radical flank effect would explain why the emer-gence of jihadist radicalization has led Western governments to see the Brothers more as more benign actors and even flirt with the idea of estab-lishing forms of partnership with them. The Western Brothers have seized this unprecedented opportunity by presenting themselves as sworn ene-mies of the jihadists and loyal partners of the state in stemming violent extremism. But according to critics like Ahmed and many others, the Brothers' real aim is to use the financial support and political legitimacy obtained by convincing Western governments that they are the moderate alternative simply to further their own agenda.

Critics of this approach argue that even assuming that engagement with the Brothers can produce some positive short-term results against jihadists, in the long term the movement's goals are incompatible with those of the state. But a partnership with them for short-term security needs risks helping the Brothers expand their reach well beyond what they might have been able to achieve on their own in spreading their views to the larger Muslim community. In the words of Alain Chouet, the former head of the General Directorate for External Security (Direction générale de la sécurité extérieure, DGSE), the now dissolved French external intelligence agency: "Al-Qaeda is only a brief episode and an expedient instrument in the century-old existence of the Muslim Brotherhood. The true danger is in the expansion of the Brotherhood, an increase in its audience. The wolf knows how to disguise itself as a sheep."[26]

As he describes these dynamics, Ahmed bemoans the "naïveté of well-meaning Westerners" and shows extreme frustration with the West's "inability to understand the threat." Yet, since leaving the Brotherhood, he has become enamored with the traditions of Western philosophy and political culture. "During these years of self-imposed exile in Greenland," he explains, "I have immersed myself in the work of Western philosophers and have become inspired by the humanist thinking of the Christian world." He devoured Spinoza, John Stuart Mill ("I cherish his point that there is no value in having freedom of ideas if you cannot express them," says Ahmed, referring to the cartoon saga), Montesquieu, and many others.

He is particularly fond of Karl Popper's concept of the Open Society. "The whole point of an Open Society," he observes, "is that it learns from its mistakes and tries to be better, never trying to live in perfection since that is a state of utopia not possible to reach. Europe learns and develops through critiques and free minds, not by fear and tyrannical control with the minds. This is why I believe in the European spirit." The concepts of change and self-improvement Ahmed found in Popper's work were the final triggers that made him change his worldview and life. "The Open Society taught me the ability to change, give space to development. Had it not been for this understanding, I would never have taken the step to change. My belief in the European spirit gave me the strength to change."

Ahmed has been very public about his personal journey. In 2014 he published a book (in Danish), *My Farewell to Islamism: The Muhammad Crisis, the Double Game, and the Fight Against Denmark*, that recounts his story. In 2018 he published another, more introspective book, *The Courage to Doubt*.[27] In it, he recounts how Western philosophy inspired him to leave Islamism and change his worldview. "It is the story of being wrong and trying to give a better contribution and how to have the courage to doubt and dare to broaden one's perspective," he explains. "Above all, it is a story of belief in the Open Society."

Ahmed has accompanied these publishing activities—despite the logistical difficulties that come with being based in a village in Greenland—with frequent media appearances, making him a household name in Denmark. His aim is to use this profile to contribute to what he believes is a necessary development: separating faith and politics in the mind of Muslims. "My dream," he says, well aware of the difficulty of the task, "is to create a counterculture in the Muslim world, one that challenges authority and dogma and democratizes religion . . . [to] create a Kierkegaard-inspired movement in the Islamic world, so that it becomes a personal approach to religion, not one based on authority. And I would like Muslims to accept Voltaire's principle that it is necessary to protect the values of people who think differently from them and that only secular societies are capable of having people with different views live together."

"My issue is not with Islam or Muslims," he continues. "They are hostages of a political game played by Islamists. I wish they understood that it is wrong to combine politics with religion, it's an unhealthy mixture engineered by people seeking political power for themselves." Ahmed, in fact, argues that most Muslims are "unaware of the political movements in their midst." He points out, "It is difficult also for Muslims to spot a Muslim Brother. I was a Brother and nobody knew that; I was just a preacher to them and they loved me. I wish Muslims understood the mechanisms of power behind this, how Islamism is all about political power, not religion, not personal salvation."

Expanding on these thoughts, Ahmed maintains that the Brothers constitute the most insidious threat to the development of cohesive, multicultural societies in the West. "Everybody is always focused on the jihadists," he argues, "but the Brothers are more dangerous in the long term; they undermine integration, they have a sophisticated ability to teach Western Muslims that they don't belong in Western society and that they are better than the others. It is the recipe for disaster in the long run." Ahmed goes so far as to draw parallels between the Brothers and the Lebanese civil war he lived through: "The way things are going, I would not be surprised if one day, in response to Islamism, the right wing will militarize to defend Europe; it is the natural progression of the culture of us versus them the Brothers are spreading among Western Muslims."

Driven by these fears, Ahmed devotes his energy to warning about the threat posed by Islamists, and by the Brothers in particular. "It is not a personal vendetta; I don't hate anybody in the Brotherhood personally," he says. But he feels that it is his duty to "make a difference and prevent Islamists from gaining further influence." Ahmed often highlights how Denmark has always treated him fairly, welcoming him both as a refugee and, most remarkably, after his actions triggering the cartoon controversy. For this reason, he feels that he has to repay this behavior by helping the country. He argues that former Islamists like him should play a pivotal role in this effort: "We are the first generation of Western-raised Islamists, we understand these dynamics better than anybody else. We can make a difference."

Unrelenting and passionate, Ahmed is driven by what he terms his "idealistic foolishness" in his effort to raise awareness about Islamism. At times he despairs about the West's ability to overcome this challenge, worrying about its own moral relativism. "Europeans no longer look at ideas," he says, "they just think that everything is about material goods and they can't conceive that other people are moved by an ideology," he explains. Nonetheless, Ahmed remains optimistic: "Today, I clearly see Europe, despite its deficiencies, as a place for the world to look up to; as said in old days: *Ut Roma cadit, sic omnis terra* [As Rome falls, so does the whole world]."

CHAPTER V

Pierre Durrani

Joining the Brotherhood

Pierre Durrani was born in Stockholm on January 20, 1972.[1] His fair skin and piercing blue eyes hide the Pakistani ancestry displayed in his last name. His father was born in Lahore in 1942, when the city was still part of colonial India and the state of Pakistan was still only a political project that would be realized five years later. Durrani's father's lineage is complex and reflects the melting pot that is Pakistan, a mixture that has always fascinated Pierre: Pashtun and Kashmiris, rich and poor, ordinary people and famous Sufi saints.

His father grew up in a poor family and had hardly any formal schooling. Nonetheless, he was, according to Pierre, a man "with high cognitive abilities, who could compensate for his lack of formal education" with his personality and intelligence. He also had an adventurous nature. Barely twenty, after seeing postcards of Sweden shown to him by a Swedish missionary couple in Lahore, he decided to make his way to the Scandinavian country. On his own, he hiked throughout the Middle East and Turkey with just a rucksack, spent some time working odd jobs in Switzerland and Germany, and eventually, by 1964, made his way to Stockholm.

At the time Sweden was still a very homogeneous country; immigration, mostly from Italy, Turkey, and the former Yugoslavia, had only recently begun. Charismatic and entrepreneurial, the "kind of guy who could easily read people and pull their strings," Pierre's father immediately found success in his new country. He worked for Swedish state television as a photographer and opened his own shop, Pakistanska (The Pakistani), which mostly sold Indian-style clothes to hippies. In 1968 he met Pierre's mother at a party. Eighteen and recently arrived in Stockholm, Gunilla was descended from a line of hardworking farmers, a member of a deeply conservative and religious family from the north of Sweden. She immediately fell in love with the charm and exoticism of Pierre's father, and the two soon married.

The couple had three children, a son (Pierre) and two daughters. They lived in the relatively affluent Kungsholmen area of Stockholm, but by the time Pierre was eight, they were divorced. Pierre's feelings toward his father, who has recently passed away, are strong but mixed. His charm and magnetic personality made him extremely popular and successful. But he also had "a dark side," tended to manipulate people, and, according to Pierre, had sociopathic tendencies and undiagnosed ADHD. Moreover, he was prone to violent outbursts—which was one of the main reasons for the divorce, according to Pierre.

After divorcing, both parents soon remarried and Pierre divided his time between them. During the week he lived with his mother and his stepfather; over the weekend he would crash at his father's shop or apartment. Pierre describes those years as difficult, particularly as he entered adolescence. He had a bad relationship with his stepfather, whom he describes as racist and closed-minded. The arguments soon turned into fistfights, and at seventeen Pierre left his mother's home. He became closer to his father, who found him an apartment near his. He "surfed through school" without studying much and became active in Stockholm's thriving punk/anarchist/alternative scene. He participated in violent protests and occupations, getting arrested once but avoiding prison because he was a minor.

"Looking back at my life now at forty-six, it was, I guess, my way of coping with internal problems, of finding my own tribe," he explains, bringing up a concept—the search for identity—that would recur often in his life. "I was quite depressed and even had suicidal thoughts, even though I never acted on them." The anarchist scene provided him with that sense of belonging for which he was desperately searching, a tribe with its own narrative and rituals that enabled him to feel part of something.

In 1990 Pierre's father, concerned about his son's physical and psychological well-being, decided to take him to Pakistan. Pierre had visited his father's country of birth on several previous occasions, but now, for the first time, he was to spend an extended amount of time there in order to get away from the demons that were haunting him back in Sweden. It was, as Pierre put it, a "culture shock." He had grown up straddling his parents' two cultures. After the divorce his mother had become a practicing Pentecostal, and until the age of sixteen Pierre had gone to Sunday school. His summer holidays were spent at his maternal grandparents' farm, immersed in "picture-perfect" Swedish nature and traditions. At the same time, he had been exposed to Islam. His father was not particularly devout but still considered Islam an important part of his life and identity. Pierre had celebrated 'Eid and other Islamic festivals, which his father saw as cultural markers. But being in Pakistan, surrounded only by Muslims, was a completely different experience.

Pierre stayed with his aunt, who lived in an old part of Lahore. His aunts, uncles, cousins, and the many relatives and friends he came to know during his stay did not live Islam in a politicized way—their Islam, as Pierre puts it, was still uncontaminated by the "Arabization" and consequent extremist trajectories that developed under President Zia ul Haqq in the 1980s. They lived Islam fully and were traditionalist but not militant or intolerant. Pierre was immediately conquered. Spending the nights on the rooftop of his aunt's house, drinking carrot juice and listening to the call to prayer, he found the solace that had eluded him in Stockholm. "I became interested in Islam not by active choice but by easing into it," he recounts. "After a couple of months it became a lifestyle; the *adan* [call to prayer] in the morning felt good, inculcating me in an environment that felt my own." It was, as he puts it, "exotic and familiar at the same time." "I had grown up in the Pentecostal Church, been a punk for a while, tried shamanism and a few other things," he wrote in 2002, "and had finally found my way to the religion I knew least about yet had roots in—Islam."[2]

Pierre felt he had finally found a tribe to belong to. He did not feel he had to formally convert, because he had always been to some extent Muslim, having grown up with a Pakistani father. But he was reluctant to call himself a Muslim or pray, an activity he actually began only during a short trip back to Stockholm. Once back in Pakistan he took his Muslim faith more seriously, praying, going to the mosque, and reading literature. Fasting for the first time during Ramadan was extremely challenging but reinforced his commitment to the religion. After ten months in Pakistan, he saw himself as a practicing Muslim. He and his father decided it was time for him to return to Sweden.

Back in Stockholm, Pierre reenrolled in school, this time selecting a more demanding field of study. For a year or so he juggled his two identities. He identified as a Muslim and continued to learn more about Islam. But he also went back to drinking beer and listening to punk rock music. Eventually, in his "perennial hunt for authenticity," his interest in and commitment to Islam prevailed. He started attending a mosque in Husby, an area of Stockholm with a large immigrant population. Worshippers came from all over the world: the Middle East, Somalia, Eritrea, Albania. Most were "ordinary Muslims," while others were "active on the Muslim scene." The distinction between various sects, currents, and organizations within Islam, with their frequent clashes and fissures, was lost on Pierre at the time. But his active presence at the mosque brought him close to the mosque's leadership. And Pierre also possessed a rare feature among the mosque's attendees: native knowledge of the Swedish language, the lingua franca of the diverse congregation. Soon he was asked by the mosque's leadership to deliver the Swedish translation of the *khutba*, the Friday sermon. At the Husby mosque Pierre got to know a group of young activists who had recently formed an organization called Swedish Young Muslims. In 1992 Pierre was elected to the board of the organization, a position he kept for the following ten years.

Pierre immersed himself in Stockholm's small but active Muslim scene. He attended various mosques, went to lectures, and tried to do as much as possible to learn about and support his new faith. In 1994 he was reportedly approached by one of the most prominent leaders on that scene, Mustafa Kharraki, and offered the opportunity to study at the European Institute for Human Sciences (IESH), the Western Brotherhood's foremost center of higher learning. Established in 1992 by Yusuf al Qaradawi and based in a castle in a bucolic part of Burgundy, IESH provides Arabic language and Islamic education to some 120 students resident on campus plus 200 students studying by correspondence each year.

Kharraki assured Pierre that all expenses for his stay in France would be covered. Pierre later found out that Kharraki had secured a grant from a Swedish government agency that provides financial support to religious organizations other than the Swedish state church. In September 1994, thanks to the support of the Swedish state, Pierre enrolled at IESH in one of the school's very first incoming classes. By his own admission, Pierre had no clue that the school was de facto the Brotherhood's school of higher learning. "I had heard of the existence of the Muslim Brotherhood," he recounts. "I kind of knew that environment was linked to it, but I didn't have the vocabulary to put it together."

Life at IESH turned out to be ideal for Pierre. "Now I have a different view [of it]," he says, "but at the time I thought it was great." Book smart and curious, he thoroughly enjoyed the intellectual challenge that Islamic theology provided him with. He describes the curriculum as "traditional and Islamist, Salafi-light." The works of Qaradawi were featured prominently, as were those of other Brotherhood ideologues. But not all texts—or all teachers—were Islamists. Pierre reminisces with particular fondness about a "more secular-minded" Arabic teacher from the Levant who transmitted his deep love for the Arabic language to him and other students.

Pierre enjoyed the social life provided at IESH no less than the intellectual stimulation. The sense of camaraderie that naturally arises among students living in a castle in the middle of the countryside suited Pierre's deep-seated desire to belong, to "find his tribe." "That was a beautiful year, very monastic in a sense," he recalls. "We stayed there, we prayed in the night, we fasted together."

Pierre became particularly close to two fellow students from the United Kingdom. Both of South Asian descent, in the UK they had been involved in youth organizations linked to Jamaat-e-Islami, the Brotherhood's "sister organization" in the Indian subcontinent.[3] And both struck Pierre as more "plugged in" when it came to activities at IESH besides the purely academic. Pierre had picked up on the fact that most of IESH's leadership and some of its students frequently met outside the classrooms or took part in activities together. Many of these meetings occurred during visits to the campus of senior scholars such as Faysal Mawlawi, the late leader of the Lebanese branch of the Brotherhood who had strong connections to the Union of Islamic Organizations in France (Union des Organisations Islamiques de France, UOIF), the main Brotherhood spawn in France (on which, see the following two chapters). Pierre also noticed that his British friends and some others at the school used the term "Harakat Muslimiya" (Islamic Movement), the name frequently used by Islamist groups like the Muslim Brotherhood and Jamaat-e-Islami to refer to themselves.

In this way, Pierre slowly came to realize that IESH was a Brotherhood institution. Its leadership and management were Brotherhood; most of its teachers belonged to or sympathized with the Brotherhood; and most of the students were Brotherhood members or promising activists handpicked by Brotherhood leaders in their countries of origin to be trained and perhaps selected to become Brotherhood members. He was therefore not surprised when, a couple of months after the start of the school year, his two British friends approached him and told him he was going to receive an invitation to join the group.

The process of swearing the oath was, as Pierre describes it, "strange, reminiscent of the Freemasons." After class Pierre was asked to go on a stroll in the countryside, and his friends walked in a different direction. Following the directions he was given, he found himself at a lush villa, which reportedly belonged to IESH's principal. Waiting for him were some fifteen people, all teachers or students at the school. He was asked to kneel down, place a hand on the Quran, and swear the oath, which "had words from the Quran that are also used when pledging allegiance to Sufi *tariqat* [orders]." He was then given a copy of the *mathurat*, a booklet with daily prayers and selected readings by Hassan al Banna.

Pierre's reasons for joining, as he recalls them, were multiple and over-lapping. Some had to do with his desire to belong. Seeing the activism of the sworn Brotherhood members at IESH "created an interest in wanting to be in the in-group environment; if something goes on in the school I want to know about it, and I want to relate to it in some sense, that was even by then one part of my thinking."

At the same time, the offer came after a long and, clearly, effective process of vetting and grooming that had operated unbeknownst to Pierre. He recounts having been increasingly included in conversations about the need to engage in organized, collective work in order to defend and spread Islam. The name of the group had been used with ever-greater frequency, and it had become clear to him that not just many of the people at IESH but also many of the people he had interacted with in Sweden were members of the Muslim Brotherhood. Therefore accepting the invitation to become a member felt to him natural, "easing in." "Most of all," he says, "I wanted to help Islam establish itself in a good way, and I thought that was a *manhaj* [methodology] that was workable in our time and age, and I had the contacts and the networks already since I was a member of the board of the Swedish Young Muslims."

Life Inside the Brotherhood

In 1995 Pierre finished his first year at IESH but decided not to continue his studies; instead, he returned to Sweden. Back in Stockholm, he immediately saw the local Muslim scene in which he had been active in a completely different way. Now a sworn Brother, albeit a low-ranking one, he found out that many of the activists he had interacted with were Brotherhood members. In his days as a young activist, before studying at IESH, he had been deeply involved in various Muslim organizations—organizing events, serving on the board of Swedish Young Muslims, making connections with various elements of Swedish society and the Swedish establishment that he, born and raised in Sweden and mostly in a "truly Swedish" family, knew better than did the activists who had arrived in the Scandinavian country as adult immigrants.

But all this had been done without any knowledge that Brotherhood activists were behind the many organizations and initiatives in which he feverishly involved himself. As he puts it, "I was basically helping an organization I didn't know the existence of." "I had heard the name [Muslim Brotherhood] because I was not stupid," he explains, "but I didn't connect the dots at all by then. . . . I had the worldview that Islam is one, that's it." Later, he explains, it became clear to him that "my whole vocabulary and way of explaining things and presenting myself and whatever texts I wrote" were unconsciously influenced by the Brotherhood's thinking. Now, as even a low-ranking Brother, Pierre had a different vantage point and could know who among the Muslims with whom he engaged in Sweden were Brotherhood members.

This dynamic described by Pierre, with a not so subtle hint of anger, of having been "used" and "shaped" by an organization without even knowing it is not uncommon in Western Brotherhood milieus. As Kamal Helbawy explained, the Brotherhood uses various organizations, particularly youth and charitable ones, for purposes ranging from advancing their political agenda to collecting funds (and, simultaneously, to spotting potential new recruits). They tend to hide and deny any link to the Brotherhood, and most activists who are involved in them are unaware of the heavy Brotherhood presence inside them.

Back in Stockholm, Pierre was soon included in a local usra, something he did not know existed before joining the group. He also found out that the Muslim Brotherhood in Sweden had a relatively sophisticated yet completely secret structure, which resembled that of the mother group in Egypt. It had, in fact, a system of usra, a shura council, and an elected emir.[4] In those years the Swedish branch of the Brotherhood also supervised Brotherhood activities in neighboring Norway and Finland (Denmark always had an independent structure).[5]

This new perspective enabled Pierre to better understand the dynamics of what he terms the "activist Muslim scene" in Stockholm and, more broadly, in Sweden. It soon became clear to him that the vast majority of organizations populating that scene had been founded or were in one way or another controlled by the small group of Brothers who had begun establishing a presence in Sweden in the late 1970s. In substance, he argues, a dozen or so individuals who belonged to various national branches of the Brotherhood in the Middle East and North Africa had managed to carve out for themselves a position of enormous influence as Islam began to organize in Sweden. The same men (and a handful of women—mostly their wives) sat on the board of dozens of mosques, charitable organizations, schools, business enterprises, and other kinds of organizations, creating a tightly knit web of connections and giving the impression of a wide network that purportedly represents the "Swedish Muslim community."

The core of that network is represented by the Islamic Federation in Stockholm, which was established in 1981 and became the more comprehensive Islamic Federation in Sweden (Islamiska Förbundet i Sverige, IFiS) in 1987.[6] IFiS is the flagship organization of the Brotherhood in Sweden, the network's most visible public face. Its headquarters are at Kapellgränd 10, a building in Stockholm's central Södermalm district, within walking distance from most Swedish political institutions and media outlets. The same building houses many other organizations that serve different purposes but are all part of the network and see the same individuals rotating through them in various leadership positions.[7]

Through his activism before he joined the Brotherhood and much more deeply afterward, Pierre came to know the "big men of Islam in Sweden," the dozen or so self-appointed leaders of the country's Muslim community. According to Pierre, one of them was the naqib of his usra, Ahmed Ghanem. Ghanem ran the Islamic Information Society (Islamiska Informationsföreningen), which published most of the network's literature. He later served as president of IFiS and currently runs the Gothenburg mosque, in the country's west. His wife, a Swedish convert, was also very active on the scene.

Abdallah Salah, another member of Pierre's usra, is also a well-known figure. Tunisian born, he was one of the founders of Swedish Young Muslims, the organization that Pierre joined before his trip to France. In addition, Salah has long been country manager for the Swedish branch of Islamic Relief Worldwide, the Brotherhood-associated charity giant described by Helbawy, and has served as vice president of IFiS and chairman of the Ibn Rushd Educational Association. He is appreciated beyond the Muslim scene and was even voted "Stockholmer of the month" in November 2015 for his work in welcoming refugees to Sweden.[8]

Pierre also had a "relatively close" relationship with another founder of Swedish Young Muslims, Chakib Ben Makhlouf. The Moroccan-born Ben Makhlouf heads various educational organizations of the Swedish Brotherhood network, including a school in northern Stockholm where Pierre briefly worked. Pierre later found out that other activists that he befriended in his pre-Brotherhood days belonged to the same network. Mustafa Kharraki, the man who invited Pierre to go to IESH, was (and still is) very engaged, having occupied leadership positions in many of the network's organizations, from Islamic Relief (where he served as president) to Ibn Rushd, from IFiS to the Muslim Council of Sweden. In keeping with Brotherhood patterns, his son Mohammed Amin is also active, having served as president of Swedish Young Muslims and later as spokesperson for IFiS.

These and a few other smart, well-educated, and motivated activists control a wide web of overlapping organizations with interlocking boards that demonstrate the ubiquity of a small clique of Swedish Brothers—or, better, their ability to project the impression of having big numbers and being representative by creating countless organizations with high-sounding names. The individuals who belong to the Swedish Brotherhood milieu have consistently denied their membership in the organization or that the milieu even exists. One notable exception is Jordanian-born Mahmoud Aldebe, one of the historical leaders of the Swedish Brotherhood milieu, who in 2013 published an open letter to reveal his involvement in the organization and to criticize its aims. He wrote:

I, Mahmoud Aldebe[,] . . . was one of those who established the Swedish branch of the Muslim Brotherhood in Sweden and who wrote its statutes. I abandoned my commitment to the Islamic Federation in Sweden (IFiS) and the Muslim Brotherhood in 2010, after over 25 years as a leading figure for the organization. I'm not saying this to besmirch anyone, but the truth should come forward.

The problem is not the movement per se, but those who rule over it. I devoted my whole adult life to defending the Islamic Federation in Sweden, but realized I was its tool—and thus decided to leave all my positions of responsibility in the federation and the Muslim Brotherhood in Sweden. This move cost me much, but I sacrificed it all to save myself from the dark tunnel. Now the truth must come to light, and I chose to go out and describe the true picture of the Islamic Federation in Sweden. . . .

. . . The problem we are facing is the double message, which is more harmful than beneficial. Dialogue is pursued with Christian and Jewish groups in official forums, but internally they spread fears regarding them. They speak of democracy, but actually do the opposite. The Federation managed to deceive those who want to have dialogue with them in Sweden.

Aldebe continued with a long list of institutions (among others, Ibn Rushd Study Association, Swedish Young Muslims, the Stockholm mosque, and the Gothenburg mosque) and individuals (Chakib ben Makhlouf, Mostafa Kharraki, Khemais Bassomi, Mohammad Amin Kharraki, Omar Mustafa, and Mahmoud Khalfi) that he, like Pierre, claimed are associated with the Brotherhood. Aldebe concluded his letter with a sharp critique of the Brotherhood:

Today, the Federation uses its conferences to prove to Swedish politicians that it controls Islam in Sweden. The Federation also works to make Sweden accept its order for Muslims. The division is sharp and clear: the enemies of Islam cannot be tolerated. Its representatives are active in large parts of organized Islam in Sweden. . . . [D]emocracy, equality, and freedom of speech are met with great dislike. They speak of democracy to achieve their own goals and to exert power over Islam in Sweden.

The Swedish Brothers' activism is also reflected in their high status in the broader family of the European Brotherhood, as Pierre discovered during his activist years. In June 1995 he participated to a conference, sponsored by the Swedish Ministry for Foreign Affairs, titled "Young Muslims in Europe." Subsidized by Swedish taxpayers, the conference was run by youth organizations of various European Brotherhood branches: Young Muslims UK, Jeune Musulmans de France, Muslimische Jugend Deutschland, and Pierre's Swedish Young Muslims.

The conference caused discomfort among some of the participants, who were unaware of its underlying aims and accepted an invitation to it because of the Swedish government's endorsement. Most notable among them was famed French scholar Gilles Kepel. "I was surprised to see how the youth conference was controlled by the Islamists," Kepel confessed to a Swedish newspaper at the time. "They are well-organized, intelligent, and have a built-up contact network throughout Europe. With this, they succeeded in taking control over the youth conference, even though they are in the minority among Muslims in Europe."[9]

The outcome of the event was the formation of the Forum of European Muslim Youth and Student Organizations (FEMYSO), the Brotherhood's pan-European youth organization. FEMYSO and its twin entity, the abovementioned FIOE, which, according to Ahmed Akkari, solved the internal dispute within the Danish Brotherhood, represent the European Brothers' lobbying arm at a pan-European level. Strategically headquartered in Brussels in two buildings located a few blocks from the European Commission and other institutions of the European Union, FIOE and FEMYSO (which for years shared its building with the World Assembly of Muslim Youth, Helbawy's organization) enjoy a degree of access to the European seats of power that no other European Muslim organization can even dream of gaining. Their leaders have often been invited to testify before the European Parliament and to represent the "Muslim point of view" in debates with policy makers.

FIOE's leaders are ambiguous about their relation to the Brotherhood. Ahmed al Rawi, the organization's former president, says that FIOE shares "a common point of view" and has a "good close relationship" with the Brotherhood.[10] Other officials deny any connection.[11] But some Middle Eastern–based affiliates of the organization proudly proclaim that FIOE's ideological and methodological identification with the Brotherhood is complete. Salem Abdul Salam Al Shikhi, a member of FIOE's European Council for Fatwa and Research, writes of FIOE that "it represents the Muslim Brotherhood's moderate thought taking into consideration European specialty, and working under European regimes and laws."[12] As usual, the terminological difficulties related to defining the nature of the Brotherhood make the identification of organizations linked to it controversial.

The Swedish Brothers' prominent role in the European network goes well beyond having hosted FEMYSO's founding meeting or the fact that IFiS is a founding member of FIOE. More tellingly, many members of the Swedish network have occupied some of the highest positions inside the Brothers' two Brussels-based organizations. Omar Mustafahas served as a FEMYSO board member and Abdirizak Waberi, discussed in more detail below, as the organization's vice president. Moreover, despite formally occupying only less visible positions related to education in Sweden, Chakib Ben Makhlouf served in the powerful position of president of FIOE until 2014—a position previously held by European Brotherhood bigwigs such as Ibrahim el Zayat and Ahmed al Rawi.

Pierre moved with ease in this milieu. Educated, eloquent, enthusiastic, and with a significantly deeper knowledge of Swedish culture, society, and language than the first-generation Brotherhood leaders, he soon became one of the main public faces of the Brotherhood-dominated organized Swedish Muslim community. He routinely gave interviews, appeared on television (there was even a documentary about him), and attended high-profile meetings with politicians and government officials. "If you forget my last name, everybody thinks I'm Swedish," the Nordic-looking Pierre says with a smile. "The Brothers loved that."

Pierre's form of Islamic activism was of the quintessential Brotherhood kind, composed of grassroots community organizing, media outreach, and engagement with the political system at all levels. He was not involved in any kind of militant or violent activity, something "I have never been interested in." And, according to him, the broader Brotherhood milieu he had become part of was similarly focused on carving out for itself a position of leadership within the nascent Swedish Muslim community in the eyes of both the Swedish establishment and the community itself.

Yet, he notes, there was a "gray area." While he was taking action in Brotherhood spaces—mosques, lectures, protests—it was not uncommon for him to come into contact with individuals who embraced more radical forms of Islamism. "I got to know people who were in Afghanistan or were injured during the Bosnia years," he says, referring to the two large jihadist mobilizations of the 1980s and early 1990s, respectively. "I knew many people who fought in jihad." He describes how he frequently interacted

with the fairly large cluster of Algerian jihadists active in Stockholm during the days of the Algerian civil war of the early 1990s, as well as with
Oussama Kassir, a veteran of the Lebanese civil war who years later was
arrested because of his attempt to set up an al Qaeda–linked training camp
in Oregon.

"In those days in the '90s," he says, "everything was connected and most
active people on the so-called Muslim scene, religious Muslims, got to
know each other, at least indirectly, or at least recognized each other. I was
part of that environment." Pierre explains that during those years Stockholm's Muslim community was small, and the active Muslim scene even
smaller. It is clear that those who attended the city's relatively few mosques
or participated to events such as pro-Palestine protests were a small cohort,
and, not surprisingly, everybody more or less knew everybody else.

But Pierre argues that such familiarity was not just a matter of casual
interactions. Unquestionably, the Brothers had their own structure, which
was clearly separate from those of other groups, and their methods were
different. But according to Pierre, in those years—unlike today, he argues,
when the boundaries are more distinct—the moments of ideological and,
at times, operational overlap between the Brotherhood and the jihadist
milieu were not insignificant. "The general idea that was conveyed to me
was that we are all brothers against the *kufar* [infidels]," he explains. "We
[the Brothers and jihadists] have differences. Some might get directly into
action, some do not. But in front of the enemy we stand united."

Leaving the Brotherhood

Once Pierre was back in Sweden as an initiated member of the group, his
active involvement in the organization lasted for only two years. It was
not long before he started having reservations about several aspects of the
Brotherhood, starting with its views on Islam and Sweden. For example,
he felt that the language used inside his usra should have been Swedish,
not Arabic, as most of the activities discussed related to Swedish society
and how to bring Islam to Sweden. To his frustration, his suggestion was
rejected.

Pierre began developing similar concerns while serving as editor of
Salaam, the first and arguably most influential among the early publications
on Islam in Swedish. *Salaam* played a key role not just in disseminating

Brotherhood-leaning writings but also in bringing some of the pioneers of the Brotherhood in Sweden together with a fairly large group of Swedish converts to Islam or, as in the case of Pierre, individuals of mixed background who had grown up in the country. Many of the converts were women who had married Brotherhood members (like the wife of the head of Pierre's usra) or others active on the Muslim scene. (For discussion of this, see chapter 8.)

By 1996, Pierre recounts, *Salaam* had become the site of an "undercover struggle" between the Brotherhood pioneers and their underlings more closely tied to Sweden. "A new generation of guys with levels of consciousness were trying to create a new hybrid form [of Islam] which they themselves, us, we called 'Blue Yellow Islam'" (a reference to the colors of the Swedish flag). "We wanted to truly integrate Islam in a Swedish context," he continues, "and do so in a way that it would have been a win–win situation for both Sweden and Islam." The goal was "an Islam that would really fit into and therefore also help Swedish society, because we thought it was the recipe for everything, for any problem: more Islam, better Islam." But, he adds, "We wanted an Islam that was Swedish not just language-wise but also in the sense that it would meet with the beautiful, old, archaic ways of Swedish culture, which are very difficult for many immigrants to get to know."

Pierre and some of the Swedish-born converts at *Salaam* found the Brotherhood leadership that headed the magazine to have little interest in understanding Swedish culture and even less in adapting some of their religious, political, and social views to it. "Blue Yellow Islam," he maintains, was a nice slogan for those wishing to be seen as moderates in the eyes of the Swedish establishment, but the pioneer Brothers dismissed outright any liberal view that conflicted with their dogma.

Moreover, and perhaps most disturbingly to Pierre, they expressed a deep contempt toward Swedish society and people. Pierre describes these attitudes as sheer racism, providing many examples of Brotherhood leaders deriding Swedish people for their perceived naiveté, loose morality, and poor personal hygiene. Pierre was equally disturbed by forms of racism within the Muslim community. He argues that the Brotherhood leadership, largely composed of Arabs, spoke disparagingly of Eritrean, Somali, and other African Muslims, shattering the ideal of color-blind brotherhood that should characterize not just the organization but the entire global community of believers in Islam.

Pierre connects these attitudes at least in part to the Brotherhood's structure. During his time as part of an usra and in the lower levels of Brotherhood's Swedish branch, Pierre witnessed a "masonic-like structure" and an obsession with secrecy that he found highly problematic and that he thinks is lost on most Western observers. "To understand the Brotherhood," he insists, "one should look at medieval guilds, religious and knights' orders from the era when Europe was more Christian, and secret societies; and understand the intermarriages, the financial links." Moreover, in his view this setup, necessary in Middle Eastern countries but completely out of place in the West, fosters victimhood, paranoia, conspiracy theories, and a constantly adversarial mind-set.

"I came to the conclusion," he says, "that these guys [the Brothers] didn't know much about Europe and they are causing more harm than good right now; they are cheating Swedish society, they are taking money which isn't theirs, they are talking internally in very racist and very xenophobic ways about the majority of the population and it's very disheartening." Such thinking naturally led him to the decision to disengage from the group.

Pierre's departure from the Brotherhood was not dramatic. By late 1996 or early 1997 he simply stopped going to his usra meetings and detached from the Brotherhood milieu, no longer identifying himself with the organization. He nonetheless remained active on the Swedish Muslim scene—particularly within the Swedish Young Muslims—working "somewhat in opposition against the Brotherhood but still working within the framework of the organization they had set up." He did not formally leave the organization, and there was not, at least as far as he knows, any acknowledgment of his departure.

The events of September 11, 2001, were "an eye-opener" for Pierre—a reaction shared by many Islamist activists throughout the West, particularly converts.[13] Bombarded with media requests, he provided the "Muslim point of view" about the attacks. While condemning them, Pierre recalls, he also made points that were "apologetic, impregnated with the Brotherhood's narrative of victimhood and grievance." He realized that his frames of reference, his way of viewing the world, had become heavily influenced by the Brotherhood's ideology. Feeling that he no longer wanted to use his position of influence as one of the most influential spokespeople for Swedish Muslims to spread the Brotherhood's narrative, albeit unwittingly, he decided to leave activism.

Like the decision to leave the Brotherhood, Pierre's departure from the activist scene was quietly made. He explains that one of the main reasons for this reticence was his desire not to cause pain to the many people he had influenced. "I was one of the most visible guys [on the activist Muslim scene]; . . . many people got inspired by my speeches, I had an audience of like 500 to 600 people and changed their emotions like that. . . . I've helped so many people enter into a more religious worldview, I didn't want to hurt or confuse them too much by saying 'Nope, I leave this, it's a waste of time, it's a mistake, goodbye.' "

This move coincided with his growing interest in the spiritual aspects of Islam, an aspect he felt the "politics-obsessed" Brothers wholly neglected. "I was one of the spiders in the web," says Pierre, describing his role in the Brotherhood-linked activist world with an analogy commonly used by Brothers and their critics alike, "but as someone who wanted to make this whole religious scene more pious. I was not the most pious guy myself; I tried my best, but my idea is that we don't need strange politics from a strange country, we need something which fulfills the spiritual vacuum of people who want to have that as part of their lives, and it's all about focusing on God, it's about prayer, it's about knowing your traditions."

By the late 1990s Pierre had begun cooperating with the networks linked to Hamza Yusuf and Muhammad al Yaqoubi, conservative preachers who traced their spiritual roots to Sufism. He later became closer to various Sufi tariqat, such as the Naqshbandiyya, the Chistiyya, and the Shadhiliyya. He found solace in these orders' deeply spiritual and esoteric forms of Islam, which rejected politics. Yet his religious fervor has waned with the years and he now only occasionally practices the faith. He recalls making *dua* (praying) during his father's funeral in Pakistan in 2014, but doing so "because whatever religion they have, that's their religion and traditions and I love parts of that, I am still emotionally attached to it in a sense," rather than out of a sense of belief.

Over the past few years Pierre has focused mostly on his personal life. He moved with his wife and two children to a rural village not far from Stockholm, where he was able to ponder and make peace with his life choices. While continuing his studies, he has also remained an attentive observer of the "Muslim scene" of which he was once an integral part. And, since 2016, he has decided to resurface in the public sphere. Like many other former activists in high-commitment movements, after a hiatus devoted to introspection and putting his personal life in order, Pierre felt ready to speak out about his personal experience. He has been participating in a collective, government-funded research project that seeks to analyze the presence of Muslim Brotherhood networks in Sweden and critiquing the Swedish establishment's approach to it. He has also begun giving interviews again, discussing his previous role in Brotherhood-linked organizations, describing how the Brotherhood milieu in Sweden works, and warning the public about the harm it does to Swedish society.

Pierre perceives this new role as a personal responsibility, makings amends for the damage he thinks he caused during his activist days. He feels that for years, thanks to his knowledge of Swedish society, he enabled the Brotherhood milieu to better infiltrate various parts of the Swedish establishment, empowering a force that harmed both relations within the Swedish Muslim community and the social cohesion of Swedish civil society at large. He now feels that it is his personal duty to warn the Swedish establishment and public about the dangers of that milieu, without employing either the excessive political correctness that often characterizes the Swedish debate on the matter or the alarmist or racist tones used by some critics of the Brotherhood.

Pierre's attempt at a balanced criticism of the Brotherhood's milieu in Sweden starts from his analysis of the organization's goals. As in most Western countries, some of the most hardline critics of the Brotherhood in Sweden argue that the group wants to turn the country into an Islamic state and impose sharia. Pierre, intimately involved in the milieu for a decade, argues that its views on the subject are significantly more sophisticated. On one hand, he argues, there is no denying that privately many members of the milieu indeed want some form of Islamic rule in Sweden. Yet there is no well-defined vision of what that system should look like—no specific view other than the conviction that such a system would somewhat magically cure all the social ills affecting Sweden. And, Pierre is clear, the ideal Islamic order that some members of the Swedish Brotherhood milieu would envision in a remote future is different from what hard-core Salafists or jihadists would like to create.

Moreover, Pierre argues, if dreams of an Islamic order are at times voiced internally, the milieu is quintessentially pragmatic and keenly aware of what it can and cannot attain in the short and middle term. It fully understands that the chances of Sweden becoming an Islamic state in the near future are nonexistent and therefore does not work on making that dream a reality. But it does concentrate, he claims, on carving out progressively larger spaces for Islam and for itself in as many aspects of Swedish life as possible: within Sweden's Muslim community, within Sweden's political and legal system, in public debate, and in any other environment in which it can gain traction and establish a foothold so that it can further its agenda.

For various interconnected reasons Pierre believes that while this strategy of gradual Islamization by infiltrating the system is common to all Brotherhood branches throughout the West, Sweden is the ideal country in which to pursue it. One basic reason, as Pierre notes, is demographic: Sweden had traditionally been a very homogeneous country, but it quickly became extremely diverse (in 2017 Statistics Sweden, the Swedish government agency responsible for producing official statistics, calculated that 24.1 percent of the country's inhabitants had a foreign background).[14]

In Pierre's view, "Swedish society was not able to cope with all of the complexities and differences coming here." When it comes to Islam, he argues that the Swedish establishment accepted at face value the false claim made by a small milieu of organized and savvy activists that they represented the entire Muslim community. Not possessing tools to understand the complex dynamics within global Islam and within the country's new yet fast-growing Muslim community, the Swedish establishment fully embraced an active minority, ignoring the many other voices that make up the mosaic of Swedish Islam. "The Brothers are the ones who explained to the Swedish state what Islam is."

According to Pierre, this ignorance goes hand in hand with two other elements of Swedish society: its emphasis on trust and its embrace of political correctness. "Swedish culture, going back to the Vikings," he argues, "values trust enormously; people do not expect duplicity and find it difficult to conceive that somebody would try to deceive them." This "blue-eyed naiveté," as Pierre terms it, has played into the hands of the Brothers, who have "not been honest about who they are and what they want" yet have rarely found their true motives questioned. At the same time, the value placed on honesty by Nordic culture also means that when trust is broken the consequences are severe. "You can use the vacuum of naiveté and blue-eyedness within the Swedish institutions for a while," he argues, "but when it closes, everything closes, so they [the Brothers] have somehow dug their own grave."

Equally propitious for the Brothers is the high level of political correctness that characterizes Swedish society. "Everybody is too scared of calling a spade a spade," sighs Pierre, bemoaning the inability of many of his countryfolk to see or, better, to publicly express any negative views about minorities, even when doing so would not be tantamount to displaying prejudice but would simply be treating them the same way they would ethnic Swedes. Moreover, he argues, the Brothers have learned how to employ the language of human rights, democracy, and multiculturalism to their own advantage without themselves truly valuing those concepts. Their ability to use the language of the contemporary Swedish Left has enabled them to be seen as a victim group and deflect any criticism as bigoted.

The final but crucial element making Sweden a very hospitable country for the Brothers is its deep embrace of multiculturalism. Sweden was the first European country to formally adopt the policy, enshrining it in a law that was unanimously passed by Parliament in 1975. Since then the country has invested heavily in promoting a strong version of multiculturalism, openly rejecting any form of assimilation and advocating the retention of identity of all minority groups. This policy, argue Pierre and the academics and experts with whom he has recently been working, creates the perfect opportunity for the Brotherhood milieu to carve out large areas of influence. They write in the study "The Muslim Brotherhood in Sweden":

> In a country like Sweden, according to World Values Survey the world's most secular nation, it would border on political suicide to be upfront with the fact that one is working for sharia to govern society or that men and women by birth are biologically predisposed to different tasks. In Sweden and other Western countries, the MB [Muslim Brotherhood] instead offered to insert its Islamic project within the ideological framework of multiculturalism. For years, ever since Mahmoud Aldebe's tenure as one of the leaders of the MB's network, the MB's activists have argued that Muslims should be recognized as a religious "minority" because they have a special way of life that must be preserved. Aldebe claimed in a letter to former MP and Social Democratic Party chair Mona Sahlin that "special legislation" (read: sharia) was an essential part of Muslim lifestyle.[15]

Pierre and his colleagues believe that the Brothers have duped the Swedish elites into buying their unsubstantiated claim to represent an imaginary homogeneous "Muslim community" and their view that "Muslims should be incorporated into society as a collective entity where everyone submits to Islam in the MB's version of what the religion requires, and that this group demands collective rights." In essence, the Brothers are exploiting the concept of multiculturalism as the best vehicle to advance their agenda of creating a parallel society, run by them and funded by the Swedish state. Whereas Qaradawi has long urged Western Brotherhood leaders to create a "Muslim ghetto" ("Try to have your small society within the larger society," the spiritual leader of the global Muslim Brotherhood has advocated, "otherwise you will melt in it like salt in water"), the Swedish Brothers are doing so with the approval and financial support of Swedish society.

These dynamics have played out on various levels over the years, but Pierre finds them particularly problematic in connection with public funding and access to the political system. The two issues are extremely complex and deeply intertwined. Neither is exclusive to Sweden, as they appear in various forms in almost all Western countries. But the degree of intensity with which both play out in Sweden appears to be well above the norm, definitely making Sweden one of the most "Brotherhood-friendly" countries in the West.

Public funding to Islamists is something Pierre has been denouncing with particular vehemence since coming back into the spotlight. Public funding of civil society activities, particularly if seen as furthering the country's multicultural project, is famously lavish in Sweden, provided through a web of public organizations such as the Commission for Government Support for Faith Communities, the Swedish Agency for Youth and Civil Society, the Public Inheritance Fund, and many other national, regional, and municipal bodies.[16] Pierre and other critics argue that organizations linked to the Brotherhood have created a block informally known as "Muslim civil society" (*Muslimska civilsamhället*) which, thanks to their superior understanding of how the system works and their tight connections to Swedish elites, has in effect monopolized access to the generous funds given by the Swedish state to the Swedish Muslim community.

Pierre calls this a perverse dynamic, with "well-meaning Swedes paying for organizations that are working against Sweden." Aje Carlbom, a Malmoe-based academic who has recently written a report about the Muslim Brotherhood in Sweden, argues that through this system, "economic resources go to a MB-associated network of politically oriented activists with ambitions to build a parallel Islamic sector governed by different values compared to the majority society." By helping MB-associated organizations develop their activities, Carlbom continues, "the state (or other funding providers) offers tax funding to a small group of actors who spread messages that undermine the dominant values in society."[17] Or, as Pierre puts it, "the welfare state pays dawa work dressed up in the language of minority rights." He adds, "They are good at getting taxpayers' money and luring different authorities to pay for different projects with the multicultural buzzwords like 'democracy,' 'women's rights,' 'human rights,' and 'cultural understanding' and what have you, because these guys are adaptable and charismatic and keen on getting their goals realized; they use whatever means there is to achieve their own goals."

Pierre is similarly concerned about the high level of penetration of the Brotherhood network inside the upper echelons of the Swedish political establishment. He remembers how in the 1990s, when the milieu was still in its relative infancy and he was intimately involved in it, the Swedish Brothers talked about the need to create solid ties to political parties. The internal debate on what party with which to ally themselves focused, according to Pierre, not so much on ideological affinities but on a cold calculation of which relationship would advance the milieu's efforts the most.

The first party with which the Brotherhood milieu formed a relationship was the Social Democrat Party (Sveriges socialdemokratiska arbetareparti, SAP), the oldest and largest political party in Sweden. Frequent contacts throughout the 1990s were formalized in 1999, when the SAP entered into an agreement with the Brotherhood-dominated Muslim Council of Sweden (Sveriges muslimska råd, SMR) with precise numerical benchmarks for the participation of Muslims as candidates for the party.[18]

The relationship between the SAP and the Brotherhood milieu has remained firm ever since. Tellingly, one of the rising stars of the milieu, Omar Mustafa (who has served as president of IFiS, director of Ibn Rushd, and vice president of Islamic Relief, besides playing active roles in many other groups), was elected to the SAP's national governing board in 2013. Media exposés of the links between the organizations he was involved in and misogynistic and anti-Semitic views forced him to resign only a few days after his election. "You can't hold an elected position within the Social Democrats," commented the embarrassed head of the SAP, Stefan Löfven, "unless you can fully stand up for the party's values that all human beings are equal and for equality between women and men." For his part, Mustafa insisted that he was the victim of "unfounded attacks and conspiracy theories about Islam, Muslims, and Muslim organizations" and vowed to continue working within Muslim civil society for "justice, equality, and human rights."[19]

Pierre claims that despite this close relationship with the Social Democrats, the Brotherhood milieu has always considered establishing alliances with other parties as well, including those with very different leanings. On one level, this strategy makes sense because the Swedish Brothers, like their counterparts throughout the West, might agree with left-wing parties on certain issues (immigration, multiculturalism, foreign policy) but tend to see eye to eye with conservative parties on others, especially social issues (abortion, gay marriage, and so on). But it could be argued that the approach is merely opportunistic, as those in the milieu seek to cover all political bases and have ties to power irrespective of political outcomes.

Whatever the reason, those in the Swedish Brotherhood have succeeded in creating solid ties to most political parties. An especially pertinent example is that of Abdirizak Waberi, a prominent member of the milieu who has served as president of IFiS, board member of SMR, and vice president of FIOE in Brussels. In 2010 Waberi was elected to the Swedish Parliament for the Moderate Party, the historical center-right rival of the Social-Democrats, and served on the Defense Committee and the Joint Parliamentary Committee on Foreign Affairs and Defense

But Pierre feels most directly involved in the case of another member of the Brotherhood milieu who rose to a high level in Swedish politics: Mehmet Kaplan. In the 1990s Pierre and Kaplan were the two main figures behind Swedish Young Muslims, holding most of the leadership positions in the organization and developing a close personal relationship. It was around that time that Pierre introduced Kaplan to Sweden's thriving environmentalist movement and to the Green Party, a scene in which Pierre had been active since before his trip to Pakistan at age eighteen. Indeed, one of Pierre's main tasks during his days inside the Brotherhood milieus was introducing members of the milieu to Swedish institutions with which they had little familiarity. "These guys didn't have a clue about Sweden," says Pierre with a smile. "And I, with my language skills and local knowledge, was good at connecting them."

Kaplan rose through the ranks of the Green Party. He served in Parliament between 2006 and 2014 and as housing minister between 2014 and 2016 in the Social Democrat–Green Party government led by Stefan Löfven—the head of the Social Democrats who, as mentioned above, had expressed his regrets about Omar Mustafa's election. Kaplan's appointment as minister elated the Brotherhood milieu. In an interview with Arabic-language media, Mahmoud Khalfi, the imam of Stockholm's IFiS-controlled mosque and, like Pierre, a graduate of IESH, called it "a breakthrough for the Islamists in Sweden" and complimented Swedish politicians for "having normalized relations with the Islamic association known for its affiliation with the Muslim Brotherhood."[20] Despite this enthusiasm, Kaplan's time in government was short and troubled. He was at the center of various media storms for comparing Swedes traveling to Syria to fight to those who fought in Finland during World War II, and the treatment of Palestinians to that of Jews in 1930s Germany. As the media uncovered his close ties to both the Turkish ultranationalist group Grey Wolves and the Islamist Millî Görüş, Kaplan was forced to resign in April 2016.[21]

After a hiatus from the public scene during which he continued to observe the developments within Sweden's Brotherhood milieu and the country's approach to it, Pierre Durrani has decided to leverage his personal experience to warn his country about what he perceives as bad decisions made over the past twenty years. He argues that out of a toxic combination of ignorance, well-meaning naiveté, and, at times, political opportunism, Sweden's elites have empowered a small group of self-appointed representatives of the country's Muslim community at the expense of all other Muslims and, more broadly, social cohesion within Swedish society.

Pierre believes that the Brothers are an obstacle to the creation of a cohesive and truly multicultural society, as their influence promotes both jihadist radicalization and right-wing extremism. Indeed, he says, that influence has "hindered the growth of a healthy conversation about Islam, Islamism, and integration, as they charge anybody who seeks to have a reasonable conversation about these issues with accusations of racism and Islamophobia." This has had a paralyzing effect on the public debate and on the ability of the Swedish state to take measures against even the most extreme fringes of the country's Islamist movement. While the Brothers have little to no role in the recent mobilization of foreign fighters going from Sweden to Syria (proportionally, one of the largest such groups in Europe), Pierre sees their influence as preventing Swedish authorities from taking substantive actions on the matter.

A direct consequence of the paralysis within Swedish society and political establishment triggered by the Brothers' use of the racism card, according to Pierre, is "the growth of a radical right" inside Sweden. Pierre argues that the Swedish state's inability to even openly discuss various issues related to immigration and Islam have inevitably led many ordinary Swedes to listen to extremist voices. He sees a very troubling future in which right-wing sentiments may take violent and authoritarian forms, in large part because of the Brothers' chilling effect on public debate.

A deep thinker with a strong sense of ethics and responsibility, Pierre engages in these debates with passion and a desire to undo what he think he did wrong in his youth—empowering a movement that he believes is damaging to both Sweden and Islam. Even though his personal story is unique, Pierre is representative of the first generation of Western-born individuals (whether born Muslims, converts, or, as in Pierre's case, of mixed background) who became active in Brotherhood networks without knowing the ideological stripes of the organizations in which they so passionately involved themselves.

His trajectory out of it, driven by a mix of reasons but primarily by ideological disillusionment with Islamism in general (and not just the Brotherhood's version of it), is not uncommon, as the stories of various current and former members of the movement suggest. Many of them, though, for reasons that vary from shame to fear of retribution to simply a desire to leave behind what they consider a bad experience, simply disengage without speaking out—as Pierre himself did in the first years after he left the movement.

CHAPTER VI

<hr>

Mohamed Louizi

Joining the Brotherhood

Mohamed Louizi was born in Casablanca on March 21, 1978, the fifth of seven children of a couple who hailed from the Moroccan countryside.[1] Upon moving to Casablanca, the sprawling commercial hub of Morocco, Mohamed's father came under the influence of conservative mosques linked to the Muslim Brotherhood, Salafists, and other Islamist currents and began embracing an interpretation of Islam that, according to Mohamed, "was not Moroccan, in the sense of blending the principles and values of Islam with Moroccan history, traditions, and culture."[2] That meant that the Louizi household, which became mockingly known in the neighborhood as the Ikhwanis, was devoid of a television, family pictures, music, and all the things forbidden by the Wahhabi-influenced form of Islam that the father adopted. Despite these deprivations, which Mohamed found hard to digest growing up, he describes his childhood as happy, characterized by a harmonious family life. His parents never forced him to attend the mosque or be active in religious activities but pushed him hard in school, a challenge he enjoyed and at which he thrived.

Mohamed's "first actual contact with Islamist structures" came in 1991, when, as a thirteen-year-old student, he was integrated into an usra of the confraternity of Abdessalam Yassine. The late Yassine is one of the godfathers of Islamism in Moroccan—the founder of a movement, Jamaat Al Adl Wa Al Ihssane (Justice and Spirituality Movement), that was independent from but deeply inspired by the Brotherhood. Mohamed began attending the group's study seminars and many of its extracurricular activities, all aimed at introducing the youth to conservative Islamic principles. He was fascinated but conflicted, at times succumbing to the lure of going to the movies and meeting a girl he liked.

A more serious commitment began the following year, when Mohamed and his family moved to Boujniba, a town of roughly 15,000 some 120 kilometers from Casablanca where his father had opened a grocery store. Mohamed, in fact, began attending the activities devoted to the youth of the Movement for Reform and Renewal (Mouvement de la Reforme et du Renouveau, MRR), another Moroccan Islamist movement similar to Yassine's. "The MRR claimed not to have any organic link with the Muslim Brotherhood," explains Mohamed, "which was not false in itself: the movement has never officially or publicly sworn allegiance to Hassan al Banna's fraternity." At the same time, Mohamed points out, the ideological ties were extensive and immediately evident in the literature disseminated by the MRR with the funding of various Gulf countries, Qatar in particular, "the main avenue of dissemination of Islamist ideology." During those days Mohamed started reading the works of Hassan al Banna, Fathi Yakan, Sayyid and Mohammed Qutb, Said Hawwa, Yusuf al Qaradawi, and Mohammed el Ghazali, the classics of Ikhwani literature.

MRR played an important role in the spread of Islamism in Morocco in the 1980s and early 1990s—it is not a coincidence that the country's last two prime ministers, Abdelilah Benkirane and Saad Dine El Otmani, were top MRR leaders on entering office.[3] While the more political aspects of the movement were not evident to Mohamed at the time, he could see the huge impact MRR had on education: it created study groups, spread literacy, and helped poor students continue their studies. Book-smart Mohamed, who ranked at the top of his class and participated in math competitions, was naturally drawn to this aspect of MRR, but he also liked the extracurricular activities it organized. A rising star in the local MRR youth wing, Mohamed organized charity drives, going door to door to collect goods and then distributing them to the poor. He also arranged for a collective circumcision of some forty children, coordinating with doctors, families, and the municipality.

These activities and responsibilities were, as he recalls, galvanizing for him as a driven teenager. He would later understand that "all those good things serve a greater goal, which is that of Islamism." In particular, it soon became clear to Mohamed that MRR's activities served the dual role of introducing the masses to a more conservative interpretation of Islam and selecting a few activists who could become full-fledged members of the movement. The latter is exactly what happened to him at age eighteen, when he was invited to "move from the rank of active sympathizer to that of active member of the movement."

The head of MRR in Boujniba summoned Mohamed and told him the leadership had observed him for years and decided his intelligence, piety, obedience, and perseverance made him the perfect candidate for the group. Mohamed had figured out that MRR was, in substance, a Brotherhood entity—"it was in the air." But the MRR leader also explained to him that the group had a structure that was significantly more complex than Mohamed had supposed. "For four years I had work incessantly for an organization I was not aware of," he says. Mohamed enthusiastically accepted and swore baya during a ceremony along with seven or eight other new members.

In June 1996, a few months after he was inducted, Mohamed and his family moved back to Casablanca. Immediately, as instructed by MRR's leadership in Boujniba, he went to introduce himself to the head of the local MRR section, an Arabic teacher who became his mentor. "It was a surprise," recounts Mohamed. "I had never imagined such a degree of organization and specialization." After handing his new mentor a reference letter from the Boujniba leaders, he was immediately inserted in the MRR's extremely large Casablanca organizational machine. Once a week he attended the meeting of his usra, and once a month a bigger meeting with members of various usras from the region. He also participated in various study groups, invariably led by a MRR member but open to students from different schools. Junior MRR members like Mohamed worked in their schools to invite new students to the study groups, where senior members began a process of observation and grooming aimed at picking the best new recruits.

For Mohamed, 1996 was a crucial year. As he puts, "It was the end of Islam and the beginning of Islamism, the end of 'Mohamed' and the beginning of 'brother Mohamed.'" It was also the year he enrolled at the faculty of electrical engineering in Mohammedia. For the following three years Mohamed increased his involvement in the activities of MRR, which by then had merged with another group and become the Movement for Unicity and Reform (MUR). He established a MUR presence on campus, continued his involvement in both the usra and the open study groups, and campaigned for Islamist candidates in local elections—an activity that revealed his propensity for political mobilization.

In November 1999 Mohamed for the first time left Morocco and headed to Europe—"not to conquer it, but to study," he jokes. A bright student, he was given the opportunity to continue his engineering studies in Lille, a prestigious university hub in northern France. The anxiety that understandably accompanied him in his first journey away from home during the long bus ride from Morocco to Lille somewhat lessened when he was met by his cousins, who had long lived in the city. After a short stay with them, Mohamed moved into his student residency in Villeneuve d'Ascq, a college town in the Lille metropolitan area.

"On the first day, after setting up in my room and exploring the dormitory," he recounts, "I went to the prayer room." The fact that a dormitory in a French city had a prayer room was the first thing that surprised Mohamed. "Many universities in Morocco did not have them," he explains, "for fear they would be taken over by Islamists." Indeed, that was the second surprise for Mohamed: while the prayer room was empty, he could browse its small library and immediately noticed it was filled with Islamist literature, mostly of the Brotherhood variety. "I could even find books I had never seen before in Morocco," he says, somewhat amused.

The third surprise came the following day, when Mohamed went back to the small prayer room for Friday prayers and saw that leading the prayer was Khalid, a fellow MUR activist he had befriended during their student days in Mohammedia. "When he saw me among his crowd," recounts Mohamed, "he smiled discreetly. After the prayer came a moment of fraternal hugs and welcomes, and he immediately introduced me to other students and other 'brothers' present." Khalid also introduced Mohamed to a significantly older man, a Tunisian named Mohamed-Taïeb Saghrouni.

Saghrouni is allegedly a central figure in the French Brotherhood milieu, and Mohamed describes him as "a huge deal, the man behind everything, the one that calls the shots behind closed doors." Saghrouni has long been active in the Lille area, which, owing in large part to the presence of various technical universities, has historically been one of the main hubs for the Brotherhood in France. He is also a longtime leader of the Union of

Islamic Organizations of France, the main public organization of the French Brotherhood milieu. Founded in 1983, UOIF is one of the largest and best-organized Brotherhood offshoots in Europe. Like all organizations of this kind, UOIF has itself spawned numerous entities, from student and youth organizations to charities, from media production companies to the European Institute for Human Sciences (discussed in chapter 5), the Brotherhood's "graduate school" in Burgundy. In 2017 UOIF changed its name to Muslims of France (Musulmans de France). As it did so, UOIF's president, Lille-based Amar Lasfar, stated that UOIF was "not part of the Muslim Brotherhood" but "ascribed to its current of thought."[4]

Saghrouni also represents a good example of head of a Brotherhood family. His wife, Hela Khomsi, is, like her husband, a board member of UOIF, where she is also in charge of family-related issues.[5] She is also the president of the French League of the Muslim Woman (Ligue Française de la Femme Musulmane, LFFM) and, at the European level, a founding member of the European Forum of Muslim Women (EFOMW), the women's branch of the Federation of Islamic Organizations in Europe.[6] Their son, Anas Saghrouni, is a rising star of the French Brotherhood milieu. After serving as president of the Muslim Students of France (Étudiants Musulmans de France, EMF), Anas Saghrouni is currently in charge of the youth portfolio for UOIF.[7] And, following a common pattern, at the European level he served as treasurer of the Forum of European Muslim Youth and Student Organisations.

Upon being introduced by Khalid, Saghrouni invited Mohamed to join the study circles organized by his milieu in the Lille area. "Very quickly," recounts Mohamed, "my integration sped up, and the meetings with the 'brothers' grew in frequency as well, on the sidelines of the collective meals to break the fast, the night prayer, the learning circles on campus, and tours to discover other mosques, especially the one in Lille-Sud of the UOIF. As time passed, a small compact group formed, mainly constituted by foreign students—almost all of Moroccan origin. The 'brothers' recruiters of the UOIF noticed it as well."

Indeed, after roughly one year of involvement in study circles and various activities of the milieu, Saghrouni reportedly approached Mohamed and asked if he wanted to join the Brotherhood. Aware that Mohamed had already pledged allegiance to MRR/MUR while in Morocco, Saghrouni told him that organizations like MRR/MUR are "good people" but not "the real Muslim Brotherhood." Mohamed, flattered and intrigued by the offer, accepted but, out of loyalty, told Saghrouni he first wanted to inform the leaders of MUR of the development. Taking advantage of the school break, Mohamed returned to Morocco and spoke with his mentors at MUR, who approved his decision to join the Brotherhood in France.

Back in France, Mohamed informed Saghrouni that there was no obstacle to his induction. Mohamed, along with a handful of young activists from the local study circles, was then asked to attend a daylong private seminar at the Lille-Sud mosque. There, the head of education for the UOIF "trained us for a day to better understand the credo of the Muslim Brotherhood," from its core beliefs to the differences with other Islamic movements. Particular emphasis was placed on the duties that membership in the organization entails. A few weeks later, on a Saturday night, Mohamed and the other inductees were summoned for a dinner at the same mosque. Attending the dinner were Amar Lasfar, one of the senior leaders of the Brotherhood milieu in Lille and currently the president of UOIF, and various local and national UOIF leaders. In his book *Why I Left the Muslim Brothers*, Mohamed describes the moment that followed:

> After we took our seats and the meeting opened with chants of a few Quranic verses, Amar Lasfar and the person in charge of education at the LIN [Ligue Islamique du Nord, Islamic League of the North] reminded the group of the reason behind the meeting. After the introduction, they invited us to stand up and create a circle by holding hands. The light wasn't very strong. The current president of the UOIF [Amar Lasfar] asked us to repeat the pledge of allegiance after him, in Arabic. I vaguely remember some sentences: "I vow before Allah, the Almighty, to rigorously observe the dispositions and precepts of Islam and to wage Jihad to defend his cause. I vow to Him to respect the conditions of my allegiance to the Muslim Brotherhood and to perform my duties toward our Brotherhood. I vow to Him to obey its leaders in ease as well as in adversity, as much as I will be able to bear, as long as the orders that are given to me do not force me to sin. I hereby pledge allegiance and Allah is my witness." It was a very special moment, and filled with emotion too![8]

Life Inside the Brotherhood

The emotional moment described above made official something that, according to Mohamed, was already de facto accomplished. "You have already acquired skills," he explains; "the mind-set, you are already indoctrinated, you cannot picture your life out of it." Of course, once officially a member, Mohamed's responsibilities to the movement grew—"and the more you progress the greater the duties," he clarifies. He began paying his fee, as a *muntazil*, of 2.5 percent of his income. He was also inserted in an usra, which met every Friday night, where he deepened his knowledge of Brotherhood ideology and inner workings

But, as Mohamed's induction ceremony indicated, the French Brotherhood milieu appeared to be characterized by an overlap of two structures. On one hand, there was the secret structure, the *jamaat*, with a hierarchy and features not disclosed to the public, like the baya and the usra. On the other hand, there was the UOIF and its many suborganizations, all of them registered with the government, with a website, a publicly known structure, and open activities. According to Mohamed, the two structures, save for minor elements, perfectly mirror each other. The leaders of the Brotherhood structure are the leaders of UOIF, with an almost complete coincidence of roles and positions. As he puts it, "there is the façade and the arrière boutique [back of the shop]," "there is the light, and there is the shadow," each serving a function but both part of the same structure and design. Some prominent members of the UOIF network may not belong to the Brotherhood structure, but those who do not will always occupy only junior positions or, if they hold very visible positions, will in reality have little power. Conversely, while some leaders of the secret structure will not appear in the UOIF network, "the façade," most will occupy leadership positions in it.

Following this logic, Mohamed was placed in the French Brotherhood's secret structure, the "arrière boutique," participating in the usra and conducting other nonpublic activities, but he was also tasked with several positions in the "façade," the web of organizations linked to the UOIF. He was inserted in both UOIF and LIN, UOIF's local affiliate, in the Lille area, focusing particularly on student outreach. And soon he became involved with the local branch of EMF, the network's student organization. Elected president of EMF's Lille branch in 2000, Mohamed revitalized it by bringing to bear his experience in political mobilization acquired in Morocco. He and his team campaigned to be elected to student unions and all sorts of bodies that, at the local or national level, influence university life. These were enormous efforts to gain a say within bodies that decide fairly trivial matters; but, seen from another perspective, they were useful exercises to hone the recently inducted Brothers' mobilization skills and attract a larger number of Muslim students to the milieu's message.

To this latter end, Mohamed's EMF branch conducted several activities. The group had organized a system to welcome incoming Muslim students, particularly from abroad, helping them with the bureaucratic process of registering for classes and obtaining housing in student residences. It ran a food bank and even distributed envelopes with small amounts of cash during Ramadan. It organized football games and field trips, barbecues and seminars. It also presented a play, written by Mohamed himself and "very much influenced by the works of the American author Noam Chomsky," on the "fabrication of consent" in the wake of the 9/11 attacks. And it made sure that the Friday sermons in the four prayer rooms of the campus of Villeneuve-d'Ascq were delivered by individuals within or approved by the Brotherhood milieu.

All these activities were open to all Muslim students and were seen positively by university administrators, who viewed them as positive signs of integration. But, claims Mohamed, the real goal of these endeavors was spotting and selecting new Brothers. EMF's outreach "aimed at integrating them, little by little, into the cells of indoctrination of the ideology of Hassan al Banna and of Sayyid Qutb, in the backstage—closed to the greater public—in the interest of preparing them to pledge allegiance to the Muslim Brotherhood and secondarily to the UOIF." This aim, clarifies Mohamed, was unknown to most EMF members, who, "for the most part, didn't suspect a thing and ignored everything—or almost everything—of this Islamic reality whose depths were kept secret."

While Mohamed and the few other inducted Brothers who ran EMF were well aware of this reality and were actually the ones organizing the activities so that the senior leadership could spot new talent, most of their fellow EMF members worked tirelessly without knowing what for. "Most of the members of EMF," adds Mohamed, "at the local level as well as national level, knew almost nothing about Hassan al Banna, Sayyid Qutb, and the ideology of the Muslim Brotherhood. And yet, there were members of the student branch of the 'brothers' of France, organized within the UOIF. The link was never evident for many militants, even if during some activities some timid linguistic references would be dropped." It was a "deliberate opacity" that enabled EMF to attract broad support while becoming a conduit to the Brotherhood for select few.

Leaving the Brotherhood

Mohamed remained active in Brotherhood networks in the Lille area for about five years. He was respected by his superiors for his intelligence and remarkable mobilization skills, which had enabled the milieu to make various breakthroughs in the university system. Nevertheless, in 2006 Mohamed abruptly left the group. After a hiatus from public life of a few years, since 2015 he has become one of France's and Europe's most public and aggressive critics of the Brotherhood, writing various books about his experience and often appearing in the media.

The reasons for his disengagement are several. From early on, Mohamed was disturbed by various incidents that, in his view, showed the "opaque decision-making process" and the "lack of internal democracy" within the French Brotherhood milieu. He objected to the UOIF's opposition to the participation of the EMF and JMF—its student and youth branch, respectively—in a trip to Auschwitz in 2003.[9] The fact that UOIF leaders sought to overrule the decision taken after a proper internal vote by two technically independent bodies frustrated him, and he bemoaned the fact that "the big wigs can call the shots with a phone call, ignoring votes, procedures, and statutes."

Over time Mohamed also began to dislike the murkiness that surrounded many Brotherhood activities in France. Though secrecy was understandable in Morocco, where authorities could at any time take highly repressive steps to crack down on the movement, France was a completely different environment, and he found the obsession with hiding all aspects of the group's life excessive. Mohamed was particularly uncomfortable with many shady financial transactions he witnessed firsthand, starting with the huge amounts of cash he saw some leaders of the group stash in their houses—a "mafia-like situation," he quips. He also soon understood that many of the businesses connected to the network were hardly transparent in their bookkeeping.

But Mohamed's progressive disenchantment with the Brotherhood accelerated rapidly after two episodes that took place between the end of 2005 and the beginning of 2006. The first occurred as he was leading an interfaith dialogue initiative with Christians in Villeneuve d'Ascq. Together with a local priest he organized a week of interfaith prayers, with sessions to be held at both a church and a mosque. Mohamed could not attend on the day prayers were scheduled at the church because his wife was giving birth to the couple's daughter. But he was informed that the service had opened with the entire congregation offering prayers for him, his wife, and his daughter, something that deeply moved him. He compared that graciousness to how the leadership of the mosque, which was part of the Brotherhood milieu, behaved. When he asked why only one person from the mosque had gone to the church prayer, he was told that "the Christians there are all old, there is no point in converting them." And when the session was held at the mosque and he asked the imam to prepare chairs for the Christian visitors, as most of them were indeed old and could not easily sit on the floor as is customary in mosques, the imam refused. After Mohamed forced him to bring out chairs, the imam delivered a sermon in front of the multifaith congregation extolling Islam as the only true religion. "I really believed in interfaith dialogue," recounts Mohamed. "This attitude was the straw that broke the camel's back for me."

It was around that time that Mohamed began reading a book titled *The Doctrine of the First Son of Adam, or The Problem of Violence in the Islamic Action*. Written by the Syrian Islamic scholar Jawdat Said, the book makes the case for the use of nonviolence by the Islamic movement, basing its arguments on religious texts. Mohamed had read the book ten years earlier, when he was a student in Morocco, but had not been impressed by it. Rereading it after ten years of militancy, he found it eye-opening. "The book was written in 1964, exactly when Sayyid Qutb wrote *Milestones*," he explains. "It argues that the Quran has its roots in nonviolence and that two roads can be taken: one that of Abel, nonviolence, and the other that of Cain, full of violence. Qutb chose the latter, but imagine if humanity, and the Islamic movement, had chosen the other."

By pure coincidence, around that time Said's son-in-law, Khaled Halabi, who himself had been a member of the Brotherhood in Syria before leaving the group and becoming a promoter of nonviolence, was giving a lecture in nearby Brussels. Mohamed attended the lecture and then invited

Halabi to give a talk in Villeneuve d'Ascq. "I already had one foot outside [of the Brotherhood]," recounts Mohamed, "but I was still running things [i.e., activities in the Brotherhood milieu] even though I had mentally checked out." Attending Halabi's talk, according to Mohamed, were Amar Lasfar and other elders of the Brotherhood milieu in the Lille, a highly unusual occurrence. And, as he had feared, the event turned into a confrontation, with members of the Brotherhood milieu verbally attacking Halabi.

After the evening, as Mohamed accompanied Halabi to his hotel, the two men had a long conversation. "Dear Mohamed," Mohamed remembers Halabi telling him, "I was with the Brotherhood in Syria, I know these people. Let me tell you, this is the wrong way." He went on: "There are three important rules. First: no to violence, always, without ifs and buts; second: no to secret activities; and third, no to *tanzim* [organization]." "These three principles," Mohamed says, "are the antithesis of the Brotherhood. I understood he was right; it was time to leave."

Mohamed's decision to quit the organization, communicated to its local leaders, was not well received. Making matters worse, he decided to start two blogs in which he began to expose and criticize both Islamist ideology and the activities of local Brotherhood networks. "The main idea behind my willingness to maintain a continual and peaceful coverage for almost ten years," he explains, "was to explain, to shed light on the 'brothers,' and to call the 'brothers' in France and elsewhere to achieve a great ethical breakthrough, in the hope that some among them could compensate with their altered humanity, and could at least spare their own children from the traps of Islamism." "I naively thought," he continues, "that I could make those 'brothers' listen to these thoughts, especially in a Republican framework where debate is always possible; yet after having witnessed their narrow-mindedness, their intolerance, and their dogmatism, I came to understand that 'there is none so deaf as he who will not hear.'"

Rather than spurring internal debate, Mohamed's blogs triggered a reaction from the Brotherhood milieu. "Following my resignation from the UOIF," he notes, "I suffered at the end of 2006 a very violent operation of excommunication from the Muslim religion." He charges, "Under the patronage of the current president of the UOIF Amar Lasfar, some local 'brothers,' who were guided by their imam, led a serious operation of blacklisting me." During a two-month period, claims Mohamed, Ahmed Miktar, the imam of the local mosque and also the president of the Association of Imams of France, gave sermons in the mosque "alerting the crowd of silent and well-behaved believers seated in front of him of the intellectual and religious 'dangers' of a group of apostates of Villeneuve-d'Ascq who in his mind represented the 'enemies of Islam,' enemies from within." Mohamed argues that the language of those sermons, framed in Islamic terms, made clear to the congregation that it was a declaration of apostasy, which under Islamic law is punishable with death.

"In parallel," he continues, "some saint 'sisters' of the UOIF concocted an almost secret plan to attempt to separate my wife from me, only a few weeks after the birth of my son Souleïmène. They pretended that they wanted to come congratulate my wife for her new baby, but were in reality planning to convince her of the 'Islamic' obligation of divorcing an apostate." Some friends within the milieu alerted Mohamed about these machinations, which he compared to what the Brotherhood in Egypt did to liberal thinkers like Nasr Hamid Abu Zayd and Nawal Saadawi.

The months immediately after his resignation were rife with tensions for Mohamed and his family. He left Villeneuve-d'Ascq for a couple of years to work as an engineer in Metz and in Luxembourg. But he continued to post vitriolic accusations against the French Brotherhood milieu and Islamism in general on his blogs. He has since been sued for defamation six times, but despite the resulting financial burden and stress he has not desisted. If anything, in recent years he has become even more vocal. The attacks of January 2015 against the satirical newspaper *Charlie Hebdo* and the subsequent terrorist attacks that have bloodied France have only reinforced his belief that Islamism, whether in its violent or its nonviolent manifestation, is a cancer that needs to be fought and strengthened his resolve to play a role in that fight.

Mohamed does not mince words when describing the threat of Islamism. In his pamphlet *Freeing Islam from Islamism* (2018), he writes:

Political Islam is incompatible with the values that shape French democracy: *laïcité* [secularism], the heritage of the Enlightenment, the rights of men and citizens, fundamental freedoms, equality of men and women. Political Islam promotes a societal counter-project, a strategic project of "Islamization" of French society, in steps and degrees, from the top and from the bottom, under the cover of "moderate Islam" or "legalistic Islam." It operates through its closed circles of ideological indoctrination, its widespread literature, its mosques and associations crisscrossing the national territory, its private schools, its public gatherings, and all the spaces it can conquer, not without the help of the state, notably through its introduction in the chaplaincies in prisons, hospitals and even the French army. This counter-project has a name: *tamkine*.[10]

The concept of *tamkine* is one that Mohamed stresses constantly. It is, in his view, "a strategic plan elaborated by the Muslim Brotherhood to reestablish the Islamic caliphate, a plan of political conquest that the Brothers frame in religious terms, justifying what is a purely political project through the use (or, better, abuse) of hadith and Quranic verses." In substance, Mohamed argues that tamkine is the end goal of the Muslim Brotherhood, a plan for global domination in stages that the group has elaborated over the past decades and that includes the West. Mohamed bases this conviction not just on conversations he heard while part of the French Brotherhood milieus but also on the fact that clear plans outlining the tamkine strategy were reportedly found in documents retrieved in searches of top Brotherhood officials in Egypt. Most famously, one was retrieved by Egyptian authorities in 1992 in the house of Khairat el Shater, one of the guiding figures of the Egyptian Brotherhood's previous generation.

Mohamed believes that tamkine is a strategic project of supremacy that the Brothers seek to advance one step at a time, without the unplanned overreach that characterizes the jihadists. And while those in the movement fully understand that dynamics vary significantly from the East to the West, they are working in both environments to advance the Brotherhood's tamkine through gradualism, a cautious approach characterized by the choice of more or less aggressive tactics based on an assessment of what works better. According the Mohamed:

Where Islamism finds a few square kilometers to conquer or to pollinate, it does not hesitate to expand its web and to put down roots by any means at its disposal. Where it seems to have the support of a majority, it asserts itself through demands and laws that originate from the Islamic Sharia in its harshest version, as well as its most backward and intolerable versions too. Where it becomes aware of its relative minority, it adapts. Popular wisdom in Morocco created a word of advice for submissive women, or beaten women. This advice recommends to them, I quote: "Tmeskeni hta tmekkeni!" In French, this would mean: "Keep a low profile and lay low until the day where you will attain power, the day where you will dominate!" I would like to highlight that, oddly, the dialect term "tmekkeni" is derived from the Arabic term tamkine.

To demonstrate that the Brotherhood has the ultimate goal of conquering the West but seeks to do so patiently and gradually, Mohamed points to an interview that the former FIOE president and Swedish Brotherhood milieu bigwig Chakib Benmakhlouf gave to the Arabic newspaper *Asharq al Awsat* in 2008.[11] Asked about the future of Islam in Europe, Benmakhlouf touted the large and established presence of Muslims on the Continent: "Thousands of mosques, thousands of minarets, and the Islamic voice is now respected." He added, "The conditions and future of the Muslims in Europe will be better, with the help of God. We are very optimistic in this regard. The Prophet, even while besieged during the Battle of the Trench, announced the victory to the Muslims." Mohamed finds this last statement very telling and asks, "What sort of 'victory' was he talking about? Against what adversary? And why precisely reference the 'Battle of the Trench,' if the Prophet motivated his troops in almost all battles? Why this particular symbol?" While it might be lost on most non-Muslims, to Muslims and, particularly to those in the Islamist milieu, the reference to the Battle of the Trench, described in the thirty-third surah of the Quran, has a particular meaning. It was, in fact, one of the most crucial wins of the prophet Mohammed and his early followers against the Meccans, and it carries various symbolic meanings that, argues Mohamed, Islamists often adapt to their situation in the West. At the Battle of the Trench, the army of the Prophet was outnumbered but better organized and therefore capable of outwitting their stronger opponents. Thus, in Mohamed's view, Benmakhlouf's reference to it is not random but applies well-known Quranic symbology to reality in the West.

Mohamed argues that deception is one of the Brothers' main tactics to achieve tamkine. For this reason, the Brothers have developed a broad variety of dissimulating rhetorical tricks to hide their real purposes. These include *taqiya*, a "sophisticated technique of double discourse and dissimulation of true beliefs, opinions, and intentions"; *moudarah*, a "form of artificial politesse aimed at imposing their views progressively, in fits and starts, and without disavowing them"; *moudahana*, "hiding one's convictions to gain the trust of a hostile environment"; and *ta'rid*, "camouflaging the truth without lying but in a way that seeks to make the interlocutor understand the opposite of the truth."[12]

Similarly deceptive and opportunistic, according to Mohamed, is the game played by the Brothers of ever-shifting alliances:

The "brothers" have very well understood the political game based on opportunistic alliances. They execute it with more or less success. A shot on the left, another to the center, and another to the right. On Palestine, they demonstrate next to far-left forces. On the so-called Islamic headscarf, they demonstrate with Salafists and "middle ground" forces. Against "equal marriage for all," they associate themselves with the right wing, or even the far right. For local elections they don't follow a political line—one time to the left, one time to the right. Everything depends on the color of the party that facilitates their Islamist projects the best.

While Mohamed views tamkine as the Brotherhood's end goal, he also points to short- and midterm goals that the group has developed. The Brotherhood in France, he argues, seeks to "penetrate the republic through various doors: education, politics, economy, military," and to address each sector it has established specific organizations. In fact, it operates in several fields. In recent years, he argues, the main focus has been on youth, an inherently crucial demographic for a group with a long-term plan. The French Brothers have therefore developed a web of private schools, which in some cases have even managed to receive funding from the French state—a remarkable achievement in a quintessentially secular country.

Equally important for the French Brothers in this phase, according to Mohamed, is building and controlling the "cathedral mosques," as he calls them, that are being built throughout the country. Over the past few years, French authorities have significantly relaxed the obstacles they put up in previous decades to the construction of large mosques and to the Brothers. Thanks to its good connections to local political establishments and ample funding often coming from abroad (see chapter 11), the French Brotherhood milieu has often been able to obtain permits to build the large mosques that have started to dot the landscape in large and midsize French cities.

Control of "cathedral mosques" enables the Brothers to influence large number of French Muslims and recruit new members. But it also enables them to make gains in another field on which they are focusing in this phase: political representation. The French Brotherhood milieu, in fact, desperately seeks to be seen as and to become the main speakers for French Muslims in the eyes of the French establishment, and one of the main avenues to do so is gaining control of bodies, like the French Council of the Muslim Faith (Conseil français du culte musulman, CFCM), created by the government to represent French Muslims.[13] Since voting rights within the CFCM have traditionally been allocated to various Muslim organizations on the basis of square footage of the mosques they control, building "cathedral mosques" is a clever way to also obtain more power in elections.

The attitude of the French state and, more broadly, French society toward Islamism is a related topic that motivates and frustrates Mohamed. He argues that France underestimates the threat, wrongly believing that it can manage it, that it can appease it, that it can find a modus vivendi with "this conquering Islam that deliberately presents itself as victim of everything and guilty of nothing."[14] He maintains that the French establishment is intellectually ill-equipped for this fight, failing to grasp the magnitude of the challenge posed by a divisive ideology that is slowly but surely corroding the very foundations of French society from within. He writes:

> Marianne [the symbol of the French republic] believes that she is offering an honorable place to Islam, and she cedes ground to Islamism. She abandons neighborhoods, and Islamism settles in. She finances schools, and Islamism spreads in them. Islamism makes progress. Marianne pulls back. Islamism knows how to complain, as the usual victim. She grants it more power. When Marianne recites the Constitution, or issues a reminder of the secular framework of republic law, Islamism lets out the cry of Islamophobia.[15]

Mohamed argues that after decades of appeasement that have empowered Islamists and, consequently, brought major fissures to French society, France needs to seriously reevaluate its relationship toward Islamism. "A frank and open debate must take place between the French Republic and Islamism," he declares, "between the secular choice forged after so many wars and so much suffering, and the projections of the Tamkine which seek to challenge all the achievements of the Republic and of secularism, and impose once again rifts, wars of religion and sufferings. . . . The distant goal of domination by the Muslim Brotherhood through their Tamkine strategies, their programs, their values, their means, their agents and their accomplices, must be examined scrupulously."

Mohamed believes that France should take various steps to correct the mistakes of the past decades. It should "liberate" French mosques, which "a little less than a thousand brothers" "colonized" through their funds and superior organizational skills. It should also stop funding Islamist mosques and schools, stop turning a blind eye to Islamist activities, and stop being willfully fooled by self-appointed community leaders out of a wish to avoid being called Islamophobes or being reminded of France's colonial past.

But these tactical moves should be accompanied by a broader strategic change in perspective. France, according to Mohamed, needs to understand the crucial difference "between Islam and Islamism, between a faith and a political ideology." "Islamism," he argues, "has managed to portray itself as the equal of Islam" and to "convince many politicians and many media outlets that their ideology is the exact equal of the Muslim religion." Mohamed's writings ceaselessly appeal to French elites and society to start making that distinction and to no longer appease a small cadre of activists pushing a divisive political ideology camouflaged as religion.

An important inspiration for that differentiation between Islam and Islamism longed for by Mohamed comes from his late grandfather. Mohamed describes him as an epitome of the traditional way of living the faith in rural Morocco and the antithesis of Islamism: no ostentatious shows of faith, no public prayer, no politics, just a private relationship with God. "He had no beard but had a heart," writes Mohamed. "He didn't preach with his voice, his behavior spoke instead." He adds, "Without telling me anything he showed me the way. As an adolescent I chose a side path and joined the Muslim Brothers. When I was 28, in 2006, I retook my freedom, deciding to march alone, like he did, toward the horizon he had showed me."[16]

CHAPTER VII

Omero Marongiu

Joining the Brotherhood

Omero Marongiu was born in Valenciennes in 1969, the last of
the seven children of Italian immigrants who in 1957 had left
their native Mediterranean island of Sardinia to settle in the
French town.[1] They were part of a large wave of migrants from southern
Europe, the Balkans, and North Africa who reached the coal-rich towns
of northern France and Belgium to work in mines. Friendly and jovial,
Omero speaks fondly about his care-free childhood and adolescence; he
recalls growing up in a neighborhood that hosted the families of these
workers and having mostly friends of Arab origin.

By the spring of 1987, he recounts, his Arab friends, who had previously
displayed no interest in religion, began to attend the local mosque. Omero
remembers accompanying them after long afternoons playing football (soccer) and sitting in the back of the mosque, watching them pray. He and his
friends began talking with increased frequency about religion. Omero, who
used to read in church, found himself at a loss for arguments when defending Christianity to his friends who compared it unfavorably to Islam. He
was also struck by the direct, intermediary-free relationship that Muslims
had with God and fascinated by the collective Muslim prayer. He began
reading about Islam and, on December 4, 1987, nine days before turning
eighteen, converted to Islam in the local mosque.

Omero's parents did not take his conversion well. His father, he recalls, saw it as a betrayal of the family's Italian roots and heritage. While friendly to fellow miners of Muslim background, his father also did not like some of their views, starting with how they spoke about non-Muslim women. Tensions with his father led Omero to leave the house. He took to the road with the Tabligh, a transnational conservative Islamic movement that encourages its adepts to travel the world to do dawa, and spent months in the group's mosques in Roubaix, Paris, and Lyon. He eventually came back to Valenciennes but not to his home, sleeping instead at the local mosque. He recalls that during those tense times, his Muslim friends urged him to patch things up with his father and told him that compromising on certain tenets of Islam (like eating *halal* meat) was acceptable if necessary to have good relations with his family. "They adopted an open and tolerant Islam," he says with a sweet smile.

Omero and his friends started attending the talks of a handful of preachers who, in those early days of Islamic activism in France, gave their talks in French and not, like most others, in Arabic. Stars of this nascent circle of preachers were Hani Ramadan and Hassan Iquioussen. The former is the son of Said Ramadan, one of the pioneers of the Muslim Brotherhood in Europe.[2] Married to Hassan al Banna's eldest daughter, Said Ramadan occupied various important positions in the Brotherhood in Egypt before being forced out of the country in the 1950s. After moving to West Germany, by the early 1960s he settled in Geneva. He then spearheaded the creation of several of the first Brotherhood-linked Islamic centers and Muslim organizations in Europe (most famously the Islamic Society of Germany, out of the Munich mosque), thanks to his close relationship to the Muslim World League and a web of wealthy donors in the Arab Gulf. His sons Hani and the more widely known Tariq, who became an internationally renowned intellectual until his downfall in 2017 following allegations of serious sexual misconduct, continued their father's work of dawa but, being Geneva-born, in French.

Hassan Iquioussen was born in 1964 near Valenciennes, Omero's hometown, the son of Moroccan parents who had arrived in the France in the 1930s with the first generation of North African immigrants. Highly educated, charismatic, and oratorically gifted, he was, as Omero puts it, "constantly reading or preaching." Iquioussen, in fact, used to travel incessantly, mostly throughout the north of France, to give talks in mosques or in private gatherings. "His lectures were not political," Omero says, "just about Islam: the miracles in the Quran, religious practices, why Christianity was theologically flawed."

The importance of Hassan Iquioussen and Hani Ramadan in re-Islamizing young French Muslims during the 1980s and 1990s—and, in some cases, leading them on the path to becoming Brothers—cannot be overemphasized. Tellingly, Farid Abdelkrim's description of the impact the two preachers had on him is virtually identical to Omero's. Born and raised in Nantes, in the west of France, Abdelkrim joined the Brotherhood in 1990, at about the same time and same age as Omero. Like Omero, he left after more than a decade, but he has been more vocal ever since, publishing an acclaimed autobiographical book (*Why I Quit Being an Islamist: Journey at the Heart of Islam in France*) that denounces the Brothers and has made him a media personality.

Abdelkrim writes that in his late teens, as he was getting more interested in Islam, "after al Banna, I discovered the existence of another Hassan: Iquioussen. A true pioneer. Itinerant preacher. Indefatigable. Tirelessly crisscrossing France and Belgium. Bringing with him the good word. His small size and *chtimi* [from the north of France] accent did not make him less of an outstanding orator in my eyes. In public he expressed himself in French but could handle Arabic references with rare ease. Without support. He was also able to have a good sense of humor. Fascinated, I decided to follow his example." Abdelkrim was also a deep admirer of Hani Ramadan: "he had a different style, but I found him equally fascinating."[3]

Similarly mesmerized by both, Omero had more frequent access to Iquioussen, who lived close to him. And soon Iquioussen took Omero under his wing, establishing a relationship that lasted fifteen years. Recognizing potential in the young, motivated, and eloquent convert, Iquioussen decided to become his personal teacher, introducing him to many aspects of Islamic theology and the art of rhetoric and public speaking. Every Wednesday Omero, who by then had begun studying sociology at the university in Lille, would "sit for three long hours with my mentor, I would have the honor of having a private course for myself only, and I would write down every word that would leave his mouth. When my mentor was not available, he would prepare an audio cassette that I would use to transcribe word for word."[4]

The private classes were not just for Omero's benefit. Iquioussen had tasked the young convert to manage a series of *halaqat* (study groups) in the Valenciennes area, which were attended every Friday by some twenty to thirty young Muslims. Omero's job was not just to organize those meetings but also to deliver the lectures he had heard from Iquioussen on Wednesday. "I had two days to put my notes in proper form," he reminisces, "and deliver in the newly created study groups of the Valenciennes region the well-memorized content word for word, sometimes down to the last comma."

"All of this was enough to establish a reputation," he writes in his short memoire posted on his blog, "and two nicknames that would stick with me for a good decade: *Omar Taliani* [Omar the Italian] and *Le petit Hassan* [The small Hassan]." Omero and Iquioussen had a strong relationship of a kind extremely common in Brotherhood circles, as the younger man deeply admired, blindly trusted, and was shaped in his knowledge and behavior by the older. It is a natural by-product of the process of selection and grooming of new Brothers, which entails years of close contact during which the mentor tests, develops, and progressively opens up to his protégé, inevitably creating a personal bond that will continue after the individual is inducted into the Brotherhood—and often last a lifetime. It is also one of the ways that the movement ensures internal discipline, as most mentees will tend to look up to and not challenge their mentors even after decades of membership in the organization.

"I owe to him my original rhetoric," writes Omero of Iquioussen; "he introduced me . . . to the techniques of the speech, to several religious disciplines, and, most importantly, guided me toward the literature of the Muslim Brotherhood." Over time Iquioussen began to assign Omero more and more books written by Brotherhood authors: Said Hawwa, Fathi Yakin, Yusuf al Qaradawi, Faysal Mawlawi. Slowly he also started introducing Omero to the history of the movement, its politics, and its vision. "He would often mention a *hadith*," Omero reminisces, "that says that every century God sends a person that revitalizes the faith; in the twentieth century that person was Hassan al Banna."

It soon became clear to Omero that the study circles he had created for Iquioussen were instruments used both to disseminate a conservative interpretation of Islam and to spot new talent. "We, young Francophones, discovered with our mentor the global process of spreading religious rhetoric and learning that started, within the Muslim Brotherhood as with the other preaching groups, with general discourses that would end, by a funnel strategy, with closed circles reserved for the initiated." Given his position as "petit Hassan," Omero served a key role of organizer of the "infrastructure of the circles of learning that would serve as the foundation for the recruitment of local professionals who will be invited to join the Muslim Brotherhood."

It was therefore unsurprising that after months running the halaqat in Valenciennes, in June 1992 Omero was invited to join the Brotherhood. "Iquioussen told me for the first time that he was a member of the Muslim Brotherhood and asked me to become a member of the Brotherhood's structure in France," he recalls. "For me, at twenty-two, it was the best thing that could have happened. I can become a member of the Brotherhood? I couldn't believe it. It was an honor, and there was the sense of intrigue, of discovering something secret, it was gripping."

Omero's actual induction took place more than a year later, in September 1993. According to Omero, he was sworn in during an informal ceremony that was held at the main Brotherhood mosque in Lille. He described it, exactly like Louizi, who also joined the Brotherhood in Lille, does, as a small seminary during which some of the Brotherhood elders explained the history of the organization, gave speeches emphasizing the necessity of working for Islam, and then asked the dozen inductees, standing in a circle and holding hands, to swear baya. The ceremony, explains Omero, allowed the new members to "penetrate at last the lair of the Brothers, to finally access the mysteries of the initiated through a handshake and the recitation of the pact of allegiance, which translated into the language of Moliere means 'I pledge to God to bind myself to Islam and to follow in an assiduous manner its fundamental precepts, to obey to the person in charge [of the Muslim Brotherhood] with what he will order me to do, and which will be consistent with what God and his Prophet agree to, in the ease as well as in the adversity.'"[5]

Omero claims he belonged to the first batch of "francophone" Brothers to be inducted. The pioneers of the Brotherhood in France had long been hesitant to accept Muslims born in France, suspicious of children of Muslim immigrants and, even more, of converts like Omero. But by the early 1990s, and not without internal debates, they decided to open their ranks to this new generation. "I became a *muntazim*," he says, "the lowest level of the Brothers in Europe, and had two main obligations: attending the usra and paying 2.5 percent of my salary." He claims that unlike in the Arab world, the Brotherhood in Europe has only two levels, *muntazim* and *amil*, the full-ranking Brother, who has all the rights of membership and has to pay 5 percent of his salary to the organization.

Life Inside the Brotherhood

During his eleven years inside the organization, Omero came to understand many of its intricate inner workings. "It soon became clear to me that the Brotherhood in France has an open structure and a secret structure," he explains. "This is similar to all European countries, and the Brothers in each of them make a choice about how much to appear as Brothers on the public scene and how much to conceal it, depending on their assessment of what it most conducive in a given country, on how the politics and circumstances are. In Sweden or in the UK they can do more; in France, with its strict secularism, they judge it to be more challenging."

Based on this assessment, the French Brothers have created, according to Omero, two synoptic structures: One, based on the classic system of selective recruitment, induction, usras, fee-paying membership, specialized committees, and collective election of a shura and an emir, is kept secret and vehemently denied (or, in some cases, described as just a thing of the past) when brought up by critics. The other structure is public and indeed publicity seeking. It has its most visible face in the Union of Islamic Organizations in France, but it also encompasses myriad organizations devoted to specific tasks, from education to politics, from charity to interfaith dialogue, that the milieu has created.

This dichotomous nature of the French Brotherhood is, according to Omero, intended to hide the true nature of the cluster's many organizations in order to increase their effectiveness. Moreover, it is structured in a way that allows those within the secret structure, the "true Brothers," to retain control of the many organizations of the cluster's public side, since many of its organizations also include among their members and, to a lesser degree, their leadership individuals with no formal affiliation with the Brotherhood.

Omero argues that the core leadership of the UOIF, in particular its president and treasurer, are always the same individuals who serve as emir and treasurer of the secret structure of the French Brotherhood. Elections for both positions are held every four years, generally before the large annual meeting held by the UOIF in Le Bourget, outside Paris. The Brothers hold their internal elections and decide their leadership. Even though the UOIF is a federation of mosques and Islamic associations, not all of which are linked to the movement, according to Omero the Brotherhood controls the UOIF's internal elections and makes sure their outcome largely matches that of the secret structure. This tight grip is also kept at the local level. Not all mosques and Islamic organizations belonging to the UOIF, Omero says, are full-fledged Brotherhood. But the Brothers make sure to have the majority of votes on the board of each of them in order to control their direction.

Upon his induction Omero became deeply involved in both the secret and public aspects of life in the French Brotherhood. He was in charge of the local branch of the Young Muslims of France (Jeunes Musulmans de France, JMF) and of the UOIF in the Valenciennes area. In keeping with the synoptic structure he described, Omero's position as head of various "public and visible" organizations in the Brotherhood's milieu coincided with his role as main coordinator of the secret structure of the Brothers in the Valenciennes area (in which he says there were some thirty inducted Brothers). Between 1993 and 1995 he ran a web of study groups in the local area, "called in our Brotherhood jargon 'introductory circles'—halaqât tamhidiyyah," that included some 250 participants (in addition to a smaller number in the town of Tourcoing, near the Belgian border) and that, as was characteristic of the Brotherhood, served the dual purposes of doing dawa and "spotting talent." He also devoted himself feverishly to his role as imam, delivering sermons regularly in various mosques of the region and beyond, and to translating into French Arabic books by Brotherhood leaders. "These texts," explains Omero, "would be used for ten years by the people in charge of the educational aspects of the UOIF within the context of seminars for integrating new militants."[6]

By his own account, the height of Omero's career as a local Brotherhood activist came when he became the imam of a mosque in Valenciennes. "This consecration," Omero notes, "was consequent to a seizure of power that we within the Muslim Brotherhood branch of the Valenciennes area had wisely orchestrated for almost four years." The story of how the small group of Brothers in Omero's area, many of them second-generation Muslims who had gone through the halaqat system created by Iquioussen and Omero himself in the Valenciennes area, typifies a modus operandi found in Brotherhood networks throughout the West.[7] This is how Omero summarizes it on his personal website:

We [local Muslim Brotherhood activists] already had two main anchorage points in the Valenciennes area, one in a mosque which would become the "fiefdom" of my mentor in Escaudain, and another in the small mosque of Raismes in which we were fifteen supporting Brothers. It was therefore rather natural for us to establish a sort of "bi-cephalous" organization by alternating our activities between those two geographical centers, in a rather pragmatic way. But before all that, a strategy of gentle "seizure of power" would have to be enacted in both mosques. . . .

. . . The first step was the unilateral creation of a cultural association, controlled by the Brothers, within the mosque—a former mine workshop. The elders consented after a few tense moments and explanations about the usefulness of the association, then they saw mostly positively our concrete involvement in the progressive transformation of this workshop into a real mosque: we tore down fairly quickly the dilapidated structure and built the new building with our own hands, with the help of a professional construction site supervisor. . . .

. . . The second step was the total takeover of the mosque, between 1999 and 2000, not without bitter exchanges nor without major arguments with the elders. Initially, the deal was simple: an elder and a young person occupied in alternation the incumbent and deputy positions, as well as the presidency and vice presidency. In a small mosque like ours, the progressive growth of membership of the Brothers and of supporters was large enough to ensure the total control of the governing positions during the elections, and some elders firmly supported this idea of "transition." Finally, we made our final move in the following general assembly by taking total control of the administrative boards of the mosque. . . .

. . . It became a year and a half of hesitation, during which the majority of the elders left the mosque, would pray in the mosques of the neighboring cities, and would at times accuse us of having betrayed them and evicted them from the mosque. In such circumstances, it is not easy to embody the role of leader; I would see those faces marked by years of work in the mines of the Valenciennes area, those bodies with declining strength, that we had murdered again.

Thanks to his accomplishments in his local area, by the late 1990s Omero had reached a relatively senior position in the Brotherhood milieu in northern France and interacted regularly with the leadership at the national level. Yet he acknowledges that he felt he was kept in the dark about many aspects of the organization, from some of its inner workings to some of its aims and tactical choices. "Some of the elders," he recounts, "would tell us that we [the younger, mostly French-born Brothers] were their gunpowder, projecting them inside French society. They would tell us that they could not tell us everything and that we needed to trust them."

Leaving the Brotherhood

In the first years that followed his induction Omero enthusiastically embraced the French Brotherhood's agenda. Yet by 1997 he began to doubt the group's ideology and his decision to join them. A series of encounters with a diverse set of individuals and organizations from various cross sections of French society led him to question the Brotherhood-dominated mind-set he had absorbed. "These interactions allowed me to open up to new thoughts," he explains, "to develop my own narrative and worldview."

One of the first interactions that gave him pause about the Brothers' philosophy came in 1996, when Omero, as part of the outreach work he was doing in Valenciennes on behalf of JMF, came in contact with a local organization raising awareness about HIV. A leader of this organization asked Omero whether the JMF would be interested in a partnership, something Omero thought would have been beneficial to the local Muslim community. But he was taken aback when the Brotherhood leadership scolded him for even suggesting the idea, arguing that a partnership with an organization that brought up uncomfortable topics such as sex, homosexuality, and drugs was completely inappropriate.

More doubts arose when he began his master's degree in sociology in Lille. For his thesis, titled "Veiled Logics: How Veiled Muslim Women Perceive Their Integration in French Society," Omero interviewed several young Muslim women who did not belong to the Brotherhood milieu. To his surprise, he discovered that many of them had no problem reconciling their piousness and desire to wear the veil with their day-to-day life in French society, which has traditionally strictly limited the presence of religious symbols in public life. "Many of them wanted to become teachers and knew that they would not be able to wear the veil inside the classroom," explains Omero, "but it was not an issue for them; they fully accepted the separation of the private and public spheres." Omero contrasted this conciliatory approach of unaffiliated Muslim women with the "confrontational, identity-based" discourse pushed by the UOIF and the Brotherhood milieu, which had made wearing the veil in schools one of its cornerstone issues. "I began to understand the difference between the Brothers' identity politics and day-to-day reality, secularized practice."

Through his academic work, Omero also came in contact with the Ligue de l'enseignement (Teaching League), a prominent and staunchly secular French organization founded in the nineteenth century to promote education, free speech, and culture.[8] "I discovered through them a new world, honest and open-minded people who were seeking to sincerely engage Muslims in order to find common ground," explains Omero. It led him to make new friends beyond the narrow and secluded world of the Brothers, as he was exposed to new ideas and visions of society.

His time at the university and with the Ligue de l'enseignement also led him to a newfound appreciation of traditional French culture and language. He came to resent the fact that Arabic was the dominant language of the Brotherhood milieus. "I have always spoken good Arabic and even translated large Arabic books into French," he elaborates, "so it was not a matter of me not understanding what was going on; but why would meetings of a supposedly French Muslim organization be held in Arabic?" He came to slowly realize that the old generation of French Brothers knew and cared little about French culture and language, something that bothered him.

These experiences led Omero to "rediscover my own identity." "I understood," he explains, "that I am not Arab. I am Muslim, but I am French, and proud of it. I have my own identity," which is broader and more complex than that promoted by the Brothers. "The Brothers," he continues, "push an all-encompassing version of Islam, one that accompanies you from when you wake up until you go to bed. It's an Islam centered on practice, on public demonstrations, on constantly showing one's identity." He adds, "The speeches of Iquioussen, the ideas of the Brothers were appealing when I was twenty-five, but after then, and particularly once I started studying sociology and understanding the world's complexities, they made less sense; they clashed with reality."

These realizations led Omero to gradually detach from the Brothers' ideology and activities. "I began to develop my own discourse, not that of 'Omero, Hassan Iquioussen's number two.'" Through this process, he became increasingly attracted to the thinking of the Bordeaux-based imam

Tareq Oubrou. Moroccan-born, Oubrou is an iconic figure of French Islam. His name is closely associated with the Brotherhood, and he is one of the founders of the UOIF. In recent years, though, his more progressive views have occasionally put him at odds with the leadership of the French Brotherhood, making him the spiritual leader of the more liberal segments of the French Islamist milieu—the post-Ikhwan, as some would dub it.

In Omero's view, "Oubrou had understood that the old discourse of the Brotherhood has its limits, that we need to think differently about Islam in a Western society, about *laïcité*, secularization." He cites the issue of the veil, which historically has caused frequent clashes between those in the French Brotherhood milieu and the French government, as a primary example of Oubrou's more nuanced and conciliatory approach. "Iquioussen would tell you that a woman needs to wear the veil everywhere and that's that," says Omero. "Oubrou would say that it is an obligation but it is not fundamental, that there is room to negotiate with society over it." It is an approach, he argues, that Mawlawi had already supported in the 1990s but that the French Brotherhood's leadership had willfully ignored.

Omero describes 2002 as the year in which tensions between the conservative old guard and the more reformist factions of the French Brotherhood reached their apex. "The UOIF's leadership wanted the JMF to conduct activities aimed at the French public reinforcing the concept of Muslim identity," he recalls, "while the youth wanted to change the discourse, be less confrontational, focus more on how to aid Muslims in their spiritual needs." The generational and priority clash culminated when the entire leadership of the JMF resigned to protest the interference of the UOIF and the Brothers.

Omero slowly came to the conclusion that his participation inside the Brotherhood had to come to an end. In 2004 he wrote resignation letters to the president of the UOIF and to the head of the education committee of the Brotherhood in the Valenciennes area. Omero, who had reached a junior leadership position in the organization, expected that he would be summoned in Paris to explain his decision or that other members would contact him to try to persuade him to change his mind. But with the exception of Nazir Hakim, the head of the Kindi high school in Lyon and an old-time UOIF official, he did not hear from any Brother. "Silence," he says, "complete silence."

What accompanied this silence, according to Omero, was unspoken but clear ostracism. The invitations to give lectures and speak at conferences—activities that for years had occupied a substantial amount of his time—suddenly halted. Most individuals who belonged to the milieu stopped talking to him. "It was a time of deep personal crisis," he say, "and my family helped me significantly during those months." Omero decided that moving to a new city would be beneficial to him and his family. He accepted a position as director of an NGO working on integration in Nantes, a city in the western part of France six hours from the Lille/Valenciennes area.

Since that time Omero has been living in Nantes with his wife, while his four adult children are working and studying across France. He frequently teaches courses on management throughout the country and has set up a charity that promotes development in the rural part of Morocco where his wife was born. He is also still deeply involved in debates about Islam in France and remains a well-known figure on the French Muslim scene, regularly publishing in high-profile French Muslim publications and speaking at conferences.

Interestingly, his break from the Brotherhood milieu has not been as dramatic as that of some other former Brothers, starting with Mohamed Louizi, whom Omero knows well from the days when they were both active in the Brotherhood scene in Lille. "Louizi has declared war on the Brothers," says Omero. "I took a different approach. It's a matter of personalities." He argues that Louizi paints an overly conspiratorial picture of the Brothers ("it was never a sect like he makes it out to be, there was more internal democracy") and wonders how a relatively low-level member like Louizi could have had access to internal strategic documents, including the one on the tamkine, which Omero never saw. Moreover, while respecting Louizi's personal courage and never questioning his honesty, Omero argues that his overly aggressive approach is not conducive to any kind of positive development within the movement or any constructive debate within France's larger Muslim community.

Omero, in contrast, has opted for a more nuanced approach. He too has been publicly critical of the Brothers, and various pages on his blog candidly recount his story of involvement with the movement. But he has never attacked with the same frequency and ferocity as Louizi. He has simply decided to move on and find his own modus vivendi with the Brotherhood. Yet he has found it challenging to achieve some accommodation. After a few years of ostracism following his resignations, Omero managed to sporadically establish ways to cooperate with the movement. He was welcomed back as a speaker on various occasions, including several times at the annual gathering in Le Bourget. He claims that he attended because he wanted to retain connections with some of the younger and more reformist activists orbiting around UOIF and because, despite its flaws, the platform provided by the Brothers remains an important one. Yet that relationship has been shaky; most recently, Omero's strong positions on the Tariq Ramadan affair and his writings on the need to interpret the Quran in its historical context have led him to become once again persona non grata in Brotherhood circles.[9]

Omero sees in his personal experience a larger issue related to French Islam. "The Brothers monopolize the public space," he observes. "It is difficult to be active and visible beyond their network; no other group has the same reach, not even remotely." He adds, "Not everybody that uses the platform of the UOIF and the Brothers is a Brother; the Brothers allow others to be active on their platform, but only as long as it serves their own goals and if certain red lines are not crossed." In substance, he argues, the Brothers are open to giving their powerful platform to all sorts of voices (Salafists, unaffiliated Islamists, leftist activists, human rights advocates, and so on) only if such cooperation benefits the movement. The Brothers calculate that, for example, a partnership with a Salafist preacher could enable them to attract some of the more conservative segments of the community, a constituency they have struggled to retain in recent years. By the same token, leftist activists might be the perfect conduits to create valuable political contacts. But all these decisions follow a strict cost-benefit analysis and are circumscribed by red lines. "The Brothers are masters at using people and then spitting them out once they no longer need them or they prove to be incompatible," Omero notes.

Omero argues that over the past few years, the debate over the presence and influence of the Muslim Brotherhood in France has intensified, partially fueled by the publication of various books and investigative reports on the subject. In response, the group's leadership has taken various defensive measures. The most dramatic to date, in early 2017, was the decision to rename the UOIF "Musulmans de France" (Muslims of France). Tareq Oubrou candidly admitted that the name change was driven by the organization's attempt to "distance itself" from the Muslim Brotherhood.[10] Interviewed on the subject, Amar Lasfar declared, "We are not part of the

Muslim Brotherhood; on the other hand, we ascribe to their current of thought."[11]

According to Omero, in reality the French Brotherhood milieu has become significantly more conservative over the past few years. "The conservative old guard, with Amar Lasfar at the helm, has won the internal battle," he maintains, "and the reformist wing has been kicked out or sidelined." Members of the old guard have tightened their grip over organizations, particularly youth and student groups, in which more progressive voices were active. In doing so they have been careful to project an image of moderation and to distance themselves from the Brotherhood. "They will put a girl who does not wear the veil on the board of one of their organizations and they will send her to meetings or to appear on TV to look secular and moderate, but the truth is that the movement has gone back twenty years [in terms of conservatism]."

The change of name and the other actions aimed at presenting a different face are, according to Omero, simply a façade. Led by its conservative old guard, the French Brotherhood is in fact simply focused on two primary goals. The first is ideological, described by Omero as "spreading the Brotherhood's area of influence." This goal entails "opening Islamic spaces" and "increasing the areas of Islamic normativity" by employing a combination of tactics: "confrontation when needed, softer ways when judged to be better." But the idea is to carve out areas in which the group can exert its influence.

Omero directly links this desire for influence and power to what he considers the French Brotherhood's second main goal: financial profit. The small cluster of leaders of the French milieu, he argues, presides over a small financial empire and is constantly seeking to expand it. It encompasses various companies (most notably GEDIS, a publishing company managed by Fouad Alaoui that also holds the trademark to the annual "Muslim fair"), interests in the growing halal food certification market,[12] travel agencies, real estate investments, and various charities. Additional sources of income include the annual fees that all organizations belonging to the UOIF have to pay. And the construction of mosques, which has significantly increased throughout France over the past few years, also provides revenue for the milieu.

Yet, warns Omero, expanding his analysis from the organization's financial dealings to all activities related to them, one should avoid painting the Brothers as bigger and better (and more dangerous) than they really are.

He points out that while the Brothers are indeed capable of raising and moving substantial amounts, they have in the past suffered severe financial setbacks. The large complex they purchased in the Paris suburb of La Cour-neuve, for example, created a major drain on their funds, which were not restored for years, according to Omero. And he mentions the group's significant management shortcomings as indications of its fallibility.

CHAPTER VIII

Pernilla Ouis

B orn in 1965, Pernilla Ouis grew up in a large Swedish family with four siblings.[1] When she was six, her mother died and her older sister "became a mother" to her. It was that sister who, years later, introduced Pernilla to Islam. A "spiritual person, a searcher," as Pernilla describes her, she had gone to study Buddhism in China; but after meeting Muslim students there, she became fascinated with Islam, which she found "more natural and egalitarian." In 1984 she came back to Sweden, "a veiled convert," and soon married an Egyptian Islamist who lived in Stockholm. "I was a teenager and I remember that my family and I thought the whole thing was very stupid," Pernilla remembers. "We were also horrified when she and her husband burned her books about Buddhism; the act of burning books recalls such bad images."

In November 1985 her sister had her first baby, and Pernilla, who lived in the university town of Lund, went to visit her in Stockholm. "In the span of a few weeks I went from thinking that this whole Islam thing was nonsense to marrying an Algerian Islamist," she says with a sardonic smile. Her brother-in-law had introduced Pernilla to a young Algerian physics student and told her that he needed to get married in order to obtain a permanent permit to stay in Sweden and avoid going back to Algeria, where he would have been drafted to serve in the army.

Pernilla lists many superficial reasons why she lightheartedly decided to marry the Algerian student: he was "nice looking, kind, and exotic";

she was "bored with university life" and this was "a fun experience"; and she thought that "Arabs were misunderstood" and this was a nice way of helping one. On a deeper level, she now believes, "I was subconsciously doing so to please my sister, to whom I had always looked up." On December 28, 1985, the couple were married in an Islamic wedding ceremony even though, from Pernilla's point of view, "it was clear it was not a real marriage."

Yet after the wedding her husband moved in with her, as he had no other place to stay, and after a few months she became pregnant. Pernilla had been adamant about her intention not to convert to Islam, but she succumbed to increased pressure from her husband, her sister, and her brother-in-law to raise the child Muslim and therefore be a Muslim herself. "Confused," she converted and adopted the name Soumaya shortly before her first child's birth.

In the summer of 1987 she traveled to Algeria for the first time to meet her husband's family. He asked her to wear the hijab, arguing that his family would not accept her if she did not. She complied but made it clear this concession was just temporary. But upon returning to Sweden, he told her that it would be a great sin to take the veil off, and she begrudgingly assented to begin wearing it permanently. "It's like the story of the boiling frog," she says. "The water gets warmer and warmer and she always tells herself she can jump out any time; but, at some point, it becomes so hot she can no longer jump and gets boiled: that was me."

At the same time, she says that her life was not unpleasant or oppressive. The couple lived in university housing in Lund, where her husband was pursuing a doctorate, and they had many friends within the campus's and town's relatively large Muslim community. She had become a practicing Muslim, but mostly because it was "a social thing." "I did not have a deep belief in Islam," she recounts. "I never felt a spiritual connection; praying felt like gymnastics." Still, she found some attractive qualities in it. "Islam was logic: you are doing the right thing, all rules are clear, there was no relativism, none of that postmodern nonsense, everything is simple and clear."

Pernilla's life revolved around her family and her husband's friends in Lund's Muslim community. But during his time in Lund, says Pernilla, her husband's views radicalized. He already had very conservative and politicized views when she first met him, but with the beginning of the civil war in his native Algeria, "his positions hardened and became more jihadi-leaning." According to Pernilla, he embarked on a radicalization process that saw him move within the most militant segments of the Swedish Islamist scene of the 1990s and included travels to Afghanistan and Pakistan.

Pernilla found her husband's views highly problematic and did not follow him on that trajectory. But she started to be more involved in Sweden's "active Muslim scene" and consequently, in 1994, became the editor of *Salaam*. Already discussed in chapter 5, *Salaam* was the main publication of the Swedish Brotherhood network in its early days. Funded by the Islamic Information Society (Islamiska Informationsföreningen, already mentioned by Pierre Durrani) and housed in offices shared with several other organizations of the network, it published Brotherhood and Islamist-leaning writings in Swedish; it was a key incubator for Brotherhood thought and leaders in Sweden.[2]

"Most of the people writing in *Salaam* were women, converts who had married Brotherhood guys," recalls Pernilla. Indeed, the first editor of the publication was Monija Sonnius, Ahmed Ghanem's wife. After 1996, right after Pernilla's tenure, the position of editor was occupied by Helena Hummasten, a Finnish convert to Islam who was married to the late Mohammed Benaouda. Hummasten later held leadership position in two key organizations of the Swedish Brotherhood milieu, Ibn Rushd and Muslim Council of Sweden (Sveriges Muslimska Råd).

Confirming Durrani's account, Pernilla describes *Salaam* as the stage of an intellectual battle between the Brotherhood pioneers who started and funded it and many of the mostly female converts who, fluent in the Swedish language, worked in it. "We wanted to write about Sufism, wanted to talk about many things, wanted to create a Blue Yellow Islam," recalls Pernilla, "but there was a lot of pushback. The Brothers just wanted us to translate [the writings of the Brotherhood leader Sayyid] Qutb and shut up."

Despite these issues, Pernilla did not mind her work at *Salaam*. She thought she was "promoting Islam in Sweden," and, like most other converts who worked there, she had no idea that *Salaam* was a Brotherhood outfit. "Had somebody told us," she says, "we would have rejected it outright and thought it was an attempt to smear Islam. We were very naïve." The one person who told Pernilla that *Salaam* was linked to the Brotherhood was her husband—a warning that, paradoxically, only made her commitment to *Salaam* stronger. Her husband, despite having been close to the Brotherhood in his early days, "despised the Brothers" and chastised her wife for working with them. "That made me see the Brothers as the good guys," Pernilla admits. "If my husband, who was an extremist, disliked them, then they were moderates."

Her perceptions began to change in 1996, as she started a Ph.D. degree in human ecology. "They teach you to deconstruct everything," says Pernilla with a smile. "University corrupted my Islamic identity." The critical thinking she adopted all day in her studies "conflicted with what I found every night at home," and the former slowly began to prevail over the latter. Her relationship with her husband increasingly deteriorated, leading her to spend more and more time outside the house.

It was around that time that Pernilla began to be drawn to a couple who would have a huge influence in her life: Anne Sofie Roald and Adly Abu Hajar. Roald is a charismatic Norwegian convert to Islam and accomplished academic who quickly became Pernilla's best friend. The two became inseparable, traveling the world to attend conferences and writing about various aspects of Islam.[3] Eleven years older than Pernilla and extremely knowledgeable about Islam, Roald became, as Pernilla puts it, her "teacher, best friend, and mentor," accompanying her on a journey that led both women away from Islamism. "By embracing a more liberal and post-ikhwan Islam," she explains, "she made her exit from Muslim Brotherhood movement."

While the two women charted their own trajectory, a crucially important influence on them was Roald's husband, Adly Abu Hajar. Born in Yaffo and raised in Jordan, Abu Hajar has been a prominent Islamic activist since he arrived in Europe in the early 1980s.[4] According to his own account, his first contact with the Brotherhood did not take place in Jordan or in Algeria, where he pursued his undergraduate studies, but in France, once he arrived in Lille to further his education in urban planning. The French college town, as noted in chapters 6 and 7, has been a Brotherhood hub since the early 1980s, and Abu Hajar immediately gravitated toward the group. He became close to Faysal Mawlawi, the leader of the Lebanese branch of the Brotherhood, who spent several years in France and played a crucial role in the founding of two French Brotherhood institutions, UOIF and IESH. Abu Hajar also became a key player in Brotherhood networks first in northern France and then across the border in Belgium, where the Brotherhood asked him to establish a presence.

Yet despite these close connections, Abu Hajar claims he never formally joined the Brotherhood, though he was asked several times to do so. He insists, "I always told them that we think alike, that we all work for Islam, but my allegiance is for Allah alone, not for any organization. I work for Islam, not for the *jamaa* ['the group,' as the Brothers often refer to the Brotherhood]." By his own account, Abu Hajar was a high-level fellow traveler of the Brotherhood, involved in very high-profile activities of the group's early days in Europe but never a formal member.

Some of Abu Hajar's most prominent activities during those days pertained to his role in the International Islamic Federation of Student Organizations. Less known than Saudi-based organizations such as the Muslim World League or the World Assembly of Muslim Youth, groups with which it cooperates closely, IIFSO has been equally important in bringing together Brotherhood leaders and activists from all over the world. It was founded in 1969 after a two-day meeting at the Bilal mosque in the German college town of Aachen. Not coincidentally, the mosque was the headquarters of Issam al Attar, a prominent leader of the Syrian Muslim Brotherhood in exile and, together with Said Ramadan and Yussuf Nada, one of the very first pioneers of the Brotherhood in the West.

Since its foundation, IIFSO has been run mostly by individuals who held prominent positions in Brotherhood student organizations in Europe and the United States—arguably evidence of how important the Western Brotherhood is globally. In the organization's early days various leaders of the U.S. branch of the Brotherhood, such Hisham al Talib and Ahmed Totonji, served as IIFSO's secretary-generals. In more recent years European Brothers have occupied leadership positions. Particularly telling in that regard is the *cursus honorum* of Khallad Swaid, an up-and-coming figure in the German Brotherhood milieu. Early in the twenty-first century, Swaid served in leadership positions inside Muslim Youth in German (Muslimische Jugend in Deutschland, MJD) and the German Brotherhood milieu's youth organization, as well as being a member of the Forum of European Muslim Youth and Student Organisations; he later became president of FEMYSO. After a stint as deputy head of the Islamic Community of Germany (Islamische Gemeinschaft Deutschland IGD), the German Brotherhood's main organization, in 2014 Swaid was elected IIFSO's secretary-general.

In the mid-1980s Abu Hajar served as IIFSO's representative in Europe, a position that enabled him to travel throughout the Continent and around the world. While he worked side by side with Brotherhood leaders and organizations on many activities, he also started his own initiatives, which at times differed from the Brotherhood's in their aims and partners. This independence led him to clash with some of the more conservative segments of the global Muslim Brotherhood, particularly in Jordan, where some Brothers lodged a formal complaint against him with the Brotherhood's international bureau—the transnational body bringing together the leaders of branches of the Brotherhood from all over the world.

The back-and-forth between Abu Hajar and the Jordanian Brothers, as summarized by Abu Hajar, epitomizes the tensions that often exist within the Brotherhood between a leadership that wants to exert almost complete control and those—whether actual members or fellow travelers, like Abu Hajar—who seek breathing room for their actions. "Priority is with the jamaa," Abu Hajar said the Jordanian Brothers would insist. "No," he would respond, "the jamaa can be wrong; Islam, never." "No," was their retort, "the jamaa is Islam, they are one and the same." "No," Abu Hajar would counter, "Islam is from Allah, the jamaa is men; they can be wrong."

Despite the supportive intercession of Mawlawi, Abu Hajar found this pressure suffocating, and by 1993 he withdrew from the Brotherhood. He continued his many activities aimed at teaching Islam to both Muslims and non-Muslims through a variety of transnational outfits he created. He also began advising Muslims and issuing fatwas, both in person and electronically, to Muslims all over Europe. He maintained good relations with many Brotherhood leaders, and it is fair to say that he shares many of their conservative and Islamist positions. Yet in many respects he has differed from them. Tellingly, for example, in 1993, a few years after relocating to Malmoe, he joined the center-right Swedish Moderate Party. He recalls how his decision to join a Swedish party shocked many Brothers, who at the time had not yet embraced participation in democratic processes in the West. Abu Hajar, on the other hand, saw it as crucially important, and in 1998 he was elected to the Malmoe City Council, where he served for twelve years.

Abu Hajar also found—and still finds—the Brothers' excessive secrecy extremely troubling. "I have been telling them for decades: why make the usra secret?" he emphatically says. "Why deny you exist? We are in a democracy." Echoing most of the former Brothers interviewed for this book, he argues that secrecy is understandable in the Middle East and was justified during the first years of the Brotherhood's presence in the West, when its members might not have been familiar with the local political dynamics. But after more than forty years in the West, Abu Hajar maintains, this secrecy makes little sense and is both a reason that many Brothers leave the group and a reason that many Westerners distrust it. But unlike other former members of the group—in whose number he does not technically belong—he does not argue that the Brothers are a threat to Sweden. Their values, he claims, are not as problematic as those of Salafists, which are "the real threat to Sweden and Europe." But their obsession with secrecy keeps them from fully participating in Swedish society, ensuring that they concentrate only on themselves.

It was this independent approach of Abu Hajar, accompanied by his knowledge and welcoming personality, as well as the friendship Pernilla developed with Roald, that led Pernilla to attach herself to the couple. Abu Hajar and Roald began organizing many activities for Muslim women, an issue both held dear. In particular Roald wrote many progressive treatises about women in Islam and dissected the concept of "Islamist feminism."

It was during one of the conferences Pernilla attended, in October 2001, that she decided to have dinner alone with one of the invited researchers who was Muslim—an extremely inappropriate act, in conservative Islamic circles—and was spotted at the restaurant by friends of her husband. Pernilla's relationship with her husband had increasingly been deteriorating, and that very same night he confronted her and divorced her Islamically (*talaq*), simply accelerating what would have probably been the natural progression of a doomed relationship. In January 2002 she moved out of the house. "That year I got divorced and obtained my Ph.D. at 37," she quips, "which is statistically the average age to do both in Sweden."

After divorcing, she recalls, "I did not break with Islam, but I became more lax about my practice." Having become a lecturer at Malmoe University focusing on gender studies, Pernilla put her days as a cog in the Swedish Brotherhood machine behind her. Though she has never spoken publicly about her involvement in the network, she has reflected on it at length. She admits that she was a marginal actor in the network, and unaware of even having that role. "The Brotherhood fooled me," she says with a smile. "They never used the term 'Muslim Brotherhood' to refer to themselves." She argues that her experience mirrors that of other Swedish, mostly female, converts whom the Brotherhood used both to translate texts into Swedish and to present reassuring façades to outsiders.

"Us converts, we were paraded," she declares. She adds:

I was traveling selling Islam and whatever we said people would buy it. We were highly educated and knew how to do it, how to

convince our Swedish interlocutors. We would use postmodern [rhe-
torical] tools to question the bases of society, relativize everything in
order to fit our agenda. . . . We knew the culture, we always had ele-
gant ways to deflect criticism, to turn the tables: if they would criticize us for the treatment of women in Islam, for its patriarchal
approach, we would bring up the divorce rate in Sweden.

"And," she adds, "we would always bring up colonialism," consistently a
winning card in Islamist rhetoric. Reflecting on this role played by converts, she declares that "none of us thought there was a strategy" on the
part of the Brotherhood to exert power within Swedish society. "We
thought we were simply defending Islam and never thought the Brothers
wanted to be gatekeepers to Swedish society but only speak to it. They did
not detach and isolate themselves from Swedish society as other more
extreme groups did. In this sense the Brotherhood seemed very progressive to me. I never saw their understanding as a way of gaining power in
the Swedish society."

Pernilla also brings up additional aspects of her time inside the Brotherhood milieu she did not like. Like Pierre Durrani, she was disturbed by
the "anti-Swedish racism" she experienced and the "sense of superiority
toward Swedes" inside the Brotherhood milieu. But as a woman, she was
also perturbed by the misogyny that existed in those circles. The subordination of women to men was one of the main issues that, by her own
account, triggered first her disengagement from the Brotherhood milieu.

Pernilla's feelings on gender discrimination inside the Brotherhood are
not idiosyncratic. Rather, they fit into a pattern commonly seen in various
Arab countries, and particularly in Egypt. Indeed, the role of women in
the organization can be viewed from two angles. On one hand, women
have arguably played an important role in the Brotherhood throughout its
history, particularly in comparison with their place in other Islamist movements. The Sisterhood has always been an integral part of al Banna's organization, with roles and powers that are clearly subordinate to those of
the men but nonetheless highly significant.[5] Sisters are the backbone of
the Brotherhood family, support their men in all their activities, and conduct a myriad of dawa activities, from cooking collective meals to preparing banners for demonstrations, from holding classes to leafleting.

While the organization is clearly run by men and women have no right
to vote in internal elections or to be elected in any official leadership

position in it—technically, membership is not available to women—the examples of women who have played or currently play a prominent role in the Brotherhood are not limited. Most prominent is, in Egypt, Zaynab al Ghazali, who was imprisoned and tortured during the Nasserist purges of the late 1960s and later played a key role in reestablishing the Brotherhood in the country—accomplishments that let her to obtain a legendary status in Brotherhood circles.[6] And also in contemporary Brotherhood circles in the West, a handful of women play crucial roles. Fitting examples are Intisar Kherigi, former president of FEMYSO and the daughter of Tunisian al Nahda's leader Rachid Ghannouchi, and Sumaya Abdel Qader, a daughter of one of the founders of the Union of Islamic Communities of Italy (Unione delle Comunità Islamiche d'Italia, UCOII), the public organization in the Italian Brotherhood milieu, who served in various positions in both FIOE and FEMYSO before being elected to the Milan City Council.

On the other hand, many Sisters have complained about the discrimination they suffered within Brotherhood circles and have left the organization, in some cases not quietly. Some, like Hassan al Banna's granddaughter Sanaa, complained not just about gender issues but also, as is more common, about the lack of internal democracy. "If I were a man, I still would have left. There's no freedom for either sex," she explained. "There's no transparency, no permission for the divergence of thoughts or critical thinking. It's their way or you're out."[7]

Other former Egyptian Sisters have disengaged because of more gender-specific reasons. In her book *My Story with the Brothers: Memoirs of a Former Sister*, Intissar Abdel Moneim argues that the Brotherhood adopts an extreme form of gender conservatism and criticizes the group's attitudes toward women, starting with strict gender segregation. "You cannot by any logic perceive all people as mere female and male sex organs that roam the streets looking for the moment of intercourse like cats," writes the former activist.[8] Moreover, she claims that the Brothers simply use females for political purposes, telling them to take off their face-covering veils when it suits their political needs to show moderation, but forcing them to wear the veils in other settings.

Pernilla was never a member of the Muslim Brotherhood. As a well-educated and enthusiastic convert, she was simply a cog in the machine of the Swedish Brotherhood milieu, translating Islamist literature into Swedish and serving as a reassuring face of the movement in engagements with

Swedish society. Her awareness of "being used" was minimal and mostly came via the attacks from her jihadist husband. For the very reason that the criticism was leveled by an extremist, she thought of the Brothers as "the good guys."

Her process of disengagement from Islamic activism seems to have been driven by a combination of factors. Many are rooted in her personal life (the divorce, university studies). But others are connected to the Brotherhood, and in some cases they echo the reasons voiced by former members: ideological misgivings, discomfort with racism, and gender discrimination. The influence of two very different but equally charismatic mentors, Anne Sofie Roald and Adly Abu Hajar, also played a key role in Pernilla's disengagement.

CHAPTER IX

The American Brothers

Abdur-Rahman Muhammad was born Kenneth William Oliveira Jr. on July 9, 1962, in Providence, Rhode Island, the descendant of whalers from Cape Verde who had long ago settled in New England.[1] Now a minority-majority city (with whites representing roughly 40 percent of the population), in the 1960s and 1970s Providence was still quite racially homogeneous, with whites in the majority by a wide margin. It also has a history of racism, which authorities and civil society have tried to reverse in recent years.

As an African American, Abdur-Rahman recounts suffering from various forms of discrimination during his youth. In some cases, the racism was overt, as when a ten-year-old Abdur-Rahman and a handful of his friends were attacked by "a white mob of parents" at the elementary school to which he was bused when authorities sought to desegregate the local school district. But other forms of discrimination were more subtle. He says, "We found out later that the school system had a soft racism and a soft segregation going on, where they had kind of like two tracks and the white kids would be sent off to classical high school and minorities went on another track." From Abdur-Rahman's perspective, the supposedly tolerant Northeast of the United States was no less racist than the South. "Malcolm X," he quips, "used to say: 'Stop talking about the South; as long as you are south of the Canadian border you're south.' New England was like that."

When Abdur-Rahman was fourteen, that racism manifested itself in a way that affected his life forever. His cousin, a year younger than him, was dating a white girl, Anne, and one "quiet Sunday afternoon" the three of them were sitting on the stairs of the back side of the Rhode Island State House, throwing rocks into the empty adjacent parking lot—"just stuff kids do." All of a sudden, the three heard the "Starsky and Hutch-like" screech of car wheels and a police car appeared in front of them. "My cousin," recounts Abdur-Rahman, "read the situation way quicker than I did" and ran away. "I was trying to process this," he continues, "and I didn't know police brutality, I was just standing there with Anne and my big afro."

According to Abdur-Rahman, two policemen walked out of the car and approached him and Anne. "Is this your girlfriend, nigger?" one of them asked. Without waiting for an answer he turned to Anne, scolding her for associating with "black motherfuckers." They sent her home and grabbed him, tossing him against the car and then kneeing him in the back seat of the car. "They started driving me around the city, terrorizing me, using all sorts of racist names and saying they will find my body at the bottom of the river." The long ride ended at the police station, where Abdur-Rahman was booked for "disturbing the peace or something—they trumped up the charges, that's what they did then, they had you in the system so if they pick you up again. . . ."

By his own account, that incident was a major turning point in Abdur-Rahman's life. "From that point on I was very angry, very angry. I changed, everyone noticed the change. It turned into a hatred of white people—probably not everyone because I liked my teachers, they were very good to me, but, you know, white people as a category," he says. This anger was accompanied by a newfound black consciousness. Growing up in a city with a small black population and having never been politically engaged, Abdur-Rahman admits that until then he had only vaguely heard of Martin Luther King, Jr., Malcolm X, and the various forms of political activism that were inflaming the African American community in the 1960s and 1970s. But after the incident, "I got militant" and "I started giving myself a self-education on black literature": the books of black activists like H. Rap Brown and Kwame Ture, the writings of Black Panthers leaders, and, more than anything else, the works of Malcolm X. Soon, "not only do I not believe in the system, I want to take it down, I want a revolution."

Abdur-Rahman's anger did not prevent him from performing well in high school and making his way to Howard University—"it was 1980 and

I was the first in my 'hood to make it to college." Founded shortly after the end of the American Civil War and located in Washington, D.C., Howard is America's preeminent historically black university. Coming from Providence, Abdur-Rahman was elated to find himself at a black university in a majority-black city, and he immersed himself in Washington's vibrant black culture. He was drawn to various black political movements and was particularly fascinated by the rhetoric of Louis Farrakhan, the leader of the Nation of Islam, an American black nationalist movement that adopts a particularistic form of Islam with little in common with traditional Sunni Islam but with a strong message of racial pride.[2] "I didn't really understand all the differences," Abdur-Rahman admits. "I just knew that I liked the image of militancy and unity and brotherhood, it was intoxicating. I listen to it now and it is nonsense, but back then, at eighteen, I was a kid, he [Farrakhan] had a booming voice, and I was spellbound."

After less than two years at Howard, though, Abdur-Rahman was forced by financial difficulties to temporarily leave. To make money in the hopes of eventually returning to school, he started a business with a fellow Howard student selling gadgets at sporting and musical events. Business was very good, but Abdur-Rahman was disturbed by the excesses and debauchery he witnessed while touring with singers and performers. "I'm starting to move in a spiritual direction," he recalls. "I'm starting to get serious about looking at becoming religious." He started frequenting a black Baptist church in Washington but was disappointed by some immoral behavior he witnessed there. He also found certain aspects of the Bible contradictory. "But in a black church," he says, "criticism of the Bible is not allowed; it's all about the singing, the preaching, collecting money, building a new building. . . . There's a really anti-intellectual strain in it that I found unsatisfying."

"It was around 1986," he continues, "and I was really disillusioned with Christianity; I thought black people are Christian but it didn't make sense to me, I saw too many contradictions." Abdur-Rahman had had several contacts with African American Muslims over the years and had always found their views fascinating. But he never seriously thought of converting until one day he picked up the Quran ("I've always had a copy"): "I opened it and it just hit me between the eyes. It was clear this was written by God, I was convinced." He immediately decided to convert. He called Kwame Pitts, a Muslim friend from Howard, and together they went to the apartment of a group of Arab students, where he recited the *shahada* (declaration of faith) and formally converted. One of the Arabs said he "looked like an Abdur-Rahman" and, without much thought, Kenneth decided to become Abdur-Rahman.

His first days as a Muslim were not easy. His father became very upset about the conversion, and fasting for Ramadan in the heat of the Washington summer was taxing. Yet Abdur-Rahman embraced his new religion with enormous enthusiasm, devouring books about it and attending mosques with assiduity. In the fall of 1987, thanks to the money he had earned through his business, he returned to Howard. But there his academics took a back seat to Islamic activism. Pitts introduced Abdur-Rahman to Johari Abdul-Malik, another African American convert who studied at Howard, and the three became inseparable. They organized lectures, collective prayers, and other events, attracting a growing number of young Muslims on campus. "Our dawa was popping," says Abdur-Rahman, "and they were calling me the dawa machine."

The success Abdur-Rahman's group was having on Howard's campus reached the ear of Abdurahman Alamoudi. An Eritrean-born biochemist, from the 1980s to the early 2000s Alamoudi was one of the most influential figures of the American Muslim Brotherhood milieu. The organization he headed, the American Muslim Council (AMC), organized events, often held in Washington's most prestigious hotels, that were attended by high-ranking politicians, media personalities, and religious leaders. The FBI praised AMC as "the most mainstream Muslim group in the United States"; the State Department appointed Alamoudi as "goodwill ambassador," routinely asking him to travel throughout the world representing American Muslims; and the Department of Defense put him in the powerful position of training and vetting the imams who attend to the religious needs of American Muslims serving in the military.

In 2003, however, an unexpected discovery during a routine customs screening at London's Heathrow Airport wiped away Alamoudi's accomplishments. He was found to have concealed $340,000 in his suitcase. An investigation revealed that Alamoudi had been illegally importing funds from Libya since 1995, and that part of the money was intended to support a murky plot—conceived by the Libyan government and two London-based Saudi dissidents linked to al Qaeda—to assassinate then Saudi crown prince Abdallah. A year later Alamoudi pled guilty to all charges and was sentenced to twenty-three years in prison. The investigation also revealed Alamoudi's financial dealings with U.S.-designated terrorist organizations such as Hamas and al Qaeda, and the Treasury Department accused him of fund-raising for them in the United States.[3]

But in the fall of 1989, when he reached out to Abdur-Rahman and his friends, Alamoudi was at the height of his power. Flattered by the attention of a celebrated figure of the Muslim community, Abdur-Rahman drove with Johari to meet Alamoudi in Herndon, Virginia, in the same suburban office building occupied by many of the companies and organizations run by the U.S. Brotherhood network that would be raided by U.S. authorities in the weeks following the 9/11 attacks for suspected links to terrorism. "Alamoudi had charisma," reminisces Abdur-Rahman. "He was a smooth dude, very charming, he made you feel like you were very important."

Abdur-Rahman replays the moments of that important encounter, which shaped his future. "He said: 'Brothers, we're hearing some very good things are happening at Howard University and we want to help you; you need a *musalla* [prayer room], you need materials, you need teachers and we're going to help you, inshallah.'" As he was saying this, Alamoudi reportedly showed Abdur-Rahman and Johari piles of Islamic books and audiocassettes, which he said were a gift to them. "I grew up in the streets," says Abdur-Rahman with a smile, "so in the back of my mind I was already waiting for the strings."

Indeed, Abdur-Rahman explains, Alamoudi had a request: "We need to know who your speakers are going to be. If you can give us a list of all the speakers you are going to have for the next year, that would be helpful." He then proceeded to pull out a list of speakers he said the Howard group should invite on campus. Finally, he suggested that they call their group the Howard Muslim Student Association, to match the name of the national organization that was the first seed of the Muslim Brotherhood in America.

Here, before continuing with Abdur-Rahman's story, we must review the history of the American Brotherhood milieu, as it is little known and often contested. Some, in fact, have questioned whether the Brotherhood ever operated in America; more have questions whether various American Muslim organizations have links to it. Mirroring debates taking place in almost all Western countries, others have exaggerated the presence of the Brotherhood in the United States and, even more controversially, its influence over both American Muslim organizations and the U.S. political establishment—at the most extreme, voicing wild conspiracy theories, prominent in some segments of the Arab media and among some fringe American right-wing commentators, that cast the Brotherhood as an all-powerful hydra controlling the U.S. government.

Leaving aside the more complex issue of assessing aims and influence, it is fair to say that ample documentary evidence, supplemented by many personal testimonials of individuals who belong or used to belong to the group, clearly demonstrates that the Brotherhood has been operating in the United States from at least the late 1950s. And it is equally fair to say that that presence has historically been large and well-organized, even in comparison to European countries, such as France and the United Kingdom, with an important Brotherhood presence. The common belief that America has traditionally hosted fewer Islamist movements than Europe does hold true for all of them. For example, the United States contains nothing like the number of jihadist militants found in many central and northern European countries. But the Muslim Brotherhood is unquestionably the exception to this rule. Confirmation of the historically large and sophisticated presence of Brotherhood networks in America also comes from Kamal Helbawy, who played an important role in establishing, uniting, and solidifying them in the early days.[4]

Two overlapping factors account for this phenomenon. One is the usual socioeconomic background of those who join the Muslim Brotherhood in the Arab world. As we have seen, the Brotherhood is a highly selective group that opens itself up to individuals that are not only committed but, in most cases, successful and highly educated. It is an organization that recruits heavily in schools and universities and attracts large numbers of high-achieving young men who are pursuing or have obtained high levels of education. Various studies have also demonstrated that the group attracts a disproportionate number of individuals who have pursued high degrees, particularly in medicine and engineering.[5]

The second factor that explains the early and large presence of Brothers in America is the size, openness, and quality of the American university system. Indeed, starting in the 1950s and as part of a deliberate Cold War strategy to counter Soviet influence in nonaligned countries, U.S. authorities began to encourage the presence of students from non-Western countries at American universities. Historians estimate that in the 1950s and the 1960s, more than half a million students from throughout the Muslim world, as well as from other parts of Asia, Africa, and Latin America, attended universities in the United States.[6]

As noted elsewhere, aside from a few exceptions such as Kamal Helbawy or Yussuf Nada, during those years the first footholds of the Muslim Brotherhood in the West were established not by those acting as part of a concerted strategy but simply by individuals who had joined or were close to the Brotherhood while at universities in their countries of origin and had decided to continue their studies in European and American universities. While no exact numbers are available, the substantially larger number of U.S. universities, from elite institutions to local community colleges, and generous U.S. student visa policies suggest that a larger number of Brothers traveled to the United States to study than to any European country.

Once they arrived on U.S. college campuses, those Brotherhood pioneers founded the first student organizations that could fulfill their basic religious needs.[7] They were scattered throughout the United States, but many were based in universities in the Midwest; it is therefore unsurprising that, in the winter of 1963, some one hundred students representing fewer than twenty Muslim student organizations from various parts of the country met on the campus of the University of Illinois at Urbana-Champaign, twin towns less than a hundred miles from Chicago, Indianapolis, and St. Louis, in the heart of the American Midwest.[8] The result of the meeting was the creation of the Muslim Student Association (MSA), America's first national Muslim student organization.

MSA was the brainchild of a small group of student activists who came from different countries of the Muslim world but were united by a common vision of Islam as inherently political. Founders of MSA included activists from various backgrounds, including several Shias, yet a crucial role was played by members and sympathizers of national branches of the Muslim Brotherhood who had settled in the United States since the 1950s.[9] While MSA was not a "pure" Brotherhood organization, its links to the Brotherhood were strong.[10] From its inception, Brotherhood members held key positions, influencing its ideology and direction. Moreover, MSA became a sort of parallel structure of the Brotherhood: despite its independence, it provided an inexhaustible recruiting pool and a perfect avenue to disseminate the Brotherhood's ideas.[11] It published Islamist literature, organized events, fundraised, and created countless subgroups along ethnic or professional lines.

The prominence of Brotherhood networks on U.S. campuses throughout the final decades of the twentieth century is widely documented by the publications of various groups; to a lesser degree, some academic writings and internal documents have been introduced as evidence by U.S.

authorities in various terrorism financing cases related to the milieu. But confirmation also comes from the testimony of a handful of individuals who—at different times, in different places, and with different roles—were active in Brotherhood circles on U.S. college campuses and who, after leaving the movement, decided to tell their stories.

One of them is Jamal al Hossani, a former member of the Muslim Brotherhood in his native United Arab Emirates who, in 2014, decided to tell his story to the Abu Dhabi–based television station Al Emarat.[12] Al Hossani recounted how he started to be active in Brotherhood circles in his own country as a teenager but understood that the groups were run by the organization only when he was summoned by the organization's leaders in Abu Dhabi on the eve of his departure to the United States to study at a university. "You have reached a stage where you are one of us," he recalls being told on that occasion.

Al Hossani claims that, once in the United States, he became involved in various organizations and activities within the U.S. Brotherhood milieu. He used many of them, like the annual event held during Christmas holidays by the Muslim Arab Youth Association and attended by some ten thousand people, to spot potential recruits among the Emirati students attending. "The conference attracted over 150 Emirati students studying in the United States," he says, and he organized outings just for them. "After I was appointed to the student union office for Emirati students in the USA, I became in charge of maintaining the union's activity, managing its elections, and keeping communication lines open with organization members when preparing so-called religious seminars, conferences, and other activities with concealed political objectives set by the leadership." According to him, the Emirati branch of the Brotherhood had a central "operations office" in the United States that had divided the country in zones determined by the distribution of Emirati students and had assigned one member to oversee each.

Al Hossani spent two decades with the Brotherhood, becoming active again in the United Arab Emirates—a country that in 2014 designated the Brotherhood as a terrorist organization—after returning from the United States. He has since become a vocal critic of the group, arguing that it deceives and manipulates young Muslims to adopt a narrative that is divisive and conducive to violence. "You become part of this organization and it's then difficult to get out," he says. "It's like a kind of brainwashing, and you start to accept things that you did not accept ten years earlier."

While al Hossani traveled to the United States as an inducted member specifically tasked to run the activities of a Middle Eastern branch of the Brotherhood—in itself a telling indicator of the movement's extensive presence in America—Mustafa Saied has a very different story.[13] Born to an affluent family in India, Saied traveled to the United States in 1990 to attend the University of Tennessee in Knoxville. On the plane, he recounts, he made a to-do list: "learn to skateboard and bungee-jump, go on road trips, hang out with girls."[14] Once in America, he thrived in class and outside of it, making friends from all backgrounds and experiencing as many aspects of American life as possible. In 1993 he spent a semester at Disney World, taking classes on Disney's business approach.

One day, back in Knoxville, he decided "on impulse" to stop at the mosque near campus—something he had never done before. He saw a group of students discussing Quranic verses and he joined the conversation. "I knew a couple of things," he recounts, "and they were so impressed." He was invited back and asked to join a study group. Within days he stopped shaving and began praying five times a day. Many of his old interests, such as movies, music, and dating, were abandoned. Saied began devouring Islamic texts, particularly those of Yussuf al Qaradawi, and participating assiduously in the activities of the study group along with a handful of other students. A gifted speaker, Saied was also allowed to give speeches inside the mosque, excoriating "Americans who indulged in alcohol and premarital sex, or celebrated 'false' holidays such as Halloween and Christmas." He also celebrated attacks against Israel: "Our view was that suicide bombings were fine."

Throughout 1994 Saied "sensed that his allegiance to radical Islam was being tested by members of his study group," although he did not understand why. Everything changed one afternoon, when a fellow student summoned him to the campus cafeteria. After sitting in a quiet corner, the student disclosed his affiliation with the Brotherhood and invited Saied to join the group. "It was a dream, because that's what you're conditioned to do—to really love the Ikhwan," he recalls. "Everything I had learned pointed to the Muslim Brotherhood being an awesome thing, the elite movement. I cannot tell you the feeling that I felt—awesome power."

As seen in other cases, after being inducted, Saied learned the names of other Brothers in the local area and was surprised to discover that several prominent figures belonged to the group. "I was shocked," he recalls. "These people had really hid the fact that they were Brotherhood." In the following months Saied immersed himself in Brotherhood literature and activities. He also traveled throughout the country to attend Brotherhood-linked events. He remembers being particularly struck by a conference held in December 1995 at hotel in Toledo, Ohio, that was organized by the Muslim Arab Youth Association, a now defunct organization of the U.S. Brotherhood milieu that was very active in the 1980s and 1990s.

Keynoting the conference was Qaradawi, and Saied had the opportunity to meet the Qatar-based cleric. "I was awestruck because he was the biggest Muslim Brotherhood figure in the world, and I had met him," he recalls. During his speech, Qaradawi laid out a vision that critics of the Brotherhood have often cited as indicative of the group's desire to work for a patient and gradualist, yet still disturbing, goal of conquering the West. "What remains, then, is to conquer Rome," said Qaradawi, referring to a well-known hadith. "The second part of the omen, 'The city of Hiraq [once emperor of Constantinople] will be conquered first, so what remains is to conquer Rome.' This means that Islam will come back to Europe for the third time, after it was expelled from it twice. . . . Conquest through Da'wa, that is what we hope for. We will conquer Europe, we will conquer America! Not through sword but through Da'wa."[15]

In Knoxville, Saied became a fund-raiser for Benevolence International Foundation (BIF), a Chicago-based charity that claimed to be raising funds for children and the poor in war-torn countries such as Bosnia and Chechnya. Saied managed to raise thousands of dollars in the community, but he later found out from a BIF emissary who had come to Knoxville that some of the funds were destined for fighters. Saied immediately stopped fundraising. In 2002 BIF was designated a terrorism financier by the U.S Treasury Department, and close ties between its founder, Enaam Arnaout, and Osama bin Laden were revealed.[16]

In 1996 Saied moved to Florida, where he continued his activism. But an encounter at a small gathering in a private home in Chicago the following year led him to reevaluate his choices. There two young American Muslims started questioning Saied's views, basing their arguments on Quranic verses. The four-hour argument left Saied defeated, "out of arguments." Later that night, rethinking the discussion, Saied concluded that he had been wrong all along. "Oh my God, what have I been doing?" he kept asking himself. Saied's doubts were reinforced by the views of his new wife, an American Muslim of Pakistani descent, who was horrified by some of her husband's positions.

By the late 1990s Saied left the Brotherhood and adopted a significantly more liberal interpretation of Islam. While still a devout Muslim, he worries about the politicization of Islam and the influence of the Brotherhood on American Muslims. "They have this idea that Muslims come first," he says, "not that humans come first." "Anti-American sentiment is usually reserved for closed-door discussions or expressed in languages that most Americans don't understand," he adds. "While such rhetoric has been drastically reduced since 9/11, it is still prevalent enough to be a cause for concern."

The examples of al Hossani and Saied stand in for many others that show the deep network of study groups, activities, and organizations that the U.S. Brotherhood network had created by the early 1990s. It is therefore not surprising that Alamoudi, one of the vital cogs in the U.S. Brotherhood machine of the era, tried to co-opt the small group that Abdur-Rahman and Johari had formed on the campus of Howard, the home of African American elites where the Brothers, according to Abdur-Rahman, had long sought to establish a presence.

Abdur-Rahman, despite being impressed by Alamoudi's image, was distrustful of his offer. "We don't need to sell out our principles," he says he told Johari on the way back from the meeting, "change our name and be under them, we're not going to be under them, under anybody." He adds, "My thing was, we were going to build black Islam, being the vanguard of Islam in the black community, and do so independently." He remembers Johari being more noncommittal.

In the following months, several problems arose for Abdur-Rahman. A Moroccan preacher, whom Abdur-Rahman believes to have been a Brotherhood member, began attracting a following on campus. Johari distanced himself from Abdur-Rahman and, according to the latter, began convening small study groups at his house without telling Abdur-Rahman. "Things were falling apart," say Abdur-Rahman, "and there was a lot of *fitna* [internal dissent]." Abdur-Rahman says that the Moroccan preacher and Johari began to spread rumors about him, which caused him to lose a significant portion of his following on campus. "It became clear that Johari was becoming a real enemy," he says. "He literally stabbed me in the back."

In 1990 the tensions on campus and problems in his personal life (he got divorced that year) led Abdur-Rahman to leave Washington and move to Winston-Salem, North Carolina, where he spent thirteen months studying Arabic and the Quran. "I went down to recharge," he says, "licking my wounds." When he returned to Washington, he found that the situation on Howard campus had completely changed. "The Ikhwan had Howard on lock, complete total lock," he says. Johari had opened the local branch of MSA, the first of various positions in the American Brotherhood milieu he would come to occupy (he later became director of outreach for the Dar Al Hijrah Islamic Center, the network's main hub in northern Virginia). And, according to Abdur-Rahman, he had "a crew around him," badmouthing and ostracizing Abdur-Rahman.

Abdur-Rahman understood that he could no longer operate on Howard's campus, but he wanted to remain active in Islamic circles. Thanks to his charisma and knowledge, which grew during his time in Salem, by 1994 he had attracted a small group of African American Muslims around himself. He also identified a small house not too far from Howard that could serve as a mosque for the congregation and as a home for him. Abdur-Rahman and his congregation did not have enough money for the down payment, however, and despite his bad experience with the Brotherhood during his university years, he decided to approach Alamoudi for help.

Abdur-Rahman and Alamoudi, in fact, had always had good personal relations, which had been cemented during a long car ride together back to Washington from an Islamic conference in Chicago. Once approached, the Brotherhood leader decided to help Abdur-Rahman and give him the money for the down payment. "That's the one thing I'll say about him," says Abdur-Rahman of Alamoudi. "If you needed help he'd give it to you; he's never going to give you enough to be independent, but he always helped, would often pull out a wad of cash and give me something that would help me spread Islam. He was something else."

On various levels, argues Abdur-Rahman, Alamoudi embodies the characteristics and modus operandi of the Brotherhood: charming and generous when necessary, but also ruthless and manipulative. Alamoudi's impressive résumé also represents the evolution of the American Brotherhood milieu. Shortly after arriving in the United States, Alamoudi became president of the Brotherhood-linked mosque in his area, the Islamic Society of Boston, and of the Muslim Student Association at the national level.[17] But by the second half of the 1980s, after having relocated to Washington, he became affiliated with two crucially important organizations of the American Brotherhood milieu in its "adult" phase: the Islamic Society of North America, where he served as regional representative for the Washington area, and the SAAR Foundation, where he was executive assistant to the president.

By the late 1970s the American Brothers, like their European counter-parts, had realized that their presence in the country (and in Canada, where the Brothers were active yet fewer, and initially subordinate to the group in the United States) was permanent and that a student organization, even one as sophisticated as MSA, was not enough to fulfill the needs of the organization. They therefore incorporated the Islamic Society of North America, an umbrella organization intended to coordinate the activities of MSA and the other groups born from the same milieu.[18] ISNA, MSA, and the North American Islamic Trust, the body that holds the deeds to the network's mosques, soon established their headquarters on a multimillion-dollar, forty-two-acre site in suburban Indianapolis.[19]

Among the various sources documenting the first years of the Brother-hood in the United States and its growth from student groups, one of the most authoritative and comprehensive is a lecture given to other Brother-hood members in Kansas City in the early 1980s by Zeid al Noman, a *masul* (official) of the Executive Office of the U.S. Muslim Brotherhood.[20] Al Noman describes a striking level of organization. Though the group had only just established a presence in the country, al Noman outlines a formal and extremely complex structure. He explains that the group had no less than twenty collegial bodies and committees that operated within a well-defined hierarchy and met regularly. While some of the committees discussed security or dawa methods, the organization's central bodies drafted and oversaw meticulous long-term plans of action. According to al Noman, the Brotherhood's Shura Council in the United States approved five-year plans for the group's activities, which the Executive Office, to which al Noman himself belonged, put together annual work programs to implement.

According to al Noman, the plan for the 1975–1980 quinquennium was simply "general work," but the 1981–1985 quinquennium unveiled a major shift in the American Brotherhood's views and perceptions of its goals. The Shura Council and the Executive Office understood that basing the move-ment's activities within a student organization was limiting, because its membership changes as students graduate. Only a permanent network of organizations could implement the quinquennial plans. "What the Move-ment should be," said al Noman, "is to become a Movement for the resi-dents." Al Noman refers to this new phase as "the settlement of the dawa."

The writings of another member of the American Brotherhood from its early days provide a glimpse of the network's focus on developing organizations. In "An Explanatory Memorandum on the Strategic Goals for the Group in North America," an eighteen-page document written in 1991, Mohammed Akram—then a member of the Shura Council of the U.S. Brotherhood—stated that "it must be stressed that it has become clear and emphatically known that all is in agreement that we must 'settle' or 'enable' Islam and its Movement in this part of the world [America]."[21] Crucially important in order to advance this goal was the development of what Akram calls "the organizational mentality," examples of which he finds in the prophet Mohammed ("the first pioneer of this phenomenon") and the Muslim Brotherhood founder Hassan al Banna ("the pioneer of contemporary Islamic Dawa"). Akram wrote to other members of the Shura Council, "We must say that we are in a country which understands no language other than the language of the organizations, and one which does not respect or give weight to any group without effective, functional and strong organizations."

In accordance with these plans, during the second phase of their presence in the United States, the Brothers began developing a web of organizations, each with its own magazine, website, annual conference, subdepartments, and regional branches but unified by common financial sources, interlocking boards of directors, and occasional participation in common initiatives.[22] The few hundred individuals who run them form a small social network united by family, business, and, most important, ideological ties. Affluent, well-connected, highly educated, and motivated, they constitute a clique of leaders with ample clout but few followers.

As in all Western countries, the relationship between these groups and the Brotherhood is often a source of debate, particularly between supporters and critics of the organization. For example, Shaker Elsayed—a top official of the Muslim American Society, one of the organizations of the cluster with closest links to the Brotherhood—admitted in 2002 that roughly 45 percent of MAS activists are members of the Brotherhood but stressed that the organization is operationally independent and "not administered from Egypt." "Ikhwan members founded MAS," notes the Egyptian-born Elsayed, "but MAS went way beyond that point of conception."[23] "We really see that our methods and means are different from the Orient," similarly insisted the American Brotherhood leader al Noman in his Kansas City lecture. "[W]e did not take or borrow a method or a means from the Orient unless it was compatible with the reality of the Islamic Movement over here."[24]

The complexity and size of the American branch of the Brotherhood in its early days are confirmed by many internal Brotherhood documents retrieved by the U.S. government and published writings of members of the milieu. They are also detailed by various individuals who had intimate knowledge of the milieu and spoke to me about it. Kamal Helbawy, a frequent visitor to the United States between the 1970s and 1990s, is one of them. Another one is a less known yet arguably even more informed insider, a former member of the American Muslim Brotherhood milieu named Hussien Elmeshad, who for the first time decided to publicly speak about his time in the Brotherhood for this book.[25]

Elmeshad grew up in a religious family in Cairo. In the 1960s, while in high school, he began to attend Brotherhood study groups. His interactions and fascination with the group continued while he pursued business studies at al Azhar. But it was only in 1978 that Elmeshad formally joined the Brotherhood (or, as he puts it, "became organized"). And, interestingly, his induction did not take place in Egypt but in Jersey City, New Jersey. Elmeshad, in fact, had moved to the United States to continue his studies, and before leaving Egypt he had been told by a local leader of the Brotherhood to introduce himself to the late head of a Jersey City mosque "controlled by the Brotherhood" to continue his process of integration in the group. Indeed, just a few weeks after connecting with the head of the Jersey City mosque, Elmeshad was formally inducted. "The process was fast," Elmeshad explains, "because I had already started it in Egypt and I had come recommended by prominent members in Egypt." Elmeshad's induction process, started in Egypt and formalized in the United States, indicates a high level of connectivity between the Brotherhood in the Arab world and that in the West.

Upon induction, Elmeshad was inserted in a complex structure that mirrored, albeit on a smaller scale, that of the Brotherhood in Egypt. He became part of a local usra in New Jersey, which was part of a complex regional and national structure. The naqib of Elmeshad's own usra was an Egyptian graduate of Columbia University who was the director of the Eastern region of the United States (which covered the eastern seaboard, from Boston to Virginia), one of the four regions into which the Brotherhood had divided the country (the others were South, Midwest, and West). Members of each region would meet regularly, often at outdoor camps. Elmeshad recalls that at some of these camps some 2,500 people were present (although the number includes not just Brothers but also their family members).

According to Elmeshad, areas like Chicago, New York/New Jersey, Washington, D.C., and California have historically been the main Brotherhood hubs in the country, but the group had a presence also in secondary cities and remote areas. "Members of the Brotherhood in America all know each other," explains Elmeshad, "we are one big family, and everybody helps each other." While national leaders constantly interact with one another, national conferences of public organizations of the milieu are the occasion in which they all come together. Similarly, these gatherings serve the purpose of reinforcing the sense of belonging on the cadres and further "bringing in" individuals who are in the process of joining the Brotherhood.

Elmeshad played an integral role in this milieu for around two decades. He was close to most of the top leaders of the American Brotherhood milieu, and top Brotherhood leaders from abroad (former murshid Mashour and Akef, among them many) often stayed at his New Jersey home when visiting America. As is common, membership in the "secret" structure of the Brotherhood coincided with roles in the "public" organizations of the milieu. Elmeshad was a member of ISNA and served as treasurer of the Muslim Arab Youth Association (MAYA) for six years. Given his business background, he was involved in many financial activities of the American Brotherhood milieu, from fund-raising for the local Brotherhood school in Jersey City to occupying key positions in various businesses linked to the organization. "From nine to five I worked as a deputy bursar at Columbia University," Elmeshad explains, "but all my free time was devoted to the Brotherhood."

By the late 1990s Elmeshad began to feel disenchanted with the Brotherhood. His reasons are very similar to Helbawy's, a man Elmeshad considers his mentor. Elmeshad is still an ardent believer in al Banna's message, which he considers "the true Islamic thought." But he argues that the current leadership of the Brotherhood, in Egypt exactly like in the United States, has swayed from the right path, losing sight of spirituality and grassroots activism to concentrate on politics and power. Obsession with secrecy and blind obedience, argues Elmeshad, are just some of the many deviations from al Banna's true message implemented by the generation currently leading the Brotherhood. In 2003, while living in Bahrain, Elmeshad formally left the Brotherhood.

As Elemshad's role indicates, access to ample financial resources was crucial to developing this network—and, as the case of Abdur-Rahman shows, to exerting influence over many individuals and organizations that espoused conservative interpretations of Islam but did not belong to the movement. To be sure, this success would not have been possible without the drive and organizational abilities of its members, but the guarantee of substantial funding is arguably the single most important determinant of the Brothers' expansion in America—as in other Western countries. "Since they were well-connected in the Middle East, they were able to bring money to build various institutions," argues Inamul Haq, a professor of religion at Benedictine University. "They were in a position to define American Islam." Without the Brotherhood, he continues, "we would have seen a more American Islamic culture rather than a foreign community living in the United States."[26]

Connections in the Middle East were indeed the key. Three of the early pioneers of the Brotherhood in America, Jamal Barzinji, Ahmed Totonji, and Hisham al Talib (the so-called three Kurds), who were the founders of many of the most prominent organizations of the networks, worked for various companies owned by the major Brotherhood financier Yussuf Nada and were introduced by the Egyptian millionaire to his network of wealthy Arab Gulf donors.[27] The three Kurds also served in leadership positions inside global Brotherhood organizations such as IIFSO and WAMY, allowing them to have access to some of the most generous sources of funding for Islamic activities of the second half of the twentieth century.

No less revealing is the active presence in the United States of top Egyptian Brotherhood financier Mahmoud Abu Saud, one of the fathers of modern Islamic banking. Ahmed Elkadi, his son-in-law, arrived in 1967. and served both as treasurer of the American Brotherhood's secret structure and as president of the North American Islamic Trust.[28] In 1990 Abu Saud founded the American Muslim Council, which was headed by Alamoudi until his arrest.[29]

Another institution in which Alamoudi was involved, the SAAR Foundation, is paradigmatic of the American Brothers' ample access to financial resources. SAAR received substantial financial backing from wealthy Arab Gulf donors—particularly the al Rajhi family, one of Saudi Arabia's wealthiest. "We asked investors to give us one large lump sum rather than smaller amounts every year," stated the SAAR vice president and former MSA president Yaqub Mirza, explaining the foundation's fund-raising mechanisms in the early 1980s. "This way we were bringing in from $10 million to $20 million a year."[30]

An investigative report by the *Washington Post* in 2002 revealed additional details about SAAR's financial activities:

> In 1984, Yaqub Mirza, a Pakistani native who received a PhD in physics from the University of Texas in Dallas, used money from the Rajhis to start SAAR in Virginia, with the goal of spreading Islam and doing charitable work. Mirza also sought out business ventures for SAAR. By investing the Rajhis' money with Washington real estate developer Mohamed Hadid, he made SAAR one of the region's biggest landlords in the 1980s. The SAAR network also became one of South America's biggest apple growers and the owner of one of America's top poultry firms, Mar-Jac Poultry in Georgia. "The funds came very easily," said a businessman who dealt with SAAR. "If they wanted a few million dollars, they called the al-Rajhis, who would send it along."[31]

With such sums floating around, it was not difficult for Alamoudi to occasionally dispense a few dollars to Abdur-Rahman, money that did not buy his allegiance but made him indebted to the network. Abdur-Rahman, in fact, regularly attended Dar al Hijrah throughout the late 1990s and into the following decade and occasionally spoke at second-tier events organized by the milieu. He was friendly with most of the leaders of the network and shared large components of the Brothers' ideology, even though his personal emphasis was always on the African American Muslim community.

"I was definitely a fellow traveler," he says. "What I didn't like about the Ikhwan," he adds, "was the deception, because I didn't see why it was necessary. Why are you acting like you are ashamed of Islam?" Abdur-Rahman maintains that he had always been disturbed by the Brothers' decision not to reveal their identity to outsiders. He recalls that some members, after years of interactions, did tell him they were Brothers, but there was always a "kind of sneakiness, like you're ashamed of something; when I brought it up with actual Ikhwan they would say it was because of the things we suffered in Egypt, in Syria, we have to dissimulate."

Abdur-Rahman claims to have had his first doubts about his adherence to Islamist ideology and, consequently, activism on the fringes of the

Brotherhood milieu after the August 1998 bombings of the U.S embassies in Kenya and Tanzania, which were both carried out by al Qaeda. He recalls the reaction to the attack in his congregation, where sympathies for Bin Laden had frequently been expressed in those years. "We saw all these Africans get killed, black people like us," he explains, "and it was like, I don't know, how do you square that circle?" To some degree, unbeknownst to Abdur-Rahman, this reaction was similar to Alamoudi's. In a phone call that was intercepted by U.S. authorities, who had long monitored his activities, Alamoudi told his interlocutor that the attack against the embassies in East Africa had been "wrong," but in his opinion only because "many African Muslims have died and not a single American died."[32]

Another episode that frustrated Abdur-Rahman was the American Brothers' support of George W. Bush during the 2000 presidential elections. "Bush had once made an offhand comment about not profiling Muslims," he says, "and they seized on it and decided he was the candidate for Muslims; they organized an event at Dar al Hijra to get all imams on the same page to get our communities to vote for Bush." Abdur-Rahman recalls having a major falling out with Alamoudi over this decision, as he believed that the Brothers had not consulted the African American Muslim community, which overwhelmingly preferred the Democratic candidate, Al Gore.

But the tipping point for Abdur-Rahman was the attacks of September 11, 2001. "9/11," he says, "was where you learned who's who and what's what, you learned who is a good person, forget religion, ideology, who is a good person. That's when you learn who is a human being and who is not." "And at that point," he added, "I had to take stock of my life, examine what I did and what I believed." In the dramatic days that followed the attacks, Abdur-Rahman was also particularly taken aback by the conspiracy theories that abounded in Brotherhood circles and that attributed the attacks to a "Jewish conspiracy." "I started seeing the hypocrisy and started seeing the dissimulation of the Ikhwan," he says, "picking up the flag and acting like they never had a hand in creating this." Abdur-Rahman says he was "disgusted" by the hypocrisy of certain Brotherhood leaders, starting with Alamoudi, who, after years of rallying against America, were outdoing one another in displays of patriotism in the tense days following the attacks.

The secrecy and the "Machiavellian approach to politics, always trumping religion," were key reasons why Abdur-Rahman distanced himself from the Brothers. An additional major factor was seeing that thousands of Americans had been killed by an organization with which the Brothers had always had an ambiguous relation, viewing them as "well-meaning brothers who were too hasty and impetuous" in pursuing a just agenda. But what led Abdur-Rahman not just to distance himself from movement but to become a vocal critic is the racism he says he discovered inside it.

Abdur-Rahman's entire adult life has been shaped by his desire to defend and empower the African American community. While for decades this commitment has been deeply intertwined with the Muslim faith, which he still practices with devotion, Abdur-Rahman has a strong sense of black identity, which arguably overshadows any other. It is for this very reason that for him, witnessing various forms of racism against blacks inside the Brotherhood milieu dealt an intolerable blow to the Brothers' image.

"The way that they propagate the religion," he says, passionately,

the way they sell it to you is that there's no racism in Islam and all Muslims are like the teeth of a comb. . . . Then you find out that it's not true, you find out it's almost of a policy of who they wanna give shahada to [who they want to convert] and who they wanna bring into the fold. First is Caucasians. First because in American society Caucasians enjoy white privilege. Obviously, since the Ikhwan are about getting power for themselves, they want to insinuate themselves through the powerful group, so they do it through marriage, buying into it. When a Caucasian becomes a Muslim, then his white privilege can become part of their project. If you marry a Caucasian their children will be white or whiter—it has value to them, it's like a currency. They can move more easily through society and gather intel and understand the society without being detected.

Abdur-Rahman basically believes that the American Brothers, seeking to infiltrate the upper echelons of American society, have made a decision to prioritize Caucasians in their dawa to non-Muslims, deeming them to be more "useful" than African Americans. Evidence supporting his argument includes an essay that he found in a decades-old publication of the Brotherhood milieu:

When the white American becomes Muslim, he is an excellent Muslim, and he represents an excellent type. This is because his social background is better than that of the black Muslim. The schools in which he studies, the environment in which he lives are at a higher level than those of the black American. This background gives the white American Muslim the possibility to comprehend and learn more than the black Muslim. But there is also a large number of black Muslims who are extremely good; they appear to be outstanding because the number of black Muslims is greater, among whom there are some who cannot grasp things quickly. The white Muslims are few in number, but when one of them becomes Muslim he is an excellent and active Muslim. We have plans for paying attention to these white Muslims and choosing certain elements among them in order to become propagators of Islam and to become effective in white society.[33]

This kind of overt racism was too much Abdur-Rahman to bear, and not long after 9/11 he broke with the Brotherhood milieu in which he had been involved for almost two decades. He has since become a strong critic of the "Immigrant Muslim Syndicate," his term intended to highlight its "foreign and mafia-like nature."[34] He still lives in Washington, D.C., where he runs a company providing tours whose theme is the life of Malcolm X and giving lectures on Islam to diverse audiences.

Abdur-Rahman's first contact with the Muslim Brotherhood in the United States came when Brothers in the Washington, D.C., area witnessed the success of his activism in the local African American Muslim community and sought to co-opt him. After his refusal, which he says cost him dearly, he maintained close relations with the milieu, participating in its activities, mobilizing for it, and receiving funds from it for some twenty years. Despite being made privy to various aspects of the organization's ideology and mechanisms, he never received an offer to join it and remained simply a fellow traveler. Although it offers admittedly limited insights into the Brotherhood, Abdur-Rahman's experience is an interesting one, as it illuminates several aspects of one of the largest and most organized branches of the Brotherhood in the West. Moreover, many of his motivations for leaving the milieu overlap with those of actual members, including its lack of transparency and internal racism.

CHAPTER X

Joining and Leaving

What the Evidence Suggests

The stories of the individuals profiled here do not constitute anything remotely close to a statistically relevant survey of former Western Brotherhood members. They are just a handful among the thousands of individuals who belong to Western Brotherhood milieus and to the unquantifiable but obviously smaller group of those who have left the organization. The evidence they provide, which I have made all possible efforts to cross-check but which in some cases is difficult to verify, is inevitably anecdotal, not empirical. Yet despite these caveats, their testimonies provide unique insights into the internal dynamics of a notoriously secretive organization, giving important insiders' perspectives on a reality virtually unknown to the outside world.

The individuals who constitute this small sample possess different characteristics. They had different socioeconomic backgrounds and personal histories when they first entered the sphere of the Muslim Brotherhood. They joined the organization in different countries, from Morocco to Sweden, and they did so at different times, from the 1950s (in the case of Kamal Helbawy) to the beginning of the twenty-first century (in the case of Mohamed Louizi). They stayed inside the organization for different lengths of time and occupied different ranks. Their stories largely reflect this heterogeneity. Yet their accounts overall are remarkably consistent, if not at times identical. From nitty-gritty details of how the Brotherhood in the West operates to the motivations that led them to disengage from the group, the individuals interviewed for this book tell stories that are similar to one another and, in many cases, to those of the few other former Western Brothers who have discussed their experiences elsewhere.

By the same token, most accounts of the individuals profiled provide a solid answer to the queries posed at the beginning of this book (chapter 2): that is, whether the dynamics of recruitment by, inner workings of, structure of, and disengagement from the Muslim Brotherhood in the West were similar to those described for the mother branch in Egypt. The information gathered from interviews, complemented by accounts of other individuals and analysis of various documents, seem to clearly indicate that many of the dynamics of how the Brotherhood operates in the East are replicated, at times with remarkable fidelity, in the West. Many aspects of Brotherhood life, in fact, seem to have been transplanted tout court—or subjected to only minor variations—from the Arab world to Europe and North America. As for reasons for leaving the organization, while some are identical in the East and the West, others are peculiar to the West.

Joining the Brotherhood

From the accounts of all the individuals profiled, the process of joining the Muslim Brotherhood, from the "spotting" of new potential members by Brotherhood recruiters to (often years later) the induction ceremony in which the new Brother swears baya, appears to be virtually identical in the Arab world and in the West. The detailed descriptions of the phases of the process provided by all interviewees have almost no differences among them and match to a T the dynamics described in chapter 2 for the Brotherhood in Egypt.

Particularly useful in this regard are the accounts of Helbawy and Louizi, the only two individuals profiled who joined the Brotherhood in the Arab world before coming to the West. Helbawy has the vantage point of one of the most senior Brotherhood leaders ever to settle in the West—and someone who, by his own account, has recruited hundreds of new members. He describes the process of joining, in all its phases, as identical in the East and the West. Louizi was a much more junior member, but he joined the Brotherhood twice, first in Morocco (although technically MRR/MUR was not the Brotherhood but a Moroccan Islamist organization modeled on it) and then in France. He describes the process he went through in both countries as largely the same.

For most individuals profiled, recruitment started when they were spotted by a Brotherhood recruiter and invited to join a study group. That was the case for Omero Marongiu, Mohamed Louizi (both in Morocco and France), Ahmed Akkari, and Kamal Helbawy (in Egypt). Pierre Durrani was not invited to a study group but at the time of his recruitment was enrolled at IESH, the Brothers' graduate school, which itself could be seen as a giant study group. All individuals began in "open" circles or study groups and then, upon being invited, entered more restricted, closed circles. In their interviews, they all clearly identified these circles as ways to disseminate Islamist viewpoints and, at the same time, to observe and select new talent for the group. All also mentioned that while they had varying degrees of suspicion (little, in the case of Ahmed Akkari), they initially were not fully aware that the study circles were vehicles for Brotherhood recruitment. When asked what was read in the study groups, they all listed the same Brotherhood authors, noting that the literature became more markedly Islamist as they progressed. They all emphasized the importance of the relationship with their mentor and the constant observation and testing to which they were subjected.

Unsurprisingly for a meticulously bureaucratic organization like the Brotherhood, many of these dynamics are not just informal practices but have been codified, in the West as well as in the Arab world. Evidence of such codification comes, for example, from internal documents of the American branch of the Muslim Brotherhood obtained by the *Chicago Tribune*.[1] An instructional booklet for recruiters advised them to scout mosques, Islamic classes, and Muslim organizations looking for individuals with the appropriate "commitment, loyalty, and obedience" to Brotherhood ideals. Fitting candidates were invited to participate in prayer groups that they were asked to keep secret. If a candidate asked about a particular meeting to which he had not been invited, the booklet instructed the recruiter to respond: "Make it a habit not to meddle in that which does not concern you." Upon initiation, new members were told that they were part of a global organization and that, according to the booklet, membership "is not a personal honor but a charge to sacrifice all that one has for the sake of raising the banner of Islam."

The process of induction is, again, identical in the accounts of the interviewees to how it is known to happen in the Arab world. All recounted receiving an offer from a senior Brother, in most cases their mentor. And although only in some cases was it preceded by a preparatory seminar, all describe a moving ceremony that culminated in their swearing baya. As for the personal reasons that led them to join, all the individuals profiled spoke of their desire to help spread Islam and their feeling of pride at having joined such an exclusive and renowned organization.

It should be noted that most of these dynamics, whether the mechanisms of recruitment or the personal motivations of those recruited, are confirmed by the accounts of a handful of other former members of the Brotherhood in the West who have written about their experiences. They include Farid Abdelkrim, who was active in the French milieu alongside Mohamed Louizi and Omero Marongiu; Michaël Privot, a former member of the Brotherhood in Belgium during the same time, who has written a book about his experience, *Quand j'étais Frère musulman* (When I was a Muslim Brother); and Mustafa Saied, an Indian American who joined the Brotherhood in Tennessee.

Life Inside the Brotherhood

The descriptions provided of the internal dynamics of the Western Brotherhood, from its structure to its regulations, point to remarkable similarities among them and with the Arab world. All the individuals profiled describe how, upon induction, they progressively began to better understand the structure of the Brotherhood. While that knowledge can be only limited for low-level members, as were most of the interviewees, all, including a senior leader like Helbawy, describe the Brotherhood in every Western country as a highly structured organization with a clear hierarchy.

From the privileged vantage point of senior leader who operated both in the East and in the West, Helbawy makes clear that the Brotherhood in each Western country replicated the structure found in Egypt and other Arab countries, just on a smaller scale. Exactly as in Egypt, Brotherhood organizations in the West have the usra as the core unit; various usras come together and meet at the regional level, and an elected leadership presides at the top. Obviously, because the number of Brothers in Western countries, even the larger ones, is relatively small, some differences exist, but many defining aspects of the Brotherhood's structure in the Arab world are reproduced in the West.

All the interviewees highlight the centrality of the usra, the nuclear cell of the Brotherhood. All recount the weekly meetings (generally on Friday nights) and the bigger meetings with members of various usras from the region once a month. The internal dynamics of the usra are also described in almost identical terms, although those usras were located in different Western countries. Interviews conducted by the scholar Hazem Kandil with members of the Egyptian Brotherhood confirm this analysis. "On a short trip to Seattle," writes Kandil, "[Egyptian Brotherhood member] Malik felt so emotionally drained that he had to inquire frantically whether there were any family [usra] meetings being held in the area. He was directed through a Brotherhood mosque to a family meeting held by a Pakistani, with an Egyptian, a Sudanese, and an American convert in attendance. Malik recounted with amazement how this meeting replicated the ones held back home to the last detail, and how those Brothers, whom he had just met, greeted him as warmly as those he had known all his life."[2]

Descriptions of other aspects of life inside Brotherhood confirm these striking similarities between the accounts and the dynamics in the Middle East. All describe paying a fee (most put the amount at 2.5 percent of their personal income, but it varied). The tarbiya curriculum appears to be virtually identical everywhere, though local leaders may introduce slight variations. All describe an important division of labor within the group, with a high degree of specialization, and highlight the importance of the different levels of membership, noting a substantial gap between junior and senior members. And they all describe an environment shaped by a deep adherence to strict rules and hierarchies, at least on the part of the more junior members.

Although in all these respects East and West appear almost identical, one dynamic seems to be a peculiarity of the West. All the individuals profiled indicate that as soon as they began their experience inside a Western branch of the Brotherhood, they understood that there was both a nonpublic or secret structure and a public one—or, in the words of Mohamed Louizi, "the façade and the arrière boutique." Helbawy authoritatively explains that while the Western Brothers fully replicated the secret structure adopted in Middle Eastern countries, they also created a large web of heterogeneous organizations that they control but that do not publicly identify as being linked to the Brotherhood. The interviewees attribute the Brothers' decision to create this binary structure to their understanding that organizations that cannot, in theory, be directly linked to the group are more effective at conducting the kind of engagement it seeks with Muslim communities and Western society.

Another feature that emerges from the accounts, and is backed by several additional sources, is the transnational nature of the Muslim Brotherhood. All the accounts describe a fluid yet extremely tight and effective network of activists spread all over the world. While a separate Brotherhood organization, with its own leadership and structure, exists in each country analyzed in depth (the United Kingdom, Sweden, Denmark, France, the United States) and in most other Western countries, the activists in them are all connected and regularly communicating and cooperating on innumerable initiatives. While many of these ties are informal, they are strengthened by family and business connections, aside from the obvious ideological ones. Various formal organizations, such as FIOE and FEMYSO, also tie them together. As the individuals profiled indicate, these connections also extend to organizations belonging to the Islamist movements that, while independent of it, adopt a worldview and a methodology similar to the Brotherhood's—chiefly Turkish (Millî Görüş and the AKP) and South Asian (Jamaat-e-Islami) Islamism.

The claim of informal connections with the global Muslim Brotherhood is not particularly controversial, but the degree to which Western Brotherhood organizations are included inside the organizational structures of the Brotherhood in the Arab world has long been disputed. The essential question is, are Western Brotherhood organizations completely independent of their mother organizations in the East? The accounts in this book do not provide a definitive answer, because most of the individuals profiled were low-level members who would have no access to such elite and therefore secret dynamics.

On one hand, it does not appear that Western Brotherhood organizations regularly receive orders from the East on what strategy to adopt and how to pursue their goals. On the other hand, various episodes point to a level of influence and connectivity that exceeds what the Western Brotherhood has at times claimed. It is quite telling, for example, that Ahmed Akkari, who had been recruited by, had joined, and was active in the Brotherhood exclusively in Denmark, could leave the organization by hand-delivering his resignation letter to the head of the Brotherhood in Lebanon. Similarly, Hussien Elmeshad formally joined the Brotherhood in New Jersey in the span of a few weeks after arriving in the United States because a senior member of the group in Egypt referred him to a contact there. Mohamed Louizi and a current Brotherhood member who wishes to stay anonymous claim that members of the Brotherhood in North Africa can join the Brotherhood in Europe simply by presenting a letter of recommendation (*tazkiya*) from the leaders of their branch to those in Europe.[3]

In light of how the individuals profiled have described the structure of the Muslim Brotherhood in each of their countries, it can be argued that the debate over determining whether a Western Muslim organization "belongs to the Brotherhood" is often incorrectly framed. In many cases, in fact, an organization's affiliation to the Brotherhood is assessed based on its connections to the Muslim Brotherhood in Egypt or, more broadly, the Arab world. Those making the charge that a specific organization is linked to the Brotherhood will say that "it is part of the Muslim Brotherhood" or use similar expressions that denote a subordination to some branch in the Middle East. Those denying that the organization has ties to the Brotherhood will emphasize said organization's independence from Cairo or, more broadly, the Middle East.

It appears that neither analysis captures the reality of the Brotherhood in the West. Unquestionably, ties to the mother branch in the Middle East are an important indicator, but they are not the key to determining whether an organization is "Muslim Brotherhood." What all individuals profiled described is a reality in which, in each of their Western countries, a small cluster of Brotherhood members created an independent Brotherhood structure, which mirrored that of the mother countries, albeit on a smaller scale. There is therefore a French Brotherhood, a Swedish Brotherhood, a British Brotherhood, an American Brotherhood, exactly as there is an Egyptian, a Jordanian, and a Syrian Brotherhood. The way to identify whether a public organization based in a Western country belongs to the Brotherhood is therefore not necessarily by uncovering possible but, in most cases, feeble ties to any Middle Eastern country. Rather, that determination is better made by assessing whether they are a direct emanation of the Brotherhood branch of the specific Western country in which it operates. While it is often true, as Western Brothers say, that their organizations and structures are independent and do not "receive orders from Cairo," that fact in itself does not indicate that they are not Muslim Brotherhood.

In an interview with Xavier Ternisien, a French expert on religions, Mohammed Akef clearly described how the Brotherhood transcends formalities such as official affiliation. "We do not have an international organization; we have an organization through our perception of things," explained the murshid. "We are present in every country. Everywhere there are people who believe in the message of the Muslim Brothers. In France, the Union of Islamic Organizations of France (UOIF) does not belong to the organization of the Brothers. They follow their own laws and rules."[4] Confirming the informality of the movement's ties, Akef elsewhere referred to the UOIF as "our brothers in France." Finally, in a 2005 interview, he explained that European Ikhwan organizations have no direct link to the Egyptian branch, yet they coordinate actions with them. He concluded the interview with a telling remark: "We have the tendency not to make distinctions among us."[5]

Another factor on which all the individuals profiled agree is the Western Brothers' ability to keep the many Muslims who interact and even work with them in the dark about the Brotherhood's aims and very existence. "I was basically helping an organization I didn't know the existence of," says Pierre Durrani of how he felt after the revelation that the organizations he had been working with in Sweden for years were offshoots of the Muslim Brotherhood. "I had heard the name [Muslim Brotherhood], because I was not stupid, but I didn't connect the dots at all," he adds. Kamal Helbawy confirms that using well-meaning Muslims (and, in some cases, non-Muslims as well) who can be useful to the organization without revealing itself to them, even after years of close interactions, is a strategy of the group.

A quintessential example of this dynamic is offered by Pernilla Ouis, who now says the Brotherhood "fooled" her. She also maintains that had somebody told her and her colleagues at *Salaam* the truth back in the day, "we would have rejected it outright and thought it was an attempt to smear Islam. We were very naïve." Mohamed Louizi writes on this issue:

> Furthermore, not all motivations and reasons to join the UOIF are the same. The level of engagement is not uniform. Some, a minority, know what they are doing and keep their sight on the Tamkine from afar, in silence and in secret. Others, more numerous this time, embark for the sake of Allah, to resemble their Prophet, to give meaning to their lives, to protect against what is unknown, to purify their hearts and feel useful, etc.
>
> They also are not naive people, far from it. They are sincere women and men, often educated, respectable, and intelligent, but who walk

behind battle-hardened Islamic leaders, with their young innocent children who are unaware of the stakes, with their own eyes blinded, their tongues atrophied, yet strangely with their hearts finding rest and filled with emotion and the satisfaction of having, as a family, accomplished their religious duties, or so they think. They are the keyboards on social media, the hands, feet, and pockets of the UOIF. They believe that they are building and maintaining a mosque for God, but they are building an HQ for the UOIF. Those people ignore everything, or almost everything, of the true planned journey. Themselves victims of a gigantic deception, of another doublespeak. I really mean this![6]

A slightly different dynamic, also described by several of the individuals profiled, is that of the conscious fellow travelers. These are individuals who are not members of the Brotherhood but work with it while aware of the true nature of their partners. Abdur-Rahman Muhammad was, during his activist days, a quintessential conscious fellow traveler, running his own activities but coordinating and receiving support from the Brothers. Omero Marongiu likewise, but to a lesser degree, attempted to find a modus vivendi with the French Brotherhood milieu and take advantage of its platform after leaving it. The relationship between Brotherhood networks and conscious fellow travelers is one of mutual advantage, and the Brothers often rely on them to counteract their small numbers.

While the accounts of how the Brotherhood works appear to be remarkably homogeneous, the individuals profiled show less uniformity of views when assessing its aims. On one end of the spectrum, former members like Mohamed Louizi, Ahmed Akkari, and Pierre Durrani strongly believe that the Brotherhood is fully committed to a strategy of subversion (which Mohamed refers to as *tamkin*) aimed at slowly undermining the very foundations of Western society, seeking eventually, even if it takes centuries, to replace them with an Islamic order. Others, like Kamal Helbawy, Hussien Elmeshad and Adly Abu Hajar, while themselves harsh critics of the Brotherhood, do not see such malign intentions. All of them—who, to be sure, still see themselves as Islamists or conservative Muslim activists—argue that the current leaders of the Brotherhood have strayed from Hassan al Banna's original message (the main reason that Helbawy and Elmeshad left it) to seek power for themselves and have failed to adapt their worldview to the reality of the West, but they do not see the Brotherhood's ideology as inherently problematic. Others among those profiled position themselves somewhere in between these two views. Capturing the thinking of many critics of the group, Omero claims that the Western Brothers do dream of making every society, including the West's, Islamic. But, being pragmatic by nature and understanding that even in the most optimistic of scenarios that outcome is possible only in a distant future, they keep it in the back of their minds and work toward more concrete goals.

This middle-of-the road assessment, arguing that the Brothers do harbor in the back of their mind lofty ideas of an Islamic conquest, albeit a peaceful one, but work on and are constrained by significantly more mundane realities, has been elegantly put forward by Hakim El Karoui, a scholar whose report on Islamism in France (2018) has been very influential in French policy circles. Writes El Karoui:

> This Tamkin project, if it exists, is more wishful thinking than a conspiracy. It describes the desire of power of a brotherhood which, because it is semi-secret and long confined in clandestinity, nourishes fantasies. On the part of the Muslim Brothers settled in Europe, there is a desire to be influential, on one hand with the European Muslim populations that it aims to supervise, on the other with the political decision makers, in order to appear, thanks to a moderate discourse, as the principal interlocutors on matters related to Islam. In short, establishing a dual hegemony, with Muslims and with power. Perhaps in the minds of some, this goal is only a step towards the Islamization of European societies and Tamkin. . . . In fact, the main question is not "What do the European Muslim Brothers want?" but "What can the European Muslim Brothers do?" Whatever their objectives, they are confronted with the realities of the society in which the Brothers are established, the sociopolitical context of the various European countries, the different reception of their discourse within Muslim communities, or the competition of other religious discourses. If there was indeed a plot, it would run into the reality.[7]

Similarly divided are the opinions on the relationship between the Brotherhood and violence. Helbawy and Abu Hajar argue that the Western Brothers completely reject violent means. Michaël Privot, a former member of the Belgian Brotherhood and FEMYSO vice president who wrote a book extremely critical of the group after leaving it but retains loose connection to the Brotherhood milieu, agrees. "Even if I was only really active six years within the Brotherhood structures," he writes, "I never encountered—nor was I ever asked to spread—antidemocratic, violent, racist, segregationist speech, nor calls for the caliphate or for the conversion of my peers. . . . I could not find any discourse calling for violence, jihad, or segregation."[8]

While none argues that the Brothers are engaged in any terrorist activity in the West, other individuals profiled for this book disagree with Privot's claim. Mohamed, Ahmed, and Pierre maintain that literature from Qutb and other Islamist authors who advocate violence features prominently in the group's tarbiya curriculum and the publications it disseminates. They also argue that the Brothers' abandonment of violence is purely practical, as the group has decided that the methods used by jihadists are not incorrect from a moral or religious point of view but solely from a tactical one. Moreover, they assert that support for the violent actions of Hamas in Palestine or other groups in territories where the Brothers claim that Muslims are "under attack" or "suffering occupation" is unanimous within the Brotherhood, a unity shown both in words and in deeds. Pierre also talks, at least in reference to the 1990s, of a "gray area"—moments of overlap between Brothers and jihadists in Stockholm. "The general idea that was conveyed to me [by the Brothers]," he recounts, "was that we are all brothers against the *kufar* [infidels]."

There is also partial agreement on how organized the Western Brothers are. All former Brothers, whether their testimony was reported directly or indirectly here, agree that despite being fairly small, the group has managed to punch above its weight and achieve the remarkable result of creating organizations that have become the main representatives of Western Muslim communities. While all acknowledge the internal inefficiencies, at times almost comical, the accounts differ on the Brothers' overall degree of efficiency. Privot writes about the "complete lack of organization within the Muslim Brotherhood of Belgium" and says that "with respect to our local usra, I think that it ranks among the most dysfunctional of the history of the Brotherhood."[9] He acknowledges that Belgium is a country where the Brotherhood had only a limited presence, and that therefore his assessment does not necessarily apply to other countries. Farid Abdelkrim argues that the UOIF and, more generally, the French Brotherhood milieu have accomplished remarkable results but warns about seeing them as an infallible machine. He views them in relation to competing Muslim organizations, whose abysmal capabilities he stresses, and thus calls them "the least disorganized Islamic organization of France."[10]

All the former Brothers, whether their testimonies appear in this book or in other publications, agree on the core characteristics of the Brothers' modus operandi, which include gradualism, patience, self-restraint, pragmatism, and levelheadedness. The constant cost-benefit analysis, the endless evaluation (not always correct, obviously) of when and how much the movement should act aggressively and push back and when it should lay low, is seen by all as a constant in the group, as well as often a source of internal frustration.

Leaving the Brotherhood

The reasons that lead individuals to leave the Muslim Brotherhood are inevitably highly complex. Each former member underwent an evolution that was deeply personal, the product of a unique thought process. Nevertheless, the accounts published here and elsewhere show a number of similarities. As is common among those who disengage from other movements to which followers are intensely committed, all spoke of frustration with both organizational and ideological matters, showing a combination of disenchantment with how the group functioned and what ideas it espoused. Though there are important differences among them, they share many criticisms both of the organization and of its ideology. Similarly, while some specifics vary with location, many of the frustrations that have led some members of the Brotherhood in the West to leave the organization are similar to those expressed by members in the Arab world.

Regarding the organization, a common complaint is the Muslim Brotherhood's lack of internal democracy. From Ahmed Akkari to Pierre Durrani, from Omero Marongiu to a senior member like Kamal Helbawy, all agree with Mohamed Louizi's assessment that "the big wigs can call the shots with a phone call, ignoring votes, procedures, and statutes." While obedience to the senior leadership is taught to each aspiring member from the very beginning of his tarbiya, the lack of transparency in the internal decision-making process and the impossibility of challenging the leadership's positions frustrates many Brothers, whether in the East or in the West. The Brotherhood's strict application of the principle of *al-sam' wa-l-tâ'a* (listening and obeying)—or, as Privot sarcastically calls it, *"shut your mouth and obey*, as a good soldier in submission to the great leader and to all the small middle-ranking leaders"[11]—is often one of the first steps on the road to disenchantment and disengagement from the organization.

"The problem is about authoritarian management of power and decision-making," lamented a Belgian Brother to Samir Amghar and Fall Khadiya-toulah. "We often consult with members and there is a debate of ideas, but it serves no purpose because the final decision always falls on the same individuals." "One of the reasons that forced me to leave is the fact that each of my initiatives or decisions had to obtain the approval of the person in charge," a French Brother explains. "Everything had to go through this person. For me, it was difficult to endure. We are of the same age and I have a Ph.D. I do have capabilities."[12] This democratic deficit and the opaque decision-making process have caused tensions and defections throughout the Arab world but are felt as particularly objectionable in the West, where most of the Brotherhood's activists have grown up in societies that encourage transparency and the expression of one's own thoughts. Moreover, because in the West the Brotherhood has never been subjected to the repression it has long faced in the Arab world, the organization's leadership there cannot cite what is often the main justification for this hierarchical obedience.

Another long-standing cause of friction and disenchantment within the Brotherhood, both in the East and in the West, is nepotism. In Europe and North America, many of the first-generation Brotherhood pioneers have propelled their wives, children, and in-laws to some of the top positions inside the milieu. While many of these individuals are unquestionably qualified and capable, the dynamic has frustrated many activists who did not belong to any prominent families and saw themselves as being, in their view, unjustly bypassed. The fact that the wives, children, and in-laws of pioneers such as Yussuf Nada, Ghaleb Himmat, Said Ramadan, Rachid Ghannouchi, and Jamal Barzinji are overly represented in various Brotherhood-related activities reinforces the view that the Western Brotherhood is composed of a small nomenklatura of interconnected activists, an "aristocratic elite" that controls everything.[13]

Examples abound, but few are more striking than that of the El Zayats. Farouk El Zayat was a midlevel member of the Egyptian Brotherhood when he settled in Germany in the 1960s, marrying a German convert to Islam and becoming the imam of a mosque in Marburg, a university town north of Frankfurt.[14] The El Zayats raised six children, most of whom have also been involved in Islamic activities, from German Muslim charities to student organizations. The most famous is Ibrahim el Zayat, who has headed various German organizations and has served in high-ranking positions in pan-European organizations linked to the Brotherhood, among them FEMYSO, IESH, Islamic Relief Worldwide, and the Europe Trust, one of the European Brotherhood's main financial nodes. Cementing his relationship with Turkish Islamism, Ibrahim el Zayat is married to Sabiha Erbakan, the niece of Turkish Islamism's godfather, Necmettin Erbakan, and the sister of Mehmet Sabri Erbakan, the former leader of Millî Görüş in Germany.

Other members of the El Zayat family are also active in Brotherhood circles. Bilal El Zayat, for example, is a founding member of the Muslimischen Jugend Deutschland (German Muslim Youth) and an officer of the Muslim Studenten Vereinigung (Muslim Students' Union). Manal El Zayat is a graduate of IESH, the Brotherhood's institution of higher learning in France, and has also been involved in various Islamic organizations in several European countries. She is married to the son of Kamal Helbawy.[15] Amina el Zayat was involved in a number of Islamic education projects in Bavaria before moving to Austria, where she married Ammar Shakar and headed the Islamisches Religion pädagogisches Akademie (IRPA), an organization that received public funding to train Austrian imams.[16]

It is telling that Ibrahim el Zayat, arguably one of the most prominent leaders of the European Brotherhood network, was the first president of the Forum of European Muslim Youth and Student Organizations after the pan-European organization was created in 1996. And FEMYSO itself has traditionally been a training ground for second-generation activists (the children of the first-generation pioneers); after taking the helm of national youth and student organizations, they are given a platform at the European level. Indeed, while FEMYSO presents itself as a grassroots organization of ordinary young European Muslims, an overwhelming majority of its leadership positions are occupied by sons and daughter of some of Europe's most senior Brotherhood members.

The Executive Committee elected by FEMYSO's Seventeenth General Assembly in June 2013 illustrates this point well, as the four most senior positions were assigned to scions of top Brotherhood families.[17] The assembly elected as president Intisar Kherigi, the daughter of al Nahda leader Rashid Ghannouchi (for more on Kherigi, see chapter 11). One vice president was Hajar al Kaddo, who had experience working with the Islamist charity Human Appeal as deputy manager in Ireland, her country of origin, and then in Turkey and Iraq.[18] She is the daughter of Nooh Edreeb al Kaddo, an Iraqi who is one of the leaders of the Irish Brotherhood milieu and a trustee of the Europe Trust and the CEO of the Islamic Cultural Centre of Ireland (ICCI) in the Dublin suburb of Clonskeagh, historically the hub of the Brotherhood in the country and the headquarters of the European Council for Fatwa and Research headed by Qaradawi.[19] The other vice president elected was Youssef Himmat, the son of Ghaleb Himmat, a Switzerland-based Brotherhood financier who is Yussuf Nada's business partner. The treasurer was Anas Saghrouni, the son of Mohamed-Taïeb Saghrouni, an éminence grise of the UOIF and the man who introduced Mohamed Louizi to the Brotherhood in France.

Khalid Chaouki, a former member of the Italian Brotherhood milieu, has provided clear examples of these dynamics, which are common throughout the West.[20] Moroccan-born and Italian-raised, Chaouki became active in the then nascent Muslim youth scene in Italy in the mid-1990s. One of his first forays in the world of activism, while still a teenager, was helping to found what was to become one of the first organizations for young Muslims in Italy, the Association of Muslim Young and Students in Italy (Associazione Giovani e Studenti Musulmani in Italia, AGESMI). This group was established under the patronage of UCOII, the Italian Brotherhood milieu's main organization, and its first board was made up of the sons and daughters of leaders of UCOII.

Chaouki remembers sitting in the conference room of a hotel in Bologna as the president of AGESMI "dictated the articles of our new bylaws and the family assembly approved them without showing a single sign of dissent." Chaouki was particularly taken aback by one of the articles, which stated that the president had to be married and that his wife had to be head of the female section. He found the proposition unacceptable on two grounds. First, it represented "an integralist view of religion."[21] Second, it was clearly "antimeritocratic," as who could guarantee that if the president, who was elected, was competent, his wife, who would automatically get the position, was also competent? It only made things worse that at the time, according to Chaouki, only one of the founding members was married, making it crystal clear that the rule was created ad hoc to guarantee his election.

AGESMI failed to gain any traction, and in 2001, days after the attacks of September 11, Chaouki and a group of activists started a new youth organization, Young Muslims of Italy (Giovani Musulmani d'Italia, GMI). GMI, writes Chaouki, wanted "absolute independence from the organizations of the adults, in particular UCOII." Yet UCOII soon began interfering, in order to control it. Chaouki was harshly attacked by "some youth supported by the heads of UCOII" because he backed the Italian government's decision to expel an imam who had publicly supported Osama bin Laden. "One always has to defend a brother," writes Chaouki, explaining the view of his critics. "I detested this logic, which in my opinion is one of the causes of the crisis of Muslim organizations throughout the West; we need to make a choice: in favor either of the sovereign state or of the ambiguity that inevitably leads you to the vision and the realization of a state within the state."

The ensuing "character assassination" against him led Chaouki to resign from GMI in 2004. After Chaouki, the leadership of GMI returned to the hands of sons of senior UCOII leaders: his immediate successor was Osama el Saghir (discussed in chapter 11), the son of a senior al Nahda official, followed by Anas Breigheche, the son of one of UCOII's founders. Chaouki has since detached himself from the Brotherhood milieu; in 2013 he became a member of the Italian Parliament (and, in 2018, the president of Rome's Great Mosque, one of the largest in Europe).

Recounting his days in the Italian Brotherhood milieu, Chaouki brings up another aspect of its lack of internal democracy, connected to but separate from nepotism: ethnic bias. Within AGESMI, GMI, and UCOII, he states, Moroccans like him were a tiny minority, almost completed dominated by activists tracing their roots to the Levant. Even though Muslims from North Africa and, to a lesser degree, the Balkans constitute the overwhelming majority of Muslims in Italy, the leadership of those organizations was monopolized by the core group of activists from Syria, Palestine, and, Jordan who had created the Italian Brotherhood milieu in the late 1970s, together with the children of those activists. Writing in 2005 about the lack of Muslims from Morocco in leadership positions at UCOII (a situation that has since undergone some change), Chaouki states:

Yet, in Italian mosques, which UCOII claims to represent, Moroccans are by far the largest group! Maybe something is wrong. Either Moroccans in Italy are all ignorant and hopeless beyond repair, as some leader of UCOII has stated, or maybe that's because of the Middle East–style pseudo-democratic rules: bylaws that change at the last second, proxies with voting rights from nonexistent people, budgets that do not know the meaning of the word transparency, assemblies of wise-men and guarantors with access rights completely unknown to all members of the organizations. The things to be said could be many, but let's limit them to this list to make the case that organizations that call themselves Islamic often betray the values of Islam in favor of the constant search for power and hegemony.[22]

Other former Brotherhood members regularly bring up the issue of ethnic bias. For many of them, it clearly reflected not just inequalities in the internal democratic process but also a deeper ethical and religious problem within the organization. That a group that touted, in its own name, brotherhood and equality among members of the ummah in effect discriminated against certain ethnic groups within the Muslim community was a major red flag for individuals like Pierre Durrani, who witnessed racism against both ethnic Swedes and non-Arab Muslims. But it was even more decisive for Abdur-Rahman, who had been launched on his own path toward Islam by racial consciousness. The realization that the Brotherhood milieu looked down on African Americans, and had even enshrined those discriminatory positions in a document, was a deal breaker for him.

Lack of internal democracy, nepotism, and ethnic biases are intertwined issues that frustrate many current and former members of the Western Brotherhood, but all those profiled and those whose stories have appeared elsewhere complain even more vigorously about a fourth, connected problem: excessive secrecy. All, without exception, agree that while the secrecy was understandable in the Middle East for the organization to survive the harsh repression of local regimes, it is absolutely unnecessary in the West, particularly in the extreme form adopted.[23] And while they all bemoan the secrecy that envelops all aspects of the group's life, the former members are most frustrated by the denial of the very existence of the Brotherhood in the West.

"We are not selling opium or drugs; we are propagating dawa," asserts Helbawy, who for decades battled to convince the upper echelons of the organization that the decision to deny the Brotherhood's existence in the West was both immoral and strategically ill-advised. Like the others, he argues that the Brothers would actually enjoy significantly more success in their efforts at engagement if they presented themselves for who they are, as the secrecy is perceived as indicating shame or an attempt to hide dark agendas. An identical case was made by Privot, a significantly more junior Brother, who repeatedly told "several European leaders of the Muslim Brotherhood that the discourse of denying belonging to the Brotherhood was just untenable and was taking all credibility away from the members, because it made them suspected of lying, and this all the more so as every Muslim is suspected right away of *taqiyya*."[24] Abdelkrim describes this secrecy as an *omerta*;[25] Abdur-Rahman, as a "kind of sneakiness, like you're ashamed of something." All agree it is a major strategic weakness and a behavior that put them off, contributing significantly to their process of disenchantment and disengagement.

While perceived flaws in the organization have been cited by all as crucial in their decision to leave, in most cases deep concerns about the ideology of the Brotherhood had even more weight. Indeed, frustrations about the organization's inner workings often planted the first seed of doubt, which then led individuals to examine fundamental issues with adherence to the Brotherhood's creed. In some cases, there was trigger moment that either sparked or culminated the process. In other cases, doubts accumulated slowly, without any peak.

The ideological issues that led each individual to disengage are complex and personal, different from case to case. All the interviewees brought up, in one way or another, their frustration at the Western Brotherhood's prioritization of politics over religion as one major cause. Some pointed to a particular incident—for example, Ahmed Akkari's understanding that the Brotherhood's leadership had simply played politics with the Danish cartoons but was not genuinely incensed by them—that made them think that the Brotherhood was merely using religion to achieve political goals. Others, like Omero and Pierre, came to question their commitment after experiencing a more gradual realization that the Brothers lacked a true spiritual side and were simply engaged in politics.

The different post-Brotherhood trajectories of the individuals analyzed above also reveal the divergent reasons that led them to leave the group. Some, like Helbawy, do not renounce Islamism altogether but simply reject the version of it adopted by the Brotherhood or, more narrowly, the Brotherhood's current leadership, who they believe have strayed from the original teachings of al Banna. For others, like Ahmed and Mohamed, the rejection of Islamism is complete, in all its manifestations and aspects, and they have instead embraced secularism and traditional forms of Islam.

CHAPTER XI

The Western Brotherhood's Future

From the Arab Spring and Beyond

While the cases analyzed in this book clearly demonstrate common patterns of discontent among the former Western Brotherhood members profiled, one should not draw generalizations. It is difficult to determine if they constitute outliers or if their stories are indicative of a larger phenomenon of dissatisfaction inside the movement. Is the Brotherhood in the West in crisis, as some argue?[1] Should the movement's success or failure be judged by the growth and the stability of its membership? Or, since the Brotherhood is a movement seeking to mobilize the masses but willing to open itself only to few selected members, should success be assessed in another way, such as ability to exert influence within Western Muslim communities and Western elite circles?

These questions cannot be answered easily. Moreover, irrespective of the metrics employed in assessing the Brotherhood, the answer is likely to differ from country to country. Yet it is clear that the 2010s have been an earth-shattering decade for the global Muslim Brotherhood movement and, consequently, for the Brotherhood in the West as well. The primary driver of change has been the so-called Arab Spring, with all its complex and still unfolding dynamics, which has had a huge impact on Brotherhood organizations in the East and the West.

The mass protests, starting in a small town in Tunisia in December 2010 and then sweeping throughout most of North Africa and the Middle East, that came to be known as the Arab Spring took Brotherhood groups—as all other political actors in the region—by surprise. The sudden fall of the regime of Hosni Mubarak and the group's emergence as Egypt's most powerful political force, culminating in the election of Mohammed Morsi as president in June 2012, were events that hardly anyone in the Muslim Brotherhood would have predicted as the protests of the early days of the Arab Spring began to unfold.[2] Yet despite its initial reluctance to join the revolution, the Brotherhood soon seized the moment and quickly became the main player in the country's new political era. Even though it had operated semiclandestinely for the better part of eight decades, the Brotherhood was by far the best organized political organization of post-Mubarak Egypt and leveraged all its mobilization and capabilities to ascend to power. It was a triumph that many in Brotherhood milieus well beyond Egypt perceived as historical and bestowed by God, the just divine reward for decades of hard work and persecution.

Similarly monumental was the rise to power of al Nahda, the Tunisian branch of the global Muslim Brotherhood family.[3] After the sudden downfall of Zine El Abidine Ben Ali, the last in a series of staunchly secular presidents to rule the country and harshly repress Islamist forces, al Nahda found itself thrust to the forefront of Tunisia's political life. Following the triumphal return to Tunisia from London of its leader, Rachid Ghannouchi, who had spent decades in exile, al Nahda swept the October 2011 elections: no longer illegal and dispersed, it was running the country as a senior partner of a coalition government. In other Arab countries, the local branches of the Brotherhood engaged in whichever activities local conditions allowed: in Jordan and Morocco that meant protesting and advocating for more democracy, while in Libya and Syria the course of action was joining the civil wars that engulfed both countries.

These events created the perception that finally the Brotherhood's moment had arrived, and they galvanized Islamists worldwide. Brotherhood milieus in the West immediately mobilized to engage in one of the main tasks of the movement, as described by Yusuf al Qaradawi in his book *Priorities of the Islamic Movement in the Coming Phase*: lobbying. Understanding that the policies adopted by Western governments in response to the unprecedented event of Islamists ascending to power in major Arab countries would enormously influence the outcome of the experiment, the Western Brotherhood began to deploy all their resources and political connections in an attempt to influence the perceptions of Western publics and administrations.

On the public front, they wrote op-eds in major newspapers, appeared in television debates, and organized talks and demonstrations. To influence more select audiences of policy makers and experts, they organized briefings and arranged meetings between their Western interlocutors and members of Islamist forces in the region. Whether carried out publicly or behind closed doors, these activities sought to convince their Western audiences that the Brotherhood was a moderate force that rejected violence and extremism and fully embraced democracy and human rights. Seeking to make an analogy that could resonate with their interlocutors, Western Brothers often compared themselves to Europe's Christian Democrats— a political force inspired by religion but fully embracing democracy.[4]

While the entire Western Brotherhood milieu was engaged in influencing Western audiences and, at the same time, mobilizing Western Muslim communities in favor of the Brotherhood's rise to power in the countries affected by the Arab Spring, a small yet significant number of its members decided to leave the West and go back to their countries of origin to directly take part in Islamist governance. The important role played in the political developments of various North African and Middle Eastern countries during the Arab Spring by individuals who had spent years—in many cases decades—in Brotherhood milieus in the West is often overlooked, but it clearly indicates the importance of those social environments. Their involvement also had practical consequences, as the political and communication skills acquired by Brotherhood activists during their time in the West significantly influenced how various Brotherhood organizations in the Arab world engaged in diplomatic and media activities, particularly with Western audiences, during the Arab Spring.

These dynamics affected Brotherhood milieus in different Western countries in different ways, largely because of the varied national origins of the individuals within those milieus. And while Western Brotherhood activists from virtually all Middle Eastern and North African countries mobilized, the phenomenon was particularly intense in three North African countries: Egypt, Tunisia, and Libya. These were countries where the revolutions managed to topple the regime and that also contained many Brotherhood activists who had settled in the West over the past decades. Each thus deserves a separate analysis.

Egypt

The excitement triggered in Western Brotherhood milieus by the fall of the Mubarak regime and the subsequent rise to power of the Brotherhood in its country of birth, the most populous and still one of the most culturally and politically influential countries in the Arab world, cannot be overemphasized. From the onset of these events, Western Brotherhood activists of all origins, and not just Egyptians, mobilized as fully as they could to support in any possible way the Egyptian Brotherhood's historic effort. It overshadowed all other causes, and it generated so much enthusiasm that some Western Brothers dropped their guard and, after years of denial, proudly admitted their Brotherhood affiliations.

But for many Western-based Brothers of Egyptian origin, the fall of the Mubarak regime meant they were finally allowed to return to their native country after a long exile in the West. In this regard, the story of Kamal Helbawy, profiled in chapter 3, is emblematic but hardly unique. Highlighting a few of those examples will provide some indication of the strength of the links between Western Brotherhood milieus and the mother group in Egypt, despite statements to the contrary by many Western Brothers. It is significant that several individuals who for years had led Western Muslim organizations (and often denied any link to the Brotherhood) jetted to Egypt to occupy senior positions in the Brotherhood–led government as soon as the group rose to power.

Arguably one of the most conspicuous of the returnees is Ayman Aly. In the early 1990s Aly moved from Egypt to the Balkans, where he was said to be active in humanitarian work during the various conflicts then plaguing the region. He served as director of the Taibah International Aid Agency, whose Bosnian branch was designated by the U.S. government in 2004 as a financer of terrorism, before settling in the peaceful Austrian town of Graz.[5] In Graz, a well-known center of activity of the Egyptian Brotherhood in Europe since the early 1970s, when Yussuf Nada spent time there, Aly became the head of the al Nur mosque, which serves as the headquarters of the Liga Kultur Verein für Multikulturellen Brückenbau, one of the most prominent organizations of the Austrian Brotherhood milieu.[6] Aly also occupied a prominent position at the European level, serving as FIOE's secretary general and focusing on expanding FIOE's activities in eastern Europe. Despite often denying having links to the Brotherhood, in August 2012 Aly was appointed to Egypt's presidential Advisory Council and served as one of Morsi's closest advisors on foreign affairs until the downfall of the regime.[7]

Similarly, prominent examples are provided by two members of the el Haddad family. Essam, the father, is the founder of Islamic Relief, which he started when he was studying for his doctorate in medicine in Birmingham, England, in the 1980s. Essam also occupied various positions in the Egyptian Brotherhood, serving as a member of its Guidance Bureau. In 2012, when still serving as chair of Islamic Relief Worldwide's board of trustees, Essam was appointed as an advisor on foreign affairs to Morsi.[8] Essam's son Gehad, who grew up between Egypt and the United Kingdom, served as the Brotherhood's media spokesman in 2013.[9] Both Essam and Gehad were arrested after the fall of the Morsi regime. After 2013 Essam's other son, Abdullah, became one of main spokespeople for the Brotherhood in London.

But the examples of Western Brothers who served in the Morsi government are plentiful—and it should be noted that Morsi himself had spent seven years in California in the 1980s, pursuing his doctorate in engineering and teaching as an assistant professor at California State University, Northridge.[10] The group's reliance on them at such a crucial juncture is unsurprising, as many Western Brothers possessed personal connections to Western elites and better communication skills than most members of the Egyptian Brotherhood. It is therefore logical that their influence was particularly evident in the Morsi government's foreign relations apparatus, where the Brotherhood desperately needed skilled communicators who knew how to interact with and persuade wary Western interlocutors. Individuals like Ayman Aly, Essam el Haddad, or Wael Haddara, who had occupied leadership positions in various Brotherhood-leaning organizations in Canada before returning to Egypt in 2012 to serve as senior campaigner for Morsi,[11] had a much better sense of which chords to strike when speaking to Western audiences than did the Brothers who had never left Egypt.

Despite the Brotherhood's best efforts, the Morsi government lasted only one year. On June 30, 2013, millions of Egyptians filled the streets to protest it; days later, Morsi was removed from power by the military, paving the way for the beginning of the regime of General Abdul Fatah al-Sisi. The reasons for this stunning development are plentiful, complex, and beyond the scope of this book.[12] Suffice it to say that the task undertaken by the Brothers—to manage a transition to democracy with an economy in tatters—were daunting. The Brothers also faced the hostility of the country's powerful bureaucratic and military establishment, and much of the business community. But they made several mistakes of their own, from refusing to share powers with other groups to appointing inexperienced (if not flat-out incompetent) officials from their cadres to strategic positions.[13] More broadly, at that delicate juncture of the country's political life, they failed to come up with a concrete vision for Egypt and unite Egyptians, thereby losing the support of many of those who had voted for the group in the hope of change. In short, in the words of Alison Pargeter, the Brotherhood displayed a "fundamental inability to turn itself from a semi-clandestine opposition movement into a credible political actor capable of dealing with the challenges that were being thrown at it."[14]

Morsi's removal from power triggered a chain of events that culminated in the forced removal of Brotherhood members and supporters who had occupied two Cairo squares, Rabaa al Adawiya and Nahda. It was a bloodbath—though the total is in dispute, at a minimum hundreds died—that shocked the Brotherhood well beyond Egypt, in one of the biggest tragedies in its tormented history. The coup also triggered a new phase, eerily reminiscent of the crackdown implemented by Gamal Abdel Nasser in the 1950s: the outlawing of the organization, mass imprisonments of its members, summary trials, and poor detention conditions.

The crackdown also involved several Western Brotherhood members, many of whom were detained in poor conditions that in some cases, according to various human rights organizations, amounted to upright torture; charged; and subjected to in summary trials. This behavior on the part of the new Egyptian regime drew stern condemnation and considerable pressure from the Western countries where the detained Brotherhood activists had gained citizenship. The imprisonment of individuals such as Khaled el Qazzaz,[15] Mohammed Sultan,[16] Ibrahim Halawa,[17] and a few other Western-born or -raised Egyptian Brotherhood activists or children of prominent members of the group also led to a mobilization of Western Brotherhood milieus, which used the stories of these individuals to rally Western Muslim communities, human rights organizations, and public opinion against the Egyptian government. While in prison and after being released, they became causes célèbres for the Western Brotherhood milieu, embodiments of the injustices suffered by the group as a whole and of the brutality of the Sisi regime.

The crackdown caused many Brotherhood members to flee Egypt. While many settled in Qatar and in Turkey, which has since become the undisputed center of gravity of the Brotherhood (and not just of its Egyptian branch), others found refuge in the West.[18] The latter settled in countries where they could claim political asylum or where, through previous connections, they already had citizenship or a residency permit. They are not very numerous, and they tend to be scattered throughout the West. But since the fall of the Morsi regime, London—which, to be sure, for decades has had a very large Brotherhood presence, both Egyptian and not—has become a major hub for the Egyptian Ikhwan.

The London-based cluster includes some of the group's most senior members, as well as some junior activists. Particularly noteworthy among the former is Ibrahim Mounir, who has long occupied one of the top positions in the Brotherhood's International Organization. Mounir, who has lived in Britain for almost forty years, is also the general supervisor of *Risalat al Ikhwan*, the Brotherhood's official magazine published in London. Less senior but arguably more publicly active is Mohammed Soudan, the former foreign relations secretary of the Freedom and Justice Party (FJP), the Brotherhood's political party, and a longtime Brotherhood member. Soudan was able to fly out of Cairo in August 2013, a few days after Egyptian authorities began arresting Brotherhood members, thanks to a personal connection at Cairo airport and a five-year British visa he had attained though his position in the FJP.[19]

These and other senior officials are supported by a small cadre of younger Brotherhood members, many of whom are students in various British universities. Initially the official spokesperson for the Brotherhood in the United Kingdom was Mona el Qazzaz, Khaled's sister. After a few months, the position was given to Abdullah el Haddad, the son of Islamic Relief founder Essam.[20] The London cluster runs a media campaign that targets both traditional media, where they seek to provide their viewpoint to the many British and international media outlets based in London, and social media. Some of these activities are run out of the Cricklewood offices of World Media Service (WMS), a company incorporated by Brotherhood member Mohammed Ghanem in 1993.[21]

The London cluster is an important cog in the machine that the Egyptian Brotherhood has been trying to re-create outside of the country and coordinates with members operating in Turkey, Qatar, and the many other countries where the organization's exiles have settled. This global network engages in a broad array of activities, from filing legal challenges against the Egyptian regimes in various national and international courts to political lobbying, from providing support to individual Brothers seeking to escape from Egypt to organizing protests to maintain global attention to their cause.

As is true of most aspects of the Brotherhood, the post-Rabaa global network has two faces, one visible and one not. Most of the individuals driving it are core Egyptian Brotherhood members, and while their concerns over the future of democracy in Egypt may be genuine, their aims are largely those of supporting their group. Yet most of the groups they run use names that invoke democracy and human rights, purposely omitting any reference to the Brotherhood. Moreover, these ad hoc organizations often include as their most visible members a few individuals who are not Brothers, arguably a tactic used to deflect accusations of being simply appendages to the Brotherhood. But as the imagery (the ubiquitous yellow flags with the Rabaa four fingers in black) and slogans adopted at most of their events clearly show, the Brotherhood's imprint on them is dominant.[22] Moreover, a deeper analysis of the themes (like the periodically organized global "tweetstorms" using hashtags such as #remember-Rabaa), timing, and advertising methods of the activities organized by these organizations, together with an investigation of who sits on their boards, clearly displays a high level of connectivity among them and with Brotherhood milieus.

Tunisia

Dynamics similar to those seen in Egypt, at least when it comes to the mobilization of Western Brotherhood milieus, are also visible in Tunisia. Before the unexpected fall of the Ben Ali regime and its surge to power, al Nahda had been de facto a movement in exile since its establishment in 1981, when it was called Movement of the Islamic Trend (Mouvement de la tendance islamique, MTI).[23] Indeed, whereas the Egyptian Brotherhood had seen many of its members spend time in the West but had always maintained its core structure, leadership, and active membership inside Egypt, most of their Tunisian counterparts spent the better part of the two decades preceding the Arab Spring outside of Tunisia. Starting with its charismatic leader, Rachid Ghannouchi, who found asylum in London in 1989 after being sentenced to life in prison in Tunisia, the bulk of Nahda's leadership had long settled outside of Tunisia—mostly in European countries (primarily Switzerland, Belgium, Italy, France, the United Kingdom, Spain, and Sweden).

Exactly as the Egyptian Brothers had done, as soon as the so-called Jasmine Revolution started, al Nahda's milieus throughout the West began to mobilize. And while some stayed in the West and provided support in various ways from afar, most returned to Tunisia. The image of Ghannouchi's triumphant return to Tunis, welcomed by thousands of supporters, captured only part of the momentous feeling that accompanied those days.

During his almost two decades in London, Ghannouchi had become a mainstay of Europe's Islamist milieus, forging close ties to Brotherhood leaders from other countries and becoming something of a spiritual leader for Western Brothers. While some supporters have claimed that life in the West had an impact on his thinking on various political matters, starting with the relationship between Islam and democracy, Ghannouchi never fully immersed himself in British life, barely learning English and focusing his hopes and thinking mainly on Tunisia.[24]

On the other hand, the London days clearly had an impact on younger members of the Ghannouchi household. His three daughters became active in various Brotherhood-related initiatives, mostly focused on the West, in the early twenty-first century and continued their involvement as the Arab Spring arrived, this time focusing mostly on Tunisia. One of them, Yusra Ghannouchi, became the international spokesperson for al Nahda and a member of its External Relations Committee.[25] Soumaya Ghannouchi, who had become a well-known organizing figure of the protests in Britain against the 2003 Iraq War and a frequent contributor to the *Guardian* and *Huffington Post*, became one of her father's closest advisors upon moving to Tunisia.[26] Following a trend common in Brotherhood milieus, Soumaya's husband, Rafik Abdesselem Bouchlaka, was appointed as Tunisia's foreign minister in the Nahda-led government. The move sparked ridicule and accusations of nepotism within Nahda circles, where Bouchlaka's limited practical experience in foreign affairs was also criticized.

Ghannouchi's third daughter, Intissar Kherigi, remained mostly in Europe. A longtime FEMYSO board member, Kherigi became a frequent commentator on Tunisian affairs, usually without mentioning the fact that she was the daughter of al Nahda's leader (an omission made easier by her choice to go by Ghannouchi's less recognizable familial surname).[27] In the early days of the revolution, for example, she appeared on BBC World TV and was introduced only as a "Tunisian activist and a specialist in human rights in Tunisia." She proceeded to attack the interim Tunisian government as "completely discredited" and praised "the many opposition parties who are out there, some of whom are in exile, who have fought for democracy for a long time and who are willing to come forward and form a united government together."[28] Similarly, in November 2011 she testified before the British Parliament and began, "I am speaking as a British Tunisian, who has long been active in the struggle for human rights and democracy in Tunisia."[29] Her affiliation with al Nahda and Ghannouchi appeared only in the printed minutes.

Kherigi's approach has been fairly common among activists close to the Brotherhood milieu, on matters related and not related to the Arab Spring. Omitting, downplaying, obfuscating, and in some cases flatly denying their involvement with the Brotherhood are tactics frequently employed by Brotherhood-linked activists when they engage with Western audiences. In interviews, meetings, and debates, they tend to present themselves simply as ordinary Tunisians, Egyptians, Syrians, or Libyans, or, when dealing with issues related to Islam in the West, ordinary Western Muslims, expressing the voice of the people. This mild deception, together with the meticulous building of connections and the development of sophisticated media operations, has helped position the Western Brothers to be mostly likely to be chosen as the "ordinary citizens" the media would interview or lawmakers would call to testify.

Aside from Ghannouchi's daughters, several other London-based Nahda activists returned to Tunisia after the Jasmine Revolution and played a major role in the group's rebirth in the country. One of them was Lotfi Zitoun, who served as senior advisor in the al Nahda government. Equally important was Said Ferjani, a close confidant of Ghannouchi who had been deeply involved in the transnational Brotherhood in the years before the revolution. Ferjani, in fact, along with Kamal Helbawy and a handful of senior Brotherhood leaders from various countries, had been one of the founders of the Muslim Association of Britain, where he worked as head of policy, media, and public relations. He also served as chair of Mosques and Imams National Advisory Board (MINAB), a government-funded advisory body aimed at improving British Muslim institutions through self-regulation. Through these experiences, Ferjani acquired invaluable skills in dealing with Western media and political leaders—skills he used after the revolution, when he became one of the main spokespeople for al Nahda.[30]

Though the United Kingdom was a major hub for senior al Nahda leaders between 1990 and 2010, the historical role played by France in the formation of al Nahda cannot be overemphasized. As a result of the strong historical and linguistic ties between France and Tunisia, French universities have traditionally been the primary destination for Tunisian graduate students, including many of the founders of MTI/al Nahda who would later occupy prominent positions in the postrevolutionary governments. Chief among them is Hamadi Jebali, who served as Tunisia's prime minister from 2011 to February 2013. In the 1970s Jebali had pursued engineering studies in Paris. It was there, he recounted in an interview, that he became close to Moncef Ben Salem, Salah Karkar, and other Tunisian students who would come to play fundamental roles in Tunisian Islamism: "We started to organize there, particularly after we received a visit for the first time by Cheikh Rached Ghannouchi."[31] After finishing his studies in Paris, Jebali became president of Movement of the Islamic Trend.

Al Nahda's experience in power was brief. In 2014, after various high-profile assassinations triggered a political crisis, the Nahda-led government voluntarily stepped down, giving way to new elections in which the group did not perform as well as it had done previously. Nonetheless, al Nahda's government came to a significantly less dramatic end than the Egyptian Brotherhood. Rather than being overthrown by military interventions and violence, it was simply ousted through the ballot box, a testament to the relatively sound state of the young Tunisian democratic experiment. By the same token, al Nahda demonstrated a remarkable acceptance of democratic outcomes, neither attempting to unduly cling to power nor seeking to retake it in any way beyond those allowed by the democratic system.[32] Although marred by endemic economic problems, widespread discontent, and occasional jihadist violence, the story of post–Arab Spring Tunisia is one of relative success, including in its model of the controversial relationship between Islamists and democracy.

Libya

The dynamics have been very different in Libya, where, unlike in Tunisia, a bloody civil conflict has plunged the country into anarchy since early

2011. Like its Tunisian counterpart, the Libyan branch of the Brotherhood barely existed as a force inside the country at the onset of the Arab Spring, having been virtually wiped out by the Muammar al-Qaddafi regime in a crackdown that began in the 1970s.[33] It operated de facto as a movement in exile, with a presence in various Arab Gulf countries and in the West. Libyan Brothers were scattered throughout various Western countries but had formed particularly large clusters in the United Kingdom, the United States, Canada, Ireland, and Switzerland.[34]

It was in Switzerland that the exiled leaders of the Libyan Brotherhood met in late January 2011 to discuss the group's position on the revolution that, at the time, appeared about to engulf their native country. They gathered in Zurich, the adoptive city of Suleiman Abdelkader, at the time general overseer of the Libyan Brotherhood.[35] The consensus was that, in typical Brotherhood style, the group should support the protests but not a full-scale revolution: an ambiguous position dictated by the uncertainty of the outcome of the protests and by the Brotherhood's desire not to jeopardize the constructive relationship it had created with the regime since Qaddafi's son, Saif al Islam, had started a dialogue with the group around 2005.[36]

However, less than three weeks later, after it had become apparent that the revolution was in full force and had a solid chance to topple the regime, the Brotherhood met again in Switzerland and fully endorsed it. Once it decided to throw its weight behind the revolution, the Libyan Brotherhood employed the superior political and mobilization skills that characterize Brotherhood branches throughout the world. Given its limited presence inside Libya, the Brothers could not establish a fighting force that could compete with some of the more powerful militias that formed in the heyday of the revolution (and that still in effect rule the country today). Many Brothers, including those who returned from the West, participated in the fighting, whether individually or with small Brotherhood militias, but they always attached themselves to other groups. In many cases the militia to which the Brothers decided to hitch their wagon had jihadist tendencies, in some cases with some not-so-loose affiliations to al Qaeda. This tactic has led some, including a number of governments in the region, to accuse the Libyan Brothers of working with terrorist groups and to argue that the line that separates the Brotherhood from terrorism is a thin one.

Though the Brothers' small numbers prevented them from playing a major military role in revolutionary Libya, politically they were able to punch well above their weight. From the onset, the Brothers managed to attract the support of the governments of Qatar and Turkey, which provided them with substantial funding and political backing.[37] The Brothers also began to establish a web of alliances with domestic forces from a range of political and religious affiliations. These remarkable political skills enabled them to get a seat at every table that matters, starting with the National Transitional Council (NTC), and to exert a disproportionate influence in the political life of Libya during the final days of Qaddafi and in the years that followed his death.

During that time Western-based leaders of the Libyan Brotherhood have taken up some of the most prominent positions in the group and in the Libyan government. For example, the group's new leader—Bashir al Kebti, elected shortly after the revolution—had lived in the United States for more than thirty years, working as an accountant.[38] And the important position of NTC's minister of economy was held by Abdullah Shamia, who joined the Brotherhood as a student in the United States.[39] Various prominent Libyan Brothers had ties to Ireland, where they held important positions within the Irish Muslim community before returning to Libya.[40]

Over the decades, however, the largest and most influential cluster of Libyan Brothers has lived in Britain, most in Manchester but with another sizable group in London. One of the pioneers of the Libyan Brotherhood in the United Kingdom is Ashur Shamis, who has lived in exile in the country since 1971. Shamis was one of the cofounders of the Muslim Welfare House, the institution mentioned by Helbawy as one of the first created by the Brotherhood in London, and was heavily involved in the British Brotherhood milieu.[41] As the Qaddafi regime fell, Shamis returned to Libya and became an advisor with the transitional government in Libya.

Other prominent British-based Libyan Brothers include Abdel Latif Karmous, a Manchester-based member of the group's Shura Council; Mohamed Gaair, the group's spokesperson;[42] Mohamed Abdul Malek, the group's representative in Europe and a prominent leader of the Manchester Muslim community who became much more widely known in the aftermath of the May 2017 Manchester suicide bombing, which was carried out by a young Manchester native of Libyan descent;[43] Salam Sheikhi, member of the European Council for Fatwa and Research;[44] and El Amin Belhaj, one of the cofounders and the first president of the Muslim Association of Britain and the brother of Abdel Hakim Belhaj, one of the most influential military commanders of post-Qaddafi Libya.[45]

Like their brethren in Egypt (and in Syria, Yemen, and all the countries affected, in various ways, by the Arab Spring), operating in the West for decades gave the Libyan Brothers a great advantage once the Arab Spring began. All Brotherhood branches could mobilize and leverage the many contacts they had managed to establish over time with important Western policy and opinion makers; travel freely around the world with the Western passports many of them had obtained; and hone the diplomatic and communication skills necessary to operate at the political heights to which the Arab Spring had suddenly launched them.

Impact of the Arab Spring on the Western Brotherhood

While the experience and presence in the West of many members had a major impact on various national branches of the Brotherhood during the Arab Spring, the opposite is also true: the Arab Spring significantly affected Western Brotherhood milieus. And while it is difficult and definitely premature to assess what this impact has been, the negative effects seem to outweigh the positive.

During the early days of the Arab Spring, the positive energy emanating from Tunisia, Egypt, and other Arab countries galvanized the Western Brothers. It also led many in the West, from policy makers to Muslim communities, to see the Brotherhood as a positive model to embrace and as the wave of the future. Even though the developments in the Arab world quickly dispelled that optimism, the connections made by the Brothers during those years with a variety of Western interlocutors, from high-ranking government officials to those in the media, from human rights organizations to large foundations, constitute an important asset that can provide leverage in the future.

Yet there appear to be many negative repercussions of the Arab Spring for the Western Brotherhood (even more complex and arguably different from country to country than those for the Brotherhood in the Arab world). First, the departure of so many experienced and charismatic leaders for their countries of origin left many Western Brotherhood milieus depleted of human capital. A document published in 2013 by the Cordoba Foundation, a prominent organization of the British Brotherhood milieu, argues: "Prior to the Arab Spring, there was a political apparatus in the UK regulating and coordinating, albeit quite loosely, the work of the Islamic movements but that is no longer the case although the need of such an apparatus now is more than ever."[46] While the phenomenon affected various countries differently, a similar analysis can be applied to several.

Arguably even more serious is the effect on younger Western activists of the return to their home countries of so many leaders of the Western Brotherhood's milieu. While never denying their understandable passion for developments in their countries of origin, since the early 1990s most Western Brotherhood pioneers had expressed a keen interest in Islam in the West, often portraying themselves as the de facto representatives of Western Muslims. Yet at the first opportunity, many of these leaders left the West for good, and those who stayed devoted all their energies to events abroad. Seeing their actions, many younger activists, most of whom are Western-born and seek to prioritize developments in the West, felt somewhat betrayed. A good number of them, whether they were directly involved in organizations of the milieu or simply sympathizers, were left disenchanted with both the milieu's leaders and its ideology.[47] Arguably, these developments have decreased the Brothers' popularity both among Western Islamists and in the larger Western Muslim population.

In some cases, these often-overlapping dynamics of human capital depletion and "abandonment" involve not first-generation Brotherhood pioneers but individuals who have grown up in the West and were touted as future leaders of Muslim communities in their adoptive countries. A telling case is that of Osama al Saghir, the son of a prominent al Nahda leader. The al Saghirs moved to Italy when Osama was eleven, and his father ran one of Rome's most influential mosques (al Huda, in the Centocelle neighborhood).[48] In 2006, at age twenty-two, al Saghir was elected president of the Young Muslims of Italy, the youth organization of the Italian Brotherhood milieu that Khalid Chaouki had headed earlier (see chapter 10).

In that decade, thanks to his intelligence and charming personality, al Saghir became a fairly well-known public figure, routinely interviewed by Italian media on various issues related to Islam and Muslim integration in the country. He was particularly vocal on the issue of changing the country's famously restrictive citizenship laws, which prevent most individuals who do not have Italian ancestry from becoming citizens even if they were born or have spent decades in the country. In 2009 al Saghir gave an interview in which he warned about the consequences of such policies, even linking them to jihadist radicalization. "The majority of young Muslims have grown up in Italy," he said, "but very few have obtained Italian citizenship and for this reason have a distorted view of democracy. I fear the risk of a serious identitarian turn among young Muslims, because if one does not belong to a nation, then he belongs to a religious community, where it is easier to pay attention to some madman who talks about Italians being infidels, or to political groups that reject democracy."[49]

In 2011 al Saghir received Italian citizenship through naturalization. Yet in that very same year he decided to run for the Tunisian elections as one of al Nahda's candidates in Italy. He, together with the daughter of another Rome-based Nahda leader, was elected, confirming al Nahda's dominance among the Tunisian electorate in Italy.[50] Some among both Italian opinion makers and the Muslim community have accused al Saghir of hypocrisy—first decrying the potential lack of attachment to Italy a restrictive citizenship policy might trigger, and then running in Tunisian elections (shortly after receiving Italian citizenship) as soon as the unexpected opportunity arose.[51]

But, more broadly, it can be argued that the deepest impact on Western Brotherhood milieus came from the outcome of the Arab Spring—and particularly the failure of the Brotherhood in Egypt and, to a lesser degree, Tunisia to retain the support of large segments of the population and govern effectively. Many Brothers, in the East as well as in the West, have reacted to the downfall of the Brotherhood (irrespective of how they interpret the vicissitudes that led to it) with introspection often bordering on self-doubt.[52] The statement from one of the spiritual leaders of the Western Brotherhood, Rashid Ghannouchi, that after the experience of the Arab Spring, his movement has "left political Islam" to "enter Muslim democracy"[53]—a shift whose contours are uncertain but that clearly indicates doubt in the traditional dogmas of Brotherhood-style Islamism—reveals the massive soul-searching taking place within the milieu.

For many Western Muslim activists close to the Brotherhood, the Arab Spring has been a major blow to their intellectual confidence and has triggered reexamination, "the opportunity to reconsider simplistic ideological perspectives that 'Islam is the solution.'"[54] As Amghar and Khadiyatoulah cogently put it, "The all-encompassing approach of the

MB—the idea of an Islamic panacea as a solution to all the problems for Muslims—clashes with the concrete experiences of the MB and is revealed to be ineffective. The European Brotherhood movement therefore suffers from the paradoxes of both its pre– and post–Arab Spring ideology."[55] Similarly, Dilwar Hussain, a prominent British Muslim activist with years of experience in Islamist milieus and a longtime proponent of liberalizing the movement in the West, argues that "a more open and embracing vision of who we are, and what Islam means to us, will be realised [once] there is a shift towards a post-Islamist paradigm among activists in the West." "But can this happen?" asks Hussain. "I would argue that it must."[56]

Geopolitical Implications

While the Arab Spring's developments brought many changes to the internal dynamics of the Western Brotherhood, the seismic geopolitical shifts it triggered had an equally great impact on the milieu. Indeed, the decade that began in 2010 has been characterized by massive changes in the ideological leanings and political positioning of many countries in the Middle East and North Africa. For the Western Brothers, aside from the developments in their countries of origin, the shift with the greatest impact has been in the policy on the Muslim Brotherhood among most of the wealthy countries of the Arab Gulf, historically the biggest financial backers of the movement both in the East and in the West.

While each Gulf Cooperation Council (GCC) country has its own specific history with the Brotherhood, most of them began some kind of cooperation with the group as early as the 1950s and 1960s, when they gave refuge to Brothers fleeing persecution from Egypt, Syria, and other countries of the region. Once in the Arabian Peninsula, some Brothers thrived in business, accumulating fortunes that they drew on to help fund the organization in their home countries. Others worked for the local governments, which were investing their new and massive oil fortunes in building the bureaucracies that their previously underdeveloped countries had lacked. Particularly important was the Brothers' role in developing the education systems of those countries, thereby gaining influence over the political and religious thinking of the region's future generations. Finally, other Brothers, as seen in the case of Kamal Helbawy, were hired to run the organizations such as MWL, WAMY, and the many charitable entities that sought to spread worldwide a blend of the politically minded brand of Islam adopted by the Brothers and the ultraconservative interpretation common in the Gulf (often known as Wahhabism, from Saudi Arabia's version).

This relationship between the Brothers and the Gulf countries of cooperation and mutual cooptation was based on a similar (though not identical) approach to the faith, but some mutual suspicions always remained. In particular, most Gulf countries have always been wary of, and in some cases flatly prohibited, the Brothers' establishing too strong an influence within their borders. While lavishly supporting their efforts outside the region, the Gulf monarchies, to varying degrees, perceived the Brothers as a threat to their power, as a potentially subversive force competing with them for their citizens' loyalty. While the dynamics varied from country to country, these fears intensified significantly with the arrival of the Arab Spring, as what appeared then to be the Brothers' unstoppable rise to power came to be seen in the royal palaces of all GCC countries—with one notable exception—as a vital threat to the survival of the established order of the regime and the entire region.

These complex dynamics have been very much at play in the region's largest and most powerful country, Saudi Arabia, for the past decades. Brothers from Egypt and many other Arab countries have been present in the kingdom since the 1950s, developing relationships that have shaped the country, the group, the region, and, without exaggeration, the development of Islam worldwide ever since. Cracks in the relationship appeared in 1991, when important segments of the Brotherhood supported Saddam Hussein's invasion of Kuwait, and throughout the 1990s, when the Brotherhood-influenced Sahwa movement challenged the legitimacy of the Saudi monarchy.[57]

After the September 11, 2001, attacks in the United States, the relationship grew even more strained, but the Saudi state had no unified response. Part of the Saudi establishment began to seriously reconsider the support the kingdom had historically provided to the group. Most famously, Prince Nayef bin Abdul Aziz Al Saud, then minister of the interior, accused the Muslim Brotherhood of being the "source of all evils" and the root of many problems in the Arab world.[58] Still, other parts of the Saudi establishment continued their financial support of the group or, in any case, refused to crack down on it. Western Brotherhood organizations, for decades among the primary beneficiaries of Saudi largesse, still received substantial financial backing from various sources in the kingdom

But the Brotherhood's victory in Egypt and, to a lesser degree, Tunisia triggered widespread fears among the Saudi ruling class that the group could destabilize the entire region, where the Saudis saw themselves as a status quo power.[59] Partially owing to what were, in hindsight, less than strategic statements by Egyptian Brotherhood leaders that hinted at their desire to undermine Saudi Arabia, the Saudis further perceived the Brothers as competing with them for the allegiance of the country's citizens and, therefore, as a threat to the survival of the Saudi state.[60] These developments culminated with the elevation of Crown Prince Mohammed bin Salman (commonly known as MBS), a young and ambitious leader determined to guide an economic, political, and cultural revolution within Saudi Arabia. The Brotherhood had no role in MBS's vision.

In March 2014 the Saudi government declared the Muslim Brotherhood to be a terrorist organization and extended the designation to groups that resemble it "in ideology, word or action."[61] There followed a variety of measures aimed at eliminating the Brotherhood's influence in the kingdom, from purging the group's supporters from its academic institutions to removing books by Brotherhood authors from Saudi schools.[62] The implementation of this new course on the Brotherhood has not been easy, for it requires reversing and undoing decades of cooperation and connections. Unsurprisingly, the policy has been applied at times inconsistently, as some sections of the Saudi nonstate establishment still engage in activities supportive of the Brotherhood.[63] Yet overall it is clear that Saudi Arabia has become a hostile country for the Brothers. This development has had a direct impact on Western Brotherhood organizations. While some individual donors within the country still fund them, the amount of money flowing to the West from the Saudi state, the Saudi establishment, and many of its citizens has severely dwindled.

An even more aggressive approach toward the Brotherhood has been adopted by Saudi Arabia's strategic partner in the region, the United Arab Emirates. Like Saudi Arabia, the UAE attracted scores of Brothers in the second half of the twentieth century, many of whom enriched themselves and played an important role in shaping the institutions of the nascent confederation. Distrust of the Brotherhood began in the 1990s, when the government started to perceive Islah, the domestic branch of the group, as a subversive threat, particularly in the poorer and more religiously conservative northern emirates.[64]

As in Saudi Arabia, the developments of the Arab Spring brought about a dramatic hardening of the Emirati attitude toward the Brotherhood, which led to the group's designation as a terrorist organization. As in Saudi Arabia, fears of domestic and regional destabilization were largely responsible for this new approach. But the UAE's hostility toward the Brotherhood, in comparison with Saudi Arabia's, seems deeper and more ideologically based. High-ranking Emirati officials have consistently made the argument that the Brotherhood is the fountainhead of terrorism: in their eyes, the extremist group has provided the core ideology that jihadist groups have simply developed to its natural conclusion. "I do not accept the hijacking of the Islamic religion by takfiri groups," Minister of State for Foreign Affairs Anwar Gargash has repeatedly stated, explaining why the UAE banned the Brotherhood. "So we must begin to fight extremist ideology."[65]

The Emiratis' opposition to the group also appears to be more consistent and proactive than the Saudis'. Tellingly, in November 2014 the UAE government decided to include on its list of eighty-two designated terrorist organizations, along with groups like al Qaeda and the Islamic State, not just the Muslim Brotherhood in general but also many Western Brotherhood entities. Indeed, the government blacklisted some of the leading Brotherhood-leaning organizations in the United Kingdom (Cordoba Foundation and MAB), United States (CAIR and MAS), Germany (IGD), France (UOIF), Denmark, Sweden, Norway, Italy, Belgium, and Finland. The list also included two transnational organizations linked to the Western Brotherhood milieu, FIOE and Islamic Relief.[66]

The UAE government's decision shocked many in the West, from Brotherhood leaders and their supporters to governments. The full impact of the designation is difficult to assess. On one hand, no Western country has taken any measure against the organizations included on the list. On the contrary, some Western governments, particularly those of the United States and Sweden, protested with their Emirati counterparts, demanding—to no avail—that the organizations based in their countries be removed from the list.[67] On the other hand, being labeled a terrorist organization by an Arab country that enjoys excellent credentials and relationships in the West has unquestionably brought negative attention to the various Western Brotherhood organizations named, arguably harming their credibility and prestige. And, without question, it has virtually eliminated the ability of Western Brotherhood organizations to fund raise in the UAE and made fund-raising more difficult throughout the Gulf.

While other GCC countries, with more or less enthusiasm, have followed the lead of Saudi Arabia and the UAE on the Brotherhood, the one notable exception has been Qatar. Since the beginning of the Arab Spring, the Qatari government has not only maintained its ties to the global Muslim Brotherhood movement but has actually strengthened them. Qatari funds have gone to support the Muslim Brotherhood in Egypt, al Nahda in Tunisia, various Islamist forces (including but not limited to the Muslim Brotherhood) in Libya and Syria, Hamas in Palestine, and a broader array of Islamist groups throughout the world—in effect picking the side opposite to that favored by its GCC partners in every country. Whereas at the onset of the Arab Spring Saudi Arabia and the UAE became the self-appointed defenders of stability and continuity in the region, Qatar actively promoted Islamist-inspired regime change. And showing another important difference, Qatar opted for a policy of détente with Iran that clashed with the hard line chosen by the rest of the GCC.

The reasons for Qatar's positions are complex. Without question, the deep historical links between the country's leadership and the Muslim Brotherhood are a factor. The status of Qaradawi, who has called Qatar home since the 1960s and has played a key role in building the country's religious education system while becoming a global theological and political celebrity (also thanks to the Qatar-funded and -based al Jazeera television channel), is just one of the many examples of the deep entrenchment of the Brotherhood in Qatari society.[68] Yet, though the links between the Brotherhood and the ruling family might be somewhat deeper in Qatar, these dynamics are common throughout the Gulf.

The difference seems to lie in a policy that Courtney Freer calls "cooperative co-optation," adopted by Qatar well before the Arab Spring.[69] Since the mid-1990s Qatar has sought to challenge Saudi–Emirati hegemony in the region and become a competing regional player.[70] Among its tactics to achieve this goal are strategic financial investments (including in the West), massive soft power (through al Jazeera and other media endeavors) and lobbying efforts, high-profile ventures to acquire maximum visibility (such as hosting the 2022 FIFA World Cup), and strong military ties with the West (epitomized by the al Udeid Air Base, which hosts a massive U.S. military presence). But Qatar's strategy also includes close cooperation with Islamist forces, mostly with ties to the Brotherhood.[71] Simply put, the

Qataris have made a calculated, strategic decision to use the Brotherhood as a tool to project geopolitical influence worldwide. As the Arab Spring began, and the Brothers initially appeared to have a winning hand, the Qataris doubled down on this policy.

This disagreement over policy on the Brotherhood (and Iran) has led to ever-increasing friction between Qatar and the other GCC countries. Tensions were already brewing in the first decade of the century, but following the Arab Spring they have escalated.[72] The first public flare-up occurred in 2014 when Qaradawi delivered a sermon on Qatari state TV in which he described the UAE as "against Islam."[73] The incident spurred an outpouring of recriminations from other Gulf countries and led the UAE, Saudi Arabia, and Bahrain to withdraw their ambassadors from Doha—an unprecedented move among GCC countries. Relations were somewhat patched up in the following months, but tensions resurfaced, in full force, in 2017. Once again Qatar stood accused of still supporting the Muslim Brotherhood and an array of Islamist forces that undermined the stability of the region, thereby violating the promises it had made to its GCC partners in 2014. The standoff culminated in June, when Saudi Arabia, the UAE, Bahrain, and Egypt decided to sever all ties with Qatar and impose a strict land, sea, and air blockade on the country.[74] Such a step had never been taken before, and it triggered an extremely tense cold war between Qatar and the other Arab countries that has been fought on the fields of politics, diplomacy, trade, espionage, and public relations—but, at least to date, not on the battlefield.

How this situation will unfold remains, at the time of writing, to be seen. But the outcome has enormous implications for the Muslim Brotherhood, in the East (not the focus here) as well as the West. It is fair to say that since the beginning of the Arab Spring, Qatar has become the Western Brotherhood's largest external sponsor. While the other Gulf countries, which for decades played a crucial role in the disproportionate growth of Western Brotherhood organizations by bankrolling them with immense sums, stopped their direct support and severely curtailed the ability of their citizens and private or semiprivate charities to provide funds to Western Brotherhood organizations, Qatar stepped in and increased its giving. Whether provided by the Qatari government directly, by organizations that are formally independent yet closely linked to the upper echelons of the Qatari establishment (e.g., the Qatar Charity or the Qatar Foundation), or by high-ranking members of the Qatari ruling family or government individually, Qatari funding has become the main financial backing of the Western Brotherhood.

A project overseen by the Qatar Charity (QC) clearly reveals these dynamics.[75] Headed by Sheikh Hamad bin Nasser bin Jassim Al-Thani, a member of the Qatari ruling family, QC is the largest charitable organization in the country. It has also a long history of accusations of links to extremism. A classified U.S. intelligence cable in 2009, made public by Wikileaks, describes QC as "an entity of concern to the USG [United States government] due to some of its suspect activities abroad and reported links to terrorism," adding that in March 2008 QC had been "listed as a priority III terrorism support entity (TSE) by the Interagency Intelligence Committee on Terrorism."[76] QC was also a member of the Union of Good, a transnational umbrella of charitable organizations linked to the Brotherhood and headed by Qaradawi that was designated as a terrorist organization by the U.S. government in 2008 for its alleged funding of Hamas.[77] At the same time, QC, particularly over the past decade, has delivered hundreds of millions of dollars to indisputably humanitarian causes and has partnered with highly respected organizations such as UNICEF, the United Nations High Commissioner for Refugees (UNHCR), and the Bill and Melinda Gates Foundation.

In 2015 QC launched a multimillion-dollar project called the Gaith Initiative to "introduce Islamic culture and strengthen its presence among Western communities in particular, and the world in general."[78] The initiative, widely publicized in the media, on QC's website, and via a specific Twitter account, has since funded dozens of projects in various Western countries, from the construction of new mosques to providing support to local Muslim organizations, from interfaith dialogue to refugee relief. Among the first projects funded or cofunded are the opening of the first Islamic center in Luxembourg (which cost 2.2 million euros), as well as the first mosque in Slovenia (12 million euros).[79]

Most of the projects of the Gaith Initiative, as well as most QC activities in the West, have been run by its London office, Qatar Charity UK, located at a prestigious Mayfair address. In October 2017, while retaining the same board, address, and activities, QC UK changed its name to Nectar Trust, stating in documents filed with the Charity Commission that "the change in name will assist them to better meet the Charity's mission, and objects, and make it easier to raise funds and form partnership with various government and non government organisations."[80] It may be no coincidence that this change was made only months after the blockade imposed on Qatar by the other Arab countries.

These documents filed with British authorities provide an interesting glimpse into Qatari funding in the West. The total income declared by the Nectar Trust for 2017 was close to twenty-eight million pounds, and in the same year it reported having spent more than eleven million pounds on charitable activities ranging from educational projects to organizing the Qatar-UK Business and Investment Forum. But some of its most significant support was given to a large number of new mosques/community centers in eight Western countries: France, Italy, Sweden, the United Kingdom, Germany, Canada, Australia, and the United States.

The annual report makes it clear that the recipients of the funds for Nectar's Trust vast mosque-building project are almost exclusively individuals and organizations that belong to the Western Brotherhood milieu.[81] Nectar Trust declares that it has three trustees, all of them European. Two, Mahfoudi Zaoui and Ayyoub Abouliaqin (who also serves as Nectar's director general), are French-based and, as the Nectar documents indicate, are also trustees of a French-based company called Passerelles. The Nectar documents further indicate that Passerelles received some eight million pounds "for two community centre projects in Mulhouse and Strasburg during 2016/17."

The background of the Nectar's two French trustees reveals the Brotherhood links. Mahfoudi Zaoui is an Algerian-born pulmonologist who sits on the board of Al Wakf France, the UOIF's financial arm (its twenty-six board members are selected by UOIF).[82] He is based in Mulhouse, where Nectar Trust is funding, through Passerelles, an Islamic center Qatari media described as "the largest such facility in Europe," strategically located on the border between France, Germany, and Switzerland.[83] The center is managed by the Muslim Association of Alsace (AMAL), the local affiliate of the UOIF. Ayyoub Abouliaqin, the other French trustee of Nectar, has in the past served as secretary general of AMAL.[84] Zaoui and Abouliaqin thus seem to be the conduits for Qatari money to the French Brotherhood milieu. And that funding goes well beyond the two above-mentioned projects in eastern France, reaching projects in Marseilles, Nantes, Villeneuve d'Ascq (the town where Mohamed Louizi and Omero Marongiu were active), and several other French cities and towns.[85] QC has also historically provided financial support to IESH, the Western Brotherhood graduate school in Burgundy.[86]

Nectar's third trustee, Mohammed Ibrahim, has a similar background in Italy. As Nectar documents state, Ibrahim is a trustee for UCOII, the public organization of the Italian Brotherhood milieu. Moreover, the Turin-based Ibrahim is also the treasurer of Alleanza Islamica (Islamic Alliance), the less high-profile organization of the Italian Brotherhood milieu that the UAE placed on its 2014 terror list.[87] According to the Nectar report, the organization was planning to provide "905.188 BP [British pounds] to UCOII for projects in Italy during 2016/17." It therefore appears that Ibrahim serves as a conduit for Qatari funds to Italian Brotherhood milieu organizations.

Qatar pays a great deal of attention to Italy. In 2016 the then president of UCOII, Florence-based Izzedin Elzir, proudly told Italian media that during the previous three years his organization secured "25 million euros in funds from the Qatar Charity." This money, he added, was "used for the construction of 43 mosques, among which [are] the ones of Ravenna (the second largest in Italy), Catania, Piacenza, Colle Val d'Elsa, Vicenza, Saronno, Mirandola."[88] The list of projects, mostly new mosques, funded by Qatar is longer in Italy than in other Western countries. QC seems to have focused particularly on Sicily (eleven projects) and on small and mid-size towns throughout the country.

This large influx of Qatari funds has been met with a mixed response in the West. Some politicians, commentators, and members of the Muslim community have criticized it, raising concerns that a country that many have accused of having, at best, an ambivalent relationship to various terrorist and extremist groups has been providing millions to organizations linked to Muslim Brotherhood, thereby enabling those groups to exert an enormous influence on the growing Western Muslim communities. Others have dismissed these concerns, arguing that they are baseless and sometimes claiming that they are motivated by political interests and Islamophobia.

Similar warnings have been voiced about Turkey, the other country that, over the past few years, has joined Qatar in providing significant support to Western Brotherhood organizations. Historically the Turkish state had been a major supporter of non-Islamist Muslim organizations operating in the Western countries where a Turkish diaspora existed. Aside from those organizations catering to Turkish ethnic-religious subgroups such as the Alevites and Kurds, Turkish Islam in the West had been traditionally characterized by competition between institutions promoted by Turkish Islamist organizations and the Diyanet—the Turkish governmental agency for religious affairs, which long supported a Turkish-centric yet moderate interpretation of Islam that emphasized the Kemalist strict separation of state and religion. The Islamist milieu was dominated by Millî Görüş, the Turkish sister organization of the Western Brotherhood that operated hundreds of mosques throughout Europe and strongly opposed Turkey's secularism.[89]

With the rise to power of Reccip Tayip Erdogan and the AKP, these dynamics have changed radically. By around 2005, as the AKP gradually solidified its hold on power in Turkey, the Turkish government made significant changes to the Diyanet's personnel and to its theological positions, which both became more Islamist.[90] And corresponding to that domestic move was a new policy in the West: Millî Görüş and Diyanet, having viciously competed for decades, were in effect brought together, as personnel moved from one to the other and undertook many joint initiatives. In effect, the AKP government managed to bring under its control the two rival apparatuses that had vied for influence in the Turkish diaspora: one, Millî Görüş, because they had always shared deep personal and ideological links and the other, Diyanet, because the AKP now dominated domestic institutions back in Turkey. This policy has a number of aims, but arguably one of the most important is to persuade as large a segment as possible of the sizable Turkish population in the West to vote for the AKP—a strategy that, judging from how Turks in Europe have voted in recent years, has succeeded.

But lately the AKP's attempts to exert influence on Western Muslim communities have gone beyond taking over Turkish diaspora organizations and extended to forming a close partnership with Western Brotherhood organizations. The links between Turkish Islamism and the Brotherhood are extensive and well documented. This book has provided examples of such connections, whether historical (see Helbawy's anecdote on WAMY's camp in Northern Cyprus in 1977[91]) or financial, personal, and organizational (all demonstrated in the case of Ibrahim El Zayat, sketched in chapter 10). In short, despite some ideological differences, the Brotherhood and Turkish Islamism (whether represented by the AKP in Turkey or by Millî Görüş in the West) are fellow travelers. The relationship has been further cemented in recent years, as Erdogan has provided refuge to hundreds of Brotherhood members fleeing Egypt after the fall of the Morsi regime and Istanbul has become the new center of gravity for the global Muslim Brotherhood.

As a result of these changes, the Turkish government or nongovernmental organizations and financial institutions close to the government and the AKP have begun to provide ever-growing support to Western Brotherhood organizations. Whether in countries with large Turkish communities (such as Germany, Austria, and the Netherlands) or without them (United States, Italy), Western Brotherhood organizations have increasingly received Turkish funding, engaged in joint activities with Millî Görüş, and vocally expressed support and lobbied for the AKP government. The relationship between some Western Brotherhood organizations and the AKP has in some cases been so close that it has made many Western Muslim activists and even various members of the Brotherhood milieu uncomfortable, whether because of the AKP's questionable reputation on democracy and human rights or because it constitutes an undue foreign influence on Muslim organizations supposedly focused on domestic matters.[92]

The Attitude of Western Governments

The question of how Western governments assess, engage with, and make decisions about Western Brotherhood milieus is complex, and it deserves a separate and much longer analysis.[93] It is worth repeating here that no Western government has adopted anything even remotely close to a clearly articulated approach to identifying and assessing Western Brotherhood organizations, let alone coherent policies on how to view and engage them. Opinions and approaches vary dramatically not just from country to country, from government to government, from political group to political group, but often from individual official to individual official in the very same office.[94]

The reasons for this inconsistency are plentiful and often intertwined. Lack of information frequently plays a role, as institutions at times engage Western Brotherhood organizations because they do not possess information (whether they lack access to it or do not bother requesting it) that would give them a clearer picture of who their interlocutors are. Cases of high-profile politicians or governmental agencies endorsing, partnering with, or providing funds to Western Brotherhood organizations only to backtrack in embarrassment once they discovered the true identify of their partners are plentiful. With notable exceptions, knowledge on Western Brotherhood organizations is very limited throughout the West, for reasons that range from the movement's complexity to the tendency of security agencies to devote little or no attention to them because they are not perceived as a security threat.

Often institutions engage with Western Brotherhood organizations when they possess sufficient information to make clear to them who their interlocutors are. Sometimes the institution (or the specific individual within the institution tasked with making that decision) finds the Western Brotherhood organization in question to be unproblematic, basically embracing what has been termed the optimist position on the Brotherhood. At other times the institution may hold the pessimist position yet still perceive engagement with the Western Brothers as a useful avenue to pursue a specific goal. It is not uncommon for these seemingly contradictory impulses to be at play at the same time within the same institution. For example, a ministry of the interior might find partnership with a Western Brotherhood organization unsuitable for integration projects but necessary to work on deradicalization.

Though it is daunting to juggle these different assessments and at times conflicting priorities, Western countries have been endeavoring to do so for the past three decades. The Arab Spring created some new dynamics. During its early days, many Western governments and institutions (in particular intelligence agencies and ministries of foreign affairs) reached out to Western Brothers to seek help in better understanding and communicating with the Brotherhood groups operating in the countries affected. While Western Brothers—leveraging their close connections to fellow Brothers in the Middle East and North Africa to establish friendly relations with Western institutions seeking to access them—have acted as gatekeepers for decades, the role obviously took on greater importance during the Arab Spring, as all Western nations rushed to better understand and, in most cases, build more solid relations with the groups that seemed to be gaining the upper hand throughout the region.

As the wave of the Brothers' successes waned and in many countries the Arab Spring took a violent turn, Western attention shifted from Islamism to jihadism. By 2014, following the Brotherhood's ouster in Egypt and Tunisia, the rise of the Islamic State in Syria and the Levant (ISIL, or ISIS; after June 2014, simply "Islamic State") and of other jihadist groups, together with the flow of Western foreign fighters to join them, became one of the top policy priorities of all Western administrations. No longer seen as the wave of the future, the Brotherhood took a backseat to jihadism in policy debates.

In attempting to insert themselves in this new phase of the post–Arab Spring debate, Western Brotherhood organizations have relied mainly on two different approaches. The first is on occasion to intercede, whether by leveraging their connections in the region or simply by making appeals to the kidnappers based on their common Islamic faith, to obtain the release of Western hostages detained by various jihadist groups in Syria and Iraq.

The second approach, which has significantly more relevance to policy, is to offer to help Western governments curtail the spread of sympathy for the Islamic State and other jihadist groups among young Western Muslims. Western governments, alarmed both by the unprecedented mobilization of thousands of their own citizens who joined jihadist groups in Syria and Iraq and by the wave of terrorist attacks that have hit Europe and North America since 2014, have been seeking ways to prevent radicalization and to deradicalize committed militants among their Muslim population. Replicating a dynamic that played out on a smaller scale during the height of the al Qaeda–linked attacks in the West a decade earlier, Western governments began to look for partners within Muslim communities that had the ability, legitimacy, and structure to help them. In several cases Western Brotherhood organizations, arguably sensing an opportunity to gain the legitimacy, contacts, and funds that often come to those who work on countering violent extremism (CVE), enthusiastically offered to partner with governments or create their own radicalization prevention programs.

The dynamics of Western Brotherhood organizations' work on CVE vary from country to country. In the United Kingdom, for example, after the experiments early in the century in which various Islamist organizations were seen as crucial partners in Prevent, the country's counterradicalization strategy, the government refused to partner with Brotherhood or any other Islamist group. In the United States, it has been organizations from the Brotherhood milieu that have refused to participate in the country's limited domestic CVE, condemning it as discriminatory and unconstitutional (even though a handful of organizations of the milieu have applied for CVE federal funding).[95] In various European countries, Brotherhood-linked organizations have enthusiastically applied for and, at times, received funding for radicalization prevention.

The decision-making process of Western governments in this area is, as usual, often inconsistent and influenced by myriad overlapping and at times contradictory factors. One unquestionably crucial element is the general assessment of the Brotherhood—whether it is perceived as part of the problem or as part of the solution, a force that favors violent radicalization or instead helps prevent it. That issue has been discussed in various parts of this book, emphasizing the complete lack of consensus among Western policy makers, including intelligence agencies. And it should be stressed that even those within the security establishment who see the Brotherhood as problematic are split on whether some small, tactical cooperation with them can be useful to counter jihadist radicalization.

The point on which security apparatuses, particularly in continental Europe, seem to agree is that the Brotherhood's activities have a negative social impact. Many of these entities traditionally possess an institutional mandate broader than their U.K. and U.S. counterparts, as they are tasked with monitoring not just direct threats to national security but also more oblique forms of subversion that might threaten the democratic order. Because of their broader remit, they have long studied the Brotherhood's presence within their jurisdictions and formed an opinion about it—almost invariably viewing it as suspicious if not unequivocally dangerous.

Germany is a good case in point. For example, the 2005 report from the Office for the Protection of the Constitution, Germany's domestic intelligence agency, describes Brotherhood-influenced organizations operating in the country as "'legalistic' Islamist groups" that "represent an especial threat to the internal cohesion of our society." It continues:

Among other things, their wide range of Islamist-oriented educational and support activities, especially for children and adolescents from immigrant families, are used to promote the creation and proliferation of an Islamist milieu in Germany. These endeavours run counter to the efforts undertaken by the federal administration and the Länder [states] to integrate immigrants. There is the risk that such milieus could also form the breeding ground for further radicalization.[96]

Belgium's domestic intelligence agency, Sûreté de l'État, described the activities of Muslim Brotherhood offshoots in the country in similarly negative terms:

The Sûreté de l'État has been following the activities of the Internationalist Muslim Brothers in Belgium since 1982. The Internationalist

Muslim Brothers have possessed a clandestine structure in Belgium for more than twenty years. The identity of the members is secret; they operate with the greatest discretion. They seek to spread their ideology within Belgium's Muslim community and they aim in particular at young, second- and third-generation immigrants. In Belgium as in other European countries, they seek to take control of sports, religious, and social associations, and they seek to establish themselves as privileged interlocutors of national and even European authorities in order to manage Islamic affairs. The Muslim Brothers estimate that national authorities will increasingly rely on the representatives of the Islamic community for the management of Islam. Within this framework, they try to impose the designation of people influenced by their ideology in representative bodies. In order to do so they were very active in the electoral process for the members of the body for the management of Islam [in Belgium]. Another aspect of this strategy is to cause or maintain tensions in which they consider that a Muslim or a Muslim organization is a victim of Western values, hence the affair over the Muslim headscarf in public schools.[97]

The AIVD, the Netherlands' domestic intelligence agency, provides an even more detailed analysis of Western Brotherhoods' tactics and aims:

Not all Muslim Brothers or their sympathizers are recognisable as such. They do not always reveal their religious loyalties and ultra-orthodox agenda to outsiders. Apparently cooperative and moderate in their attitude to Western society, they certainly have no violent intent. But they are trying to pave the way for ultra-orthodox Islam to play a greater role in the Western world by exercising religious influence over Muslim immigrant communities and by forging good relations with relevant opinion leaders: politicians, civil servants, mainstream social organizations, non-Islamic clerics, academics, journalists and so on. This policy of engagement has been more noticeable in recent years, and might possibly herald a certain liberalisation of the movement's ideas. It presents itself as a widely supported advocate and legitimate representative of the Islamic community. But the ultimate aim—although never stated openly—is to create, then implant and expand, an ultra-orthodox Muslim bloc inside Western Europe.[98]

While these are views published by intelligence agencies in official reports meant to inform policy makers and the general public, in recent years similar assessments have shaped the outcome of specific court cases in various European countries, further indicating that security establishments consider the Brotherhood's positions to be incompatible with democracy—and that the courts have in many cases accepted this position. In a telling case, an Austrian court decided on the petition of the wife of Ayman Aly, the former FIOE leader who left Graz to serve as an advisor in the Morsi government, as mentioned above.[99] In one document, the court summarized the views of the security services as follows:

The Muslim Brotherhood is not institutionalized under this name in Austria; however, it characterizes the public depiction of Islam through its intellectual and personal strength. The Muslim Brotherhood does not maintain membership registers; its members are kept secret in all countries to protect them from being identified by the authorities. Nevertheless, there is an accurate set of rules within the Muslim Brotherhood stating what is allowed and what is banned. As soon as loyalty is pledged, all instructions needs to be implemented. There are distinct categories of supporters who have pledged loyalty—from sympathisers to full members.

The court's assessment of the Brotherhood's goals and compatibility with the Austrian state and society continued: "The political system aimed at [by the Muslim Brotherhood] is reminiscent of a totalitarian system, which guarantees neither the sovereignty of people nor the principles of freedom and equality." It declared, "Such a fundamental position is incompatible with the legal and social norms of the Republic of Austria."

The court expressed its views on one of the core organizations of the Austrian Muslim Brotherhood milieu in greater detail: "The Liga Kultur Verein für multikulturellen Brückenbau in Graz is an association of the Muslim Brotherhood, insofar as it is allowed to spread only their ideology, which in its core contradicts the Western democratic understanding of coexistence, equality of men and women, the political order, and the fundamental principles of the Constitution of the Republic of Austria." It was due mostly to her involvement in the Liga Kultur that the court turned down the petition of Ali's wife to obtain Austrian citizenship. In doing so it stated that "owing to her close relationship to or membership in the

Muslim Brotherhood, the First Applicant [Soha Ghonem] cannot accept those rules of the Republic of Austria which are contrary to the divine order of the Islamic laws; thus, she cannot provide assurance for the assumption that she actually affirms the Republic and that she is a threat neither to public peace, order, and security nor to the interests mentioned in art. 8 sec. 2 ECHR."

A similar view was expressed by a German court in 2017 when it turned down the application for naturalization of a Palestinian man who was active in Brotherhood milieus in Germany. While the man possessed all other "naturalization requirements," he lacked, in the court's opinion, the "required constitutional loyalty." The court explicitly stated that the man's nearness to the Brotherhood was reason enough to find him unsuitable for German citizenship, because the Brotherhood and its affiliated organizations pursued "anticonstitutional aspirations."[100]

Despite these commonalities among continental European countries, none has yet reached a consistent assessment of the Western Brotherhood or its impact on social cohesion. The one country that has made a systematic attempt to do so is the United Kingdom. In 2014 then prime minister David Cameron ordered a government-wide review of "the philosophy, activities, impact and influence on UK national interests, at home and abroad, of the Muslim Brotherhood and of government policy towards the organisation."[101] Given the many areas in which the Brotherhood has an impact, this review entailed pulling together knowledge from a wide range of entities within the government, from the Foreign Office to the intelligence agencies, from the Charity Commission to the Department of Education.[102]

Led by Sir John Jenkins, a high-ranking British diplomat with decades of experience in the Middle East and North Africa, the review team was divided into two groups, one focusing on the Brotherhood in the Arab world and the other looking at its presence inside the United Kingdom.[103] Looking beyond, given the demographics of the British Muslim community, the latter team also analyzed the efforts of various Islamist groups of South Asian background that have an ideology and employ tactics similar to the Brotherhood's.

The process went on for months, not without controversies and difficulties, and a report (said to be more than two hundred pages long) was presented to the prime minister. Even though the entire report has not been released, in December 2015 the British government published an executive summary of its findings.[104] The document is arguably one of the most comprehensive assessments of the Muslim Brotherhood ever made public by any Western government, touching on many aspects of the group's history, tactics, and ideology. And particularly when it comes to the Brotherhood in the West, it largely concurs with the negative assessments that intelligence agencies in continental Europe have long produced. In one of its key sections, it argues:

> The Muslim Brotherhood have been publicly committed to political engagement in this country. Engagement with Government has at times been facilitated by what appeared to be a common agenda against al Qaida and (at least in the UK) militant salafism. But this engagement did not take account of Muslim Brotherhood support for a proscribed terrorist group and its views about terrorism which, in reality, were quite different from our own; aspects of Muslim Brotherhood ideology and tactics, in this country and overseas, are contrary to our values and have been contrary to our national interests and our national security.

Despite having been commissioned specifically to create a cohesive assessment of and engagement policy toward the Brotherhood for the entire British government, the "Muslim Brotherhood Review" has had, at best, mixed fortunes. Stopping short of recommending designation as a terrorist group, it attracted the ire of some the Brotherhood's most ardent critics, particularly in the Arab world. At the same time, many of the group's supporters criticized its adoption of the pessimistic view on the Brotherhood, attacking the review as poorly researched and marred by external influences. One of the strongest rebukes came from the British Parliament's Foreign Affairs Committee, which organized several hearings and published a report attacking several of the review's findings.[105]

Moreover, few practical actions seem to have been generated from the process. The British government did follow the review's recommendation to establish a permanent body, called the Extremism Analysis Unit (EAU). Housed in the Home Office and staffed with civil servants from various sections of government, it was tasked with continuing and expanding the work of the review. But it appears that the EAU has been understaffed from the onset, and its tasks eventually expanded to the monitoring of groups other than the Brotherhood. Also reducing the impact of the report was the change in the occupant of Downing Street: the government led by Theresa May appeared to have had less interest in this issue than that of David Cameron. Thus the "Muslim Brotherhood Review," the result of an effort unparalleled among other Western governments to get a sophisticated understanding of and develop a coherent policy toward the Brotherhood and political Islam more generally, has remained largely toothless.

The dynamics in the United States have been quite different. The American debate on the Muslim Brotherhood, at least regarding its domestic branch, has been extremely polarized, with much clearer divisions along political lines than in most European countries. Pessimism about the Brotherhood, at times escalating into wild conspiracy theories, has been a virtual monopoly of the right. On the other hand, most on the left (with some notable exceptions) have dismissed accusations against the U.S. Brotherhood milieu, even those that are well documented, as preposterous fabrications motivated by Islamophobia. The U.S. debate seems to be sorely lacking that middle-of-the-road approach, characterized by a healthy skepticism that does not degenerate into paranoia, which has become common in most European countries in recent years.

Another element unique to the American debate on the Brotherhood is its heavy focus on security. Most European countries, in contrast, while not completely overlooking the potential security-related implications of the Brotherhood, have concentrated on how their activities affect social cohesion. It is telling that in the United States, from 2014 to 2017, five separate bills seeking to start the process of designating the Brotherhood as a terrorist organization were introduced in Congress.[106] Most of the bills highlighted the involvement in terrorism of various elements of the global Muslim Brotherhood (from the alliance of its Libyan branch with jihadist militias to the extensive ties of its Yemeni branch to al Qaeda) and the links of U.S. organizations such as ISNA and CAIR to the Brotherhood. All were sponsored and supported almost exclusively by Republicans, and none progressed very far in the legislative process.

Where Is the Western Brotherhood Headed?

The Arab Spring has brought many opportunities and arguably an even greater number of challenges to the Muslim Brotherhood in the West. It is too early to fully assess all the implications of these tumultuous years and see where the Western Brotherhood is headed. But it fair to say that just as is true of the Brotherhood in the Arab world, there is a Western Brotherhood before the Arab Spring and one after it. This distinction is accentuated by another completely coincidental yet extremely important factor: the widespread generational change—occurring somewhat differently in different countries—that the Western Brotherhood is currently undergoing, as mostly Western-born activists are joining, and in some cases replacing, the first generation of pioneers at the helm of the milieu's organizations.

At this critical juncture, various dynamics appear to be emerging. On one hand, the Western Brotherhood seems to have lost the magnetic appeal it had arguably exercised on many. The failures of the Arab Spring have created ample self-doubt, and the actions of the Western Brothers themselves have supplied additional reasons for dwindling enthusiasm. Over the past decades, as we have seen, the Western Brotherhood has put a priority on becoming trusted interlocutors of Western governments and elites—in many cases achieving that goal. But in order to do so, it has inevitably been forced to compromise some of its principles and smooth some of its rough edges. As Samir Amghar and Fall Khadiyatoulah put it, "Faced with the reality of Muslim faith management, [Western Brotherhood] activists lost their initial utopian impetus and no longer challenged the state framework or the dominant political system."[107] Essentially, not all Brotherhood activists clearly see an Islamic light at the end of the tunnel of the countless interfaith meetings, fund-raising banquets, media sensitivity seminars, and myriad other activities to which the organization devotes most of its energies. Some are also puzzled by tactics such as alliances with feminist or LGBT organizations that, while internally explained as useful means to an end, nonetheless seem to substantially deviate from what is Islamically acceptable.

As a result, Western Brotherhood organizations suffer in competition with Salafists, whose more uncompromising approach has attracted many conservative Muslims who previously would have gravitated toward the Brothers. In the words of a Belgian Brotherhood activist, "Ever since we decided to be more consensual on certain religious issues and ever since we began discussing issues with public authorities, some of our members could no longer recognize themselves in our choices and we have lost quite a lot of people."[108]

At the same time, many Western-born Muslims are increasingly finding alternative platforms for mobilizing on the basis of their Muslim identity. Many young Muslim activists, whether they started their trajectory
in organizations belonging to the Western Brotherhood milieu or not, are
no longer constrained by the group's monopoly on Muslim identity and
freely operate in the mainstream. In fact, Western Muslim activists who
have points of contact with Brotherhood milieus are often active outside
the group's structure and achieve high positions in Western political parties and civil society, particularly on the left. The closeness of the contacts between those freelancers and the Brotherhood milieu depends on
the specific case, but it is clear that the Brothers increasingly are no longer the only avenue for Muslims seeking to be politically engaged in the
West.

Though all these dynamics and the stories of the individuals profiled in
this book (irrespective of how representative they are of a broader trend)
suggest that the Western Brotherhood is weakening, there are reasons to
think that the opposite might also be true. More entrenched in Western
society and increasingly run by new members—often scions of prominent
Brotherhood families with strong ties to one another—Western Brotherhood organizations can be seen as simply entering a new and even more
successful phase of their history in the West. On this account, the new leadership now understands how to smooth some rough edges and better present itself, making it more likely to achieve its short- and long-term goals.
New blood and more refined tactics thus may make the group more
effective.

One core issue that will determine the future of the Brotherhood in the
West is whether the new leadership will retain the movement's core ideology. Some argue that we are entering in an era of post-Ikhwanism, and
that the Western Brothers, on the pattern of European Communists in the
1970s and 1980s, will eventually shed the most radical aspects of their ideology and melt into the system. Others disagree. Ahmed Akkari, for example, believes that "the history of the Brotherhood clearly shows that despite
divisions and contradictions, the Brotherhood core always managed to
bring in new supporters and keep the conservative ideological line intact;
when some parts of the movement become too estranged to the ideological core and even break free, the old guard always manages to restructure
the organizational top and middle layer to stay supportive."[109]

It is impossible at this stage to predict in what direction the Western Brotherhood will go, whether it will melt into the system or continue to work within it but with the idea of eventually changing it. Indeed, there are indicators that point in both directions: perhaps different individuals and organizations belonging to the network will take opposite trajectories over time. Irrespective of these developments, it appears clear that for years to come, the Brotherhood will remain a crucial actor in the future of Islam in the West.

Notes

1. What Is the Muslim Brotherhood in the West?

1. Kamal Helbawy is a former member of the Egyptian Muslim Brotherhood's Guidance Office, former official spokesperson of the Muslim Brotherhood in the West, and cofounder of the Muslim Association of Britain.
2. "Interview with MB Deputy Chairman in *al Ahrar Daily*," Ikhwanweb .com, June 16, 2008. Ikhwanweb is the official website of the Muslim Brotherhood.
3. Alison Pargeter, *The Muslim Brotherhood: The Burden of Tradition* (London: Saqi Books, 2010), 96–132.
4. Cited in Hillel Fradkin, "The History and Unwritten Future of Salafism," *Current Trends in Islamist Ideology*, November 25, 2007, https://www.hudson .org/content/researchattachments/attachment/1338/fradkin_vol6.pdf.
5. Mohammed Akef interview in *Asharq Al-Awsat*, December 11, 2005.
6. Interview with Yussuf Nada, July 2008, Campione d'Italia; interview with Abd El Monem Abou El Fotouh, December 2008, Cairo.
7. Brigitte Maréchal, *The Muslim Brothers in Europe: Roots and Discourse* (Leiden: Brill, 2008), 56–82.
8. Muslim scholars have traditionally debated the two concepts, often developing subcategories and diverging opinions. See, for example, Khaled Abou El Fadl, "Striking a Balance: Islamic Legal Discourse on Muslim Minorities," in *Muslims on the Americanization Path?*, ed. Yvonne Yazbeck Haddad and John L. Esposito (New York: Oxford University Press, 2000).

9. Wasif Shadid and Pieter Sjoerd van Koningsveld, "Loyalty to a Non-Muslim Government," in *Political Participation and Identities of Muslims in Non-Muslim States*, ed. W. A. R. Shadid and P. S. van Konignsveld (Kampen: Kok Pharos, 1996); Xavier Ternisien, *Les Frères Musulmans* (Paris: Fayard, 2005), 190–92, 198–99.

10. Brigitte Maréchal, "The European Muslim Brothers' Quest to Become a Social (Cultural) Movement," in *The Muslim Brotherhood in Europe*, ed. Edwin Bakker and Roel Meijer (New York: Oxford University Press, 2013), 91.

11. Interview with Kamal Helbawy, London, December 2008; interview with Lhaj Thami Breze (then president of UOIF), La Courneuve, France, May 2009.

12. Yusuf al Qaradawi, *Priorities of the Islamic Movement in the Coming Phase* (Swansea, U.K.: Awakening Publications, 2000), 7.

13. Qaradawi, *Priorities of the Islamic Movement*.

14. Qaradawi, *Priorities of the Islamic Movement*.

15. Qaradawi, *Priorities of the Islamic Movement*.

16. See, for example, Alexandre Caeiro and Mahmoud al-Saify, "Qaradawi in Europe, Europe in Qaradawi? The Global Mufti's European Politics," in *The Global Mufti: The Phenomenon of Yusuf Al-Qaradawi*, ed. Bettina Gräf and Jakob Skovgaard-Petersen (New York: Columbia University Press, 2009), 111, 116, 117.

17. Olivier Roy, *Secularism Confronts Islam* (New York: Columbia University Press, 2007), 94–98.

18. The expression is used, for example, by the British member of Parliament Michael Gove in his book *Celsius 7/7* (London: Phoenix, 2006), 84–113.

2. Joining and Leaving the Brotherhood

1. The most detailed descriptions of how one joins the Brotherhood and how the organization is structured are in Khalil al Anani, *Inside the Muslim Brotherhood: Religion, Identity, and Politics* (Oxford: Oxford University Press, 2016); and Hazem Kandil, *Inside the Brotherhood* (Malden, Mass.: Polity Press, 2014). Equally interesting and well researched but covering only the early days of the organizations are Brynjar Lia, *The Society of the Muslim Brothers in Egypt: The Rise of an Islamic Mass Movement 1928–1942* (Reading, U.K.: Ithaca Press, 1999); and the classic by Richard P. Mitchell, *The Society of Muslim Brothers* (New York: Oxford University Press, 1969).

2. Anani, *Inside the Muslim Brotherhood*, 67.

3. Eric Trager, "The Unbreakable Muslim Brotherhood: Grim Prospects for a Liberal Egypt," *Foreign Affairs* 90, no. 5 (September–October 2011): 114–26.

4. Carrie Rosefsky Wickham, *Mobilizing Islam: Religion, Activism and Political Change in Egypt* (New York: Columbia University Press, 2002), 130.

5. Trager, "Unbreakable Muslim Brotherhood."

6. Kandil, *Inside the Brotherhood.*

7. Anani, *Inside the Muslim Brotherhood,* 93.

8. Kandil, *Inside the Brotherhood,* 1.

9. Anani, *Inside the Muslim Brotherhood,* 84, 68.

10. The usra is the bottom layer of the Brotherhood's pyramidal structure. A cluster of usra forms a division (*shu'ba*). After various intermediary levels, at the top one finds an elected body, the Majlis al Shura (Shura Council), a high executive body, the Makhtab al Irshad (Guidance Bureau), and the *murshid al'am* (supreme guide). The activities of and among all these bodies are regulated by rules and bylaws, with committees overseeing their application.

11. Anani, *Inside the Muslim Brotherhood,* 67.

12. Kandil, *Inside the Brotherhood,* 70.

13. Noha El Hennawy, "A Split in the Muslim Brotherhood? Not So Easy," *Egypt Independent,* April 17, 2011.

14. Kandil, *Inside the Brotherhood,* 48.

15. Eric Trager, *Arab Fall: How the Muslim Brotherhood Won and Lost Egypt in 891 Days* (Washington, D.C.: Georgetown University Press, 2016), 51.

16. Kandil, *Inside the Brotherhood,* 71.

17. For a comprehensive overview of the literature on the subject, see Anja Dalgaard-Nielsen, "Promoting Exit from Violent Extremism: Themes and Approaches," *Studies in Conflict and Terrorism* 36, no. 3 (2013): 99–115. See also Omar Ashour, *The De-Radicalization of Jihadists: Transforming Armed Islamist Movements* (Routledge, 2009); Tore Bjørgo and John G. Horgan, eds., *Leaving Terrorism Behind: Individual and Collective Disengagement* (London: Routledge, 2008); Froujke Demant et al., *Decline and Disengagement: An Analysis of Processes of Deradicalisation* (Amsterdam: IMES, 2008); John Horgan, *Walking Away from Terrorism: Accounts of Disengagement from Radical and Extremist Movements* (London: Routledge, 2009); Michael Jacobson, "Terrorist Dropouts: Learning from Those Who Have Left," Washington Institute for Near East Policy, January 2010; Emma Disley et al., "Individual Disengagement from Al Qa'ida-Influenced Terrorist Groups: A Rapid Evidence Assessment to Inform Policy and Practice in Preventing Terrorism," RAND Europe, 2011; Christian Davenport, *How Social Movements Die: Repression and Demobilization of the Republic of New Africa* (Cambridge: Cambridge University Press, 2014).

18. Jacquelien van Stekelenburg and Bert Klandermans, "Individuals in Movements: A Social Psychology of Contention," in *Handbook of Social Movements Across Disciplines,* ed. Bert Klandermans and Conny Roggeband, 103–39 (New York: Springer US, 2010).

19. Bjørgo and Horgan, *Leaving Terrorism Behind*; John Horgan et al., "Walking Away: The Disengagement and De-radicalization of a Violent Right-Wing Extremist," *Behavioral Sciences of Terrorism and Political Aggression* 9, no. 2 (2017): 63–77.

20. Steven Windisch et al., "Disengagement from Ideologically-Based and Violent Organizations: A Systematic Review of the Literature," *Journal for Deradicalization* 9 (Winter 2016/17): 1–38.

21. Donatella della Porta, "Leaving Underground Organizations: A Sociological Analysis of the Italian Case," in *Leaving Terrorism Behind: Individual and Collective Disengagement*, ed. Tore Bjørgo and John Horgan (London: Routledge, 2008), 49–65.

22. Caryl E. Rusbult, Christopher Agnew, and Ximena Arriaga, "The Investment Model of Commitment Processes." Department of Psychological Sciences Faculty Publications, Paper 26, 2011.

23. Anja Dalgaard-Nielsen, "Promoting Exit from Violent Extremism: Themes and Approaches," *Studies in Conflict and Terrorism* 36, no. 2 (2013): 99–115.

24. Kandil, *Inside the Brotherhood*, 68.

25. Lauren Bohn, "The Muslim Brotherhood Comes to America," CNN.com, April 6, 2012.

26. Sara Abou Bakr, "Interview with Tharwat El-Kherbawy: An Insider's Look at the Muslim Brotherhood," *Egypt Daily News*, November 20, 2012.

27. Kandil, *Inside the Brotherhood*, 19.

28. Interview with unnamed Egyptian Brotherhood member, Istanbul, January 2015.

29. Samir Amghar and Fall Khadiyatoulah, "Disillusioned Militancy: The Crisis of Militancy and Variables of Disengagement of the European Muslim Brotherhood," *Mediterranean Politics* 22, no. 1 (2017): 54–70.

30. Carnegie Endowment for International Peace, "Interview with Abul Ila Al Madi," *Arab Reform Bulletin*, December 2005, https://carnegieendowment.org /2005/12/15/arab-reform-bulletin-december-2005-pub-17786.

31. "A Talk with EX-MB Leader Ibrahim El Zafarani," *Asharq Al-Awsat*, July 29, 2012, https://eng-archive.aawsat.com/theaawsat/features/a-talk-with-ex-mb -leader-ibrahim-el-zafarani.

32. Marc Lynch, "Islam Divided Between Salafi-Jihad and the Ikhwan," *Studies in Conflict and Terrorism* 33, no. 6 (2010): 480.

33. Lynch, "Islam Divided," 480.

34. See the study by Ahmed Mubaraz, Milo Comerford, and Emman El-Badawy, "Milestones to Militancy: What the Lives of 100 Jihadists Tell Us About a Global Movement," Tony Blair Institute for Global Change, April 2016.

35. Thomas Hegghammer, "Abdallah Azzam, Imam of Jihad," in *Al Qaeda in Its Own Words*, ed. Gilles Kepel and Jean-Pierre Milelli, trans. Pascale Ghazaleh (Cambridge, Mass.: Belknap Press of Harvard University Press, 2008).

36. Hassan Hassan, "Bin Laden Journal Reveals He Was Shaped by the Muslim Brotherhood," *National* (Abu Dhabi), November 2, 2017.

37. William McCants, "The Believer: How an Introvert with a Passion for Religion and Soccer Became Abu Bakr Al-Baghdadi, Leader of the Islamic State," *Brookings Essay*, September 1, 2015.

38. Meir Hatina, "Redeeming Sunni Islam: Al-Qa'ida's Polemic Against the Muslim Brethren," *British Journal of Middle Eastern Studies* 39, no. 1 (2012): 105.

39. Mokhtar Awad, "The Rise of the Violent Muslim Brotherhood," *Current Trends in Islamist Ideology*, November 6, 2017.

40. See, for example, Marc Galanter, "Unification Church ('Moonie') Dropouts: Psychological Readjustment After Leaving a Charismatic Religious Group," *American Journal of Psychiatry* 140, no. 8 (August 1983): 984–89; Stuart A. Wright, "Reconceptualizing Cult Coercion and Withdrawal: A Comparative Analysis of Divorce and Apostasy," *Social Forces* 70, no. 1 (September 1991): 125–45.

41. Hennawy, "A Split in the Muslim Brotherhood?"

42. Hennawy, "A Split in the Muslim Brotherhood?"

43. Kandil, *Inside the Brotherhood*, 50.

44. In 2012 Abdel Gelil al-Sharnouby, who had recently left the organization after twenty-nine years of membership, accused it of being behind an assassination attempt against him that took place when anonymous gunmen fired at his car near Qalyubiya. The Brotherhood strongly denied any involvement in the incident, and Secretary General Mahmoud Hussein stated that "assassinations are not the way of the Muslim Brotherhood, and Sharnouby himself knows that." See "Former Brotherhood Member Says Group Tried to Kill Him," *Egypt Independent*, November 6, 2012.

45. Hennawy, "A Split in the Muslim Brotherhood?"

46. Hennawy, "A Split in the Muslim Brotherhood?"

47. Al Masry al Youm, *Egypt Independent*, February 21, 2010, https://today.almasryalyoum.com/article2.aspx?ArticleID=244740.

48. Daniel Steinvorth and Volkhard Windfuhr, "Morsi's Grab for Power: Egyptian Revolutionaries Take on Radical Islam," *Spiegel Online*, November 26, 2012, http://www.spiegel.de/international/world/egypt-at-a-crossroads-after-morsi-grants-himself-sweeping-powers-a-869291.html.

49. Tharwat El Kherbawy, *From Preaching to the Secret Organization*; Sameh Fayez, *Jannat Al-Ikhwan* (The Brotherhood Paradise: The Story of My Exit).

50. See Alison Pargeter, *The Muslim Brotherhood: The Burden of Tradition* (London: Saqi Books, 2010); Brigitte Maréchal, *The Muslim Brothers in Europe: Roots and Discourse* (Leiden: Brill, 2008); Edwin Bakker and Roel Meijer, *The Muslim Brotherhood in Europe* (New York: Oxford University Press, 2013);

Martyn Frampton, *The Muslim Brotherhood and the West: A History of Enmity and Engagement* (Cambridge, Mass.: Harvard University Press, 2011); Gilles Kepel, *Allah in the West: Islamic Movements in America and Europe* (Stanford, Calif.: Stanford University Press, 1997); Lorenzo Vidino, *The New Muslim Brotherhood in the West* (New York: Columbia University Press, 2010).

51. See Farid Abdelkrim, *Pourquoi j'ai cessé d'être islamiste: Itinéraire au coeur de l'islam en France* (Paris: Les Points sur les i, 2015); Ahmed Akkari, *Min afsked med islamismen: Muhammedkrisen, dobbeltspillet og kampen mod Danmark* (N.p.: Art-People, 2014); Mohamed Louizi, *Pourquoi j'ai quitté les Frères Musulmans* (Paris: Michalon, 2016); Michaël Privot, *Quand j'étais Frère musulman* (Paris: La Boîte à Pandore, 2017).

52. Kate Barrelle, "Pro-integration: Disengagement from and Life After Extremism," *Behavioral Sciences of Terrorism and Political Aggression* 7, no. 2 (2015): 129–42.

53. For some literature on the use of interviews in scholarly work, see Rosalind Edwards and Janet Holland, *What Is Qualitative Interviewing?*, ed. Graham Crow (London: Bloomsbury Academic, 2013), 36, 77; Orit Karnieli-Miller, Roni Strier, and Liat Pessach, "Power Relations in Qualitative Research," *Qualitative Health Research* 19, no. 2 (2009): 280–81; Karl Nunkoosing, "The Problems with Interviews," *Qualitative Health Research* 15, no. 5 (2005): 699; Lorne L. Dawson and Amarnath Amarasingam, "Talking to Foreign Fighters: Insights Into the Motivations for *Hijrah* to Syria and Iraq," *Studies in Conflict and Terrorism* 40, no. 3 (2017): 192; Mira Crouch and Heather McKenzie, "The Logic of Small Samples in Interview-Based Qualitative Research," *Social Science Information* 45, no. 4 (2006): 486–87, 491; Shirley M. Matteson and Yvonna S. Lincoln, "Using Multiple Interviewers in Qualitative Research Studies: The Influence of Ethic of Care Behaviors in Research Interview Settings," *Qualitative Inquiry* 15, no. 4 (2009): 667–68; James Khalil "A Guide to Interviewing Terrorists and Violent Extremists," *Studies in Conflict and Terrorism* 42, no. 4 (2019).

3. Kamal Helbawy

1. I interviewed Kamal Helbawy for this book on two separate occasions (May and December 2017) at his London home. We have been interacting for over a decade.

2. Basil El-Dabh, "The Brotherhood 'Deviated' from Original Focus, Prioritised Politics Over Revolution: Kamal Helbawy," *Daily News Egypt*, June 2, 2014.

3. Muslim World League and World Assembly of Muslim Youth, part of the Muslim Networks and Movements in Western Europe Project, September 15,

2010, http://www.pewforum.org/2010/09/15/muslim-networks-and-move
ments-in-western-europe-muslim-world-league-and-world-assembly-of-muslim
-youth/.

4. Jamal Barzinji, Ahmed Totonji, and Hisham al Talib left Iraq as students in
the 1960s, living first in the United Kingdom and then moving to the United
States. Once in America "the three Kurds" involved themselves in high-
profile roles in Brotherhood-linked organizations both in the United States
and worldwide. Totonji and al Talib served as secretary general of the International Islamic Federation of Student Organizations (IIFSO), a Kuwaiti-
based umbrella organization for worldwide Muslim student organizations
linked to the Brotherhood. Al Talib later also served as secretary general of
WAMY. Domestically, the three Kurds were no less active. Aside from their
involvement in the daily management of the Muslim Student Association,
the first Brotherhood-leaning organization created in America (of which
Barzinji served as president and chair of its Planning and Organization
Committee, Totonji as chairman, and al Talib as founding member), they also
masterminded the creation of a web of affiliated organizations. In 1973 they
set up the North American Islamic Trust (NAIT), an entity initially headed
by al Talib and Barzinji whose purpose was to financially support the activities of the MSA. The three also played a key role in the foundation of the
International Institute of Islamic Thought (IIIT), a Virginia-based think
tank for the global Brotherhood with branches on various continents.

5. Ayman al Zawahiri, *Knights Under the Prophet's Banner*.

6. Helbawy made this point to me in various conversations in the late 2000s,
when he was still a member of the Brotherhood.

7. For more on the founding of MAB, see Innes Bowen, *Medina in Birmingham,
Najaf in Brent: Inside British Islam* (London: Hurst, 2014), 107–11.

8. Ian Johnson, *A Mosque in Munich: Nazis, the CIA, and the Rise of the Muslim
Brotherhood in the West* (Boston: Mariner Books, 2011).

9. Noreen S. Ahmed-Ullah, Sam Roe and Laurie Cohen, "A Rare Look at
Secretive Brotherhood in America," *Chicago Tribune*, September 19, 2004,
https://www.chicagotribune.com/news/chi-0402080265feb08-story.html. A
prominent physician, el Kadi was involved with the Muslim American Society and the Islamic Circle of North America (ICNA) and served as president
of the NAIT. He died in Panama City, Florida, in 2009.

10. Gamal Nkrumah, "Zaghloul El-Naggar: Scientific Being," *Al Ahram Weekly*,
undated, http://weekly.ahram.org.eg/Archive/2005/769/profile.htm, accessed
October 29, 2018.

11. Egyptian Brotherhood members interviewed by Khalil al-Anani stated that
"lower-income members pay 1 to 2% of their income; medium-income members pay 3 to 5%; and higher-income members pay 5 to 7%." See Khalil

al-Anani, *Inside the Muslim Brotherhood: Religion, Identity, and Politics* (Oxford: Oxford University Press, 2016), 83.

12. For more on the Muslim Welfare House, see Martyn Frampton, *The Muslim Brotherhood and the West: A History of Enmity and Engagement* (Cambridge, Mass.: Harvard University Press, 2018), 366–67.

13. The term "paramosque" was coined by Larry Poston. See Larry Poston, *Islamic Da'wah in the West* (New York: Oxford University Press, 1992), 94–97; see also Carrie Rosefsky Wickham, *Mobilizing Islam: Religion, Activism, and Political Change in Egypt* (New York: Columbia University Press, 2002), 98.

14. Mohammed Akram, An Explanatory Memorandum on the Strategic Goals for the Group in North America, Government Exhibit 003-0085 in United States v. Holy Land Foundation et al., 3:04-cr-240 (ND, Tex.).

15. Islamic Relief UK, "About Us," https://www.islamic-relief.org.uk/about-us /history/, accessed February 9, 2018.

16. For more on the relationship between Islamic Relief and the Brotherhood, focusing mostly on the early days, see Marie Juul Petersen, "For Humanity or for the Umma? Ideologies of Aid in Four Transnational Muslim NGOs," thesis, University of Copenhagen, 2011, 169.

17. Confirming this analysis, writes Petersen of Islamic Relief and Muslim Aid, a British-based charity influenced by Jamaat-e-Islami: "While the boards of trustees is by and large unchanged, and many first generation staff members have remained in the organisation, in recent years, both Islamic Relief and Muslim Aid have increasingly incorporated a new generation of staff. First of all, and contrary to the older generation, many of the new staff members have relevant development education and experience. Some have a degree in development studies, others in e.g. journalism, nutrition, politics, or sociology. Many people, in particular among country office staff, have previously worked in national, non-Muslim, NGOs such as BRAC, just like several move on to work in transnational development NGOs such as CARE, Oxfam or Save the Children. They work in Islamic Relief and Muslim Aid, because they want to work in a development NGO, not because they want to work in a religious organisation." Petersen, "For Humanity or for the Umma?," 179. She also adds that several staffers at Islamic Relief are non-Muslims.

18. Osama Diab, "A Brother and a Scholar," *Egypt Today*, November 2009.

19. Diab, "A Brother and a Scholar."

20. El-Dabh, "Brotherhood 'Deviated' from Original Focus."

21. Mohamed Elmeshad, "Profile: Kamal al-Helbawy, a Defector of Conscience," *Egypt Independent*, April 9, 2012.

22. The theory was put forward to me by two senior Egyptian Brotherhood leaders. Their names are withheld at their request. The two were interviewed

separately, in the United Kingdom in 2015 and the United States in 2017, respectively.

23. Incidentally, it should be noted, al Shater too spent substantial time in the United Kingdom (in his case, to pursue postgraduate studies).

24. El-Dabh, "Brotherhood 'Deviated' from Original Focus."

25. Elmeshad, "Profile: Kamal al-Helbawy."

26. El-Dabh, "Brotherhood 'Deviated' from Original Focus."

27. Akef spent several years in Europe and served as director of the Islamic Center of Munich, Germany.

28. For an analysis of these dynamics, see Anani, Inside the Muslim Brotherhood, 146–49.

29. Hesham Al-Awadi, The Muslim Brothers in Pursuit of Democracy (London: I. B. Tauris, 2014), 243.

30. Elmeshad, "Profile: Kamal al-Helbawy."

31. El-Dabh, "Brotherhood 'Deviated' from Original Focus."

4. Ahmed Akkari

1. I interviewed Ahmed Akkari over three days in June 2018 in Qaqortoq, Greenland.

2. Tabligh Eddawa is a transnational Islamic movement whose main activity is reintroducing fellow Muslims to a conservative form of Islam.

3. Filings with the Erhvervs- og Selskabsstyrelsen (Danish Commerce and Companies Agency), April 7, 1983; annual reports of the International Islamic Bank, 1982–1996, Erhvervs- og Selskabsstyrelsen.

4. Sururism is the name often used to refer to an informal movement, whose intellectual forefather was Syrian Brotherhood activist Muhammad Surur, which combines "the organisational methods and political worldview of the Muslim Brotherhood with the theological puritanism of Salafism." Assaf Moghadam and Brian Fishman, eds., Fault Lines in Global Jihad: Organizational, Strategic, and Ideological Fissures (New York: Routledge, 2011), 187.

5. Al Farra died in October 2015. Bilal Assaad, "Sh. Abu Abdel-Alim, Jihad Al-Farra er gået bort," Det Islamike Trossamfund, October 6, 2015, https://wakf.com/index.php?option=com_content&view=article&id=1206:sh-abu-abdel-alim-jihad-al-farra-er-gaet-bort&catid=15&Itemid=118&lang=da.

6. Asked separately, Helbawy confirmed to me being involved in the dispute resolution but did not recall any details.

7. For more on the alleged links between FIOE and the Brotherhood, see chapter 5.

8. Flemming Rose, "Why I Published Those Cartoons," *Washington Post*, February 19, 2006.

9. Quoted in Christian F. Rostbøll, "Autonomy, Respect, and Arrogance in the Danish Cartoon Controversy," *Political Theory* 37, no. 5 (October 2009): 623–48.

10. Ayman Qenawi, "Danish Muslims 'Internationalize' Anti-Prophet Cartoons," *IslamOnline*, November 18, 2005.

11. On this, see Carrie Rosefsky Wickham, *The Muslim Brotherhood: Evolution of an Islamist Movement* (Princeton, N.J.: Princeton University Press, 2012).

12. "Day of Muslim Fury Over Cartoons," *IslamOnline*, February 3, 2006.

13. Danish Cartoon Controversy timeline by the *New York Times*, undated, https://www.nytimes.com/topic/subject/danish-cartoon-controversy, accessed October 29, 2018.

14. For more on the complex and contested relationship between the Brotherhood and violence, see Alison Pargeter, *The Muslim Brotherhood: From Opposition to Power* (London: Saqi Books, 2010), 179–210.

15. See, for example, Joyce M. Davis, *Between Jihad and Salaam: Profiles in Islam* (New York: St. Martin's Press, 1997), 219–33.

16. Yusuf al Qaradawi, *Islamic Awakening Between Rejection and Extremism* (Herndon, Va: International Institute of Islamic Thought, 1991), 149, 15, 149, 85, 88–89.

17. Yusuf al Qaradawi, *Priorities of the Islamic Movement in the Coming Phase* (Swansea, U.K.: Awakening Publications, 2000).

18. Qaradawi's criticism of Qutb dates back to the 1980s. See Husan Tammam, "Yusuf Qaradawi and the Muslim Brothers: The Nature of a Special Relationship," in *The Global Mufti: The Phenomenon of Yusuf Al-Qaradawi*, ed. Bettina Gräf and Jakob Skovgaard-Petersen (New York: Columbia University Press, 2009).

19. "New Muslim Brotherhood Leader: Resistance in Iraq and Palestine is Legitimate; America Is Satan, Islam Will Invade America and Europe," Middle East Media and Research Institute (MEMRI) Special Dispatch No. 655, February 4, 2004.

20. Investigative Project on Terrorism, Profile, Yusuf al-Qaradawi, MAYA Conference, 1995, Toledo, Ohio, http://www.investigativeproject.org/profile/167/yusuf-al-qaradawi.

21. "Leading Sunni Sheikh Yousef al-Qaradhawi and Other Sheikhs Herald the Coming Conquest of Rome," MEMRI, Special Dispatch No. 447, December 6, 2002.

22. See Lorenzo Vidino, *The New Muslim Brotherhood in the West* (New York: Columbia University Press, 2010).

23. For a fairly nuanced analysis of "civilizational" aims of the Brotherhood, see Brigitte Maréchal, *The Muslim Brothers in Europe: Roots and Discourse* (Leiden: Brill, 2008), 244–63.

24. Maréchal, *Muslim Brothers in Europe*, 269.

25. Doug McAdam, "Studying Social Movements: A Conceptual Tour of the Field," Program on Nonviolent Sanctions and Cultural Survival, Weatherhead Center for International Affairs, Harvard University, 1992; Herbert H. Haines, "Black Radicalization and the Funding of Civil Rights: 1957–1970," in *Social Movements*, ed. Doug McAdam and David A. Snow (Los Angeles: Roxbury, 1997), 440–41.

26. As quoted in Caroline Fourest, *Frère Tariq: Discours, stratégie et méthode de Tariq Ramadan* (Paris: Grasset & Fasquelle, 2004), 103.

27. Ahmed Akkari, *Mod til at Tilve* (Oslo: Gyldendal, 2018).

5. Pierre Durrani

1. I interviewed Pierre Durrani over several meetings between 2017 and 2018 in Stockholm and Malmoe.

2. Pierre Durrani, "Leaving the Religious Sandpit," in *Yalla! Let's Redecorate the Tree—Sweden and the Muslim Cultural Sphere*, ed. Gustav Adolphs, 120–22 (Stockholm: Swedish Ministry for Foreign Affairs, 2002).

3. For more on the relationship between the Brotherhood and Jamaat-e-Islami in the United Kingdom, see Innes Bowen, *Medina in Birmingham, Najaf in Brent: Inside British Islam* (London: Hurst, 2014), 83–114.

4. See also Magnus Norell, Aje Carlbom, and Pierre Durrani, "The Muslim Brotherhood in Sweden," report commissioned by MSB (Swedish Civil Contingencies Agency), November–December 2016.

5. This division is independently confirmed by Ahmed Akkari in the previous chapter.

6. Information on the organizations linked to the network are taken directly from the website of the IFiS: https://web.archive.org/web/20120823055805/http://islamiskaforbundet.se/sv/om-ifis/ifis-historia.html, accessed April 10, 2018.

7. The dynamic is common throughout the West. In Austria, for example, many Brotherhood-leaning organizations operate out of the same building on Vienna's Eitnergasse. In London many organizations are headquartered in Cricklewood Broadway (mostly Egyptian) or in office buildings in West London (Crown House and Westgate House). In the United States they operate out of a suburban office building in Herndon, Virginia.

8. Islamic Relief Selvige, https://www.facebook.com/IslamicReliefSverige/photos/a.125539617481308.9334.121702404531696/920334318001830/?type=1& theater, accessed October 29, 2018.

9. Kepel quoted in Aje Carlbom, "Islamic Activism in a Multicultural Context—Ideological Continuity or Change?," report by the Swedish Civil Contingency Agency and Malmö University, 2017, 23.

10. Ian Johnson, "How Islamic Group's Ties Reveal Europe's Challenge," *Wall Street Journal*, December 29, 2005.

11. Interview with a FIOE representative, Brussels, June 2008.

12. "The Muslim Brotherhood in Europe and a Course of Reviews, UK an Example," *Ikhwanweb*, August 12, 2008, http://www.ikhwanweb.com/article.php?id=17575.

13. For more on this, see chapter 9.

14. Statistics Sweden, http://www.statistikdatabasen.scb.se/ErrorGeneral.aspx?aspxerrorpath=/pxweb/en/ssd/START__BE__BE0101__BE0101Q/UtlSv BakgTot/, accessed October 29, 2018.

15. Norell, Carlbom, and Durrani, "The Muslim Brotherhood in Sweden," 20.

16. Norell, Carlbom, and Duranni, "The Muslim Brotherhood in Sweden."

17. Carlbom, "Islamic Activism in a Multicultural Context."

18. "Slovar att samarbeta med Sveriges muslimska råd," *Expressen* (Stockholm), January 29, 2014.

19. "Social Democrats Force Out Mustafa Over 'Values,'" *Local* (Stockholm), April 13, 2013.

20. Aje Carlbom, "Mångkulturalismen och den politiska mobiliseringen av islam," in *Centrum för Danmarksstudier*, ed. Ulf Hedetoft, Bo Betersson, and Lina Sturfelt, 26–65 (Stockholm: Makadam Förlag, 2006).

21. "Sweden's Housing Minister Quits After Extremism Row," *Local* (Stockholm), April 18, 2016.

6. Mohamed Louizi

1. I interviewed Mohamed Louizi in Lille in April 2018. I draw substantial information about his life from Louizi's book *Pourquoi j'ai quitté les Frères Musulmans* (Paris: Michalon, 2016).

2. Louizi, *Pourquoi j'ai quitté les Frères Musulmans*, 23.

3. "Biographie de M. Abdelilah Benkirane, nouveau chef du gouvernement," Agence Maroccaine de Presse, October 10, 2016; "Biographie du Dr Saad Dine El Otmani," on the Moroccan government's official website, http://www.pm.gov.ma/fr/fichier.29.34.Biographie (accessed October 29, 2018); and Abdeslam Maghraoui, "Morocco: The King's Islamists," report by the Wilson Center, August 27, 2015.

4. Élise Racque, "L'Union des organisations islamiques de France change de nom pour redorer son image," *La Croix*, April 17, 2017.

5. Union des Organisations Islamiques de France, "UOIF Actualites," http://www.uoif-online.com/equipe-de-direction/, accessed October 29, 2018.

6. European Forum of Muslim Women, "Positively European," http://www.efomw.eu/www.efomw.eu/index9fco.html?p=475&lang=en, accessed October 29, 2018.

7. UOIF, "UOIF Actualites."

8. Louizi, *Pourquoi j'ai quitté les Frères Musulmans*, 109–10.

9. Farid Abdelkrim also cites the incident as a source of frustration in his autobiography *Pourquoi j'ai cessé d'être islamiste: Itinéraire au coeur de l'islam en France* (Paris: Les Points sur les i, 2015), 179–80.

10. Mohamed Louizi, *Liberer l'Islam de l'Islamisme* (Paris: Fondation pour l'Innovation Politique, 2018), 9.

11. "Interview with Chakib Benmakhlouf," *Asharq Al-Awsat*, May 20, 2008, http://archive.aawsat.com/details.asp?section=17&article=471438&issueno=10766#.W3bdG-hKg2x.

12. Louizi, *Liberer l'Islam de l'Islamisme*, 20.

13. See Bernard Godard and Sylvie Taussig, *Les Musulmans en France: Courants, institutions, communautés: Un état des lieux* (Paris: Laffont, 2007).

14. Louizi, *Liberer l'Islam de l'Islamisme*, 13.

15. Louizi, *Liberer l'Islam de l'Islamisme*, 11.

16. Louizi, *Liberer l'Islam de l'Islamisme*, 55.

7. Omero Marongiu

1. I interviewed Omero Marongiu in Lille in April 2018.

2. For more on Ramadan, see Ian Johnson, *A Mosque in Munich: Nazis, the CIA and the Rise of the Muslim Brotherhood in the West* (Boston: Houghton Mifflin Harcourt, 2010); and Steffan Meining, *Eine Moschee in Deutschland: Nazis, Geheimdienste und der Aufstieg des politischen Islam im Westen* (Munich: Beck Verlag, 2011).

3. Farid Abdelkrim, *Pourquoi j'ai cessé d'être islamiste: Itinéraire au coeur de l'islam en France* (Paris: Les Points sur les i, 2015), 150, 152.

4. Omeru Marongiu-Perria, "Omero Marongiu-Perria: Ab esse ad posse valet, a posse ad esse non valet consequentia," blog, http://omeromarongiu.unblog.fr/, accessed October 29, 2018.

5. Marongiu-Perria, "Omero Marongiu-Perria."

6. Marongiu-Perria, "Omero Marongiu-Perria."

7. For example, a similar dynamic that took place in a Chicago area mosque is meticulously described in Noreen S. Ahmed-Ullah et al., "Struggle for the Soul of Islam: Hard-liners Won Battle for Bridgeview Mosque," *Chicago Tribune*, February 8, 2004.

8. La Ligue de L'Enseignment, "Qui Sommes-Nous?," https://laligue.org/qui-sommes-nous/, accessed October 29, 2018.

9. Omero Marongiu-Perria, "La stratégie suicidaire des ramadanien.ne.s," Oumma.com, February 17, 2018.

10. Loup Besmond de Senneville, "L'UOIF devient 'Musulmans de France,'" *La Croix*, February 28, 2017.

11. Élise Racque, "L'Union des organisations islamiques de France change de nom pour redorer son image," *La Croix*, April 17, 2017.

12. In this regard, see Florence Bergeaud-Blackler, *Le marché halal ou l'invention d'une tradition* (Paris: Seuil, 2017).

8. Pernilla Ouis

1. I interviewed Pernilla Ouis in Malmoe in April 2018.

2. For more on the role of *Salaam*, see Jonas Otterback, *Islam på svenska: tidskriften Salaam och islams globalisering*, Lund Studies in the History of Religion (Stockholm: Amqvist & Wiksell, 2000). Also available at https://lup.lub.lu.se/search/ws/files/8593272/Islam_pa_svenska.pdf.

3. For example, Pernilla Ouis and Anne Sofie Roald, *Muslim i Sverige* (Stockholm: Wahlström & Widstrand, 2003).

4. I interviewed Adly Abu Hajar in Malmoe in April 2018.

5. Omaima Abdel-Latif, "In the Shadow of the Brothers: The Women of the Egyptian Muslim Brotherhood," Occasional Paper, Carnegie Endowment for International Peace, October 31, 2008, http://carnegieendowment.org/2008/10/31/in-shadow-of-brothers-women-of-egyptian-muslim-brotherhood/ifm; and Mona Kamal Farag, "Evolving Female Participation in Egypt's Muslim Brotherhood," doctoral dissertation, University of Exeter, April 2013, https://ore.exeter.ac.uk/repository/bitstream/handle/10871/14681/FaragM.pdf;sequence=1.

6. For more on al Ghazali's influence in Brotherhood circles, with an emphasis on Europe, see Brigitte Maréchal, *The Muslim Brothers in Europe: Roots and Discourse* (Leiden: Brill, 2008), 137–43.

7. Lauren Bohn, "The Muslim Brotherhood Comes to America," CNN.com, April 6, 2012.

8. Noha El Hennawy, "In Memoir, Ex-Muslim Sister Paints an Unflattering Picture," *Egypt Independent*, January 16, 2012.

9. The American Brothers

1. I interviewed Abdur-Rahman Muhammad in Washington, D.C., in January 2018.

2. For more on the Nation of Islam, see Edward E. Curtis, *Islam in Black America* (Albany: State University of New York University Press, 2002); Robert Dannin, *Black Pilgrimage to Islam* (New York: Oxford University Press, 2002); and Aminah Beverly McCloud, *African American Islam* (New York: Routledge, 1994).

3. Mary Beth Sheridan, "Government Links Activist to Al Qaeda Fundraising," *Washington Post*, July 16, 2005.

4. Interview with Kamal Helbawy, December 2017.

5. Diego Gambetta and Steffen Hertog, *Engineers of Jihad: The Curious Connection Between Violent Extremism and Education* (Princeton, N.J.: Princeton University Press, 2016).

6. Islamic Society of North America, *History of ISNA*, documentary, http://www.isna.net/ISNAHQ/pages/Documentary.aspx, accessed October 29, 2018.

7. Aslam Abdullah and Gasser Hathout, *The American Muslim Identity: Speaking for Ourselves* (Los Angeles: Multimedia Vera International, 2003), 25–30; Karen Leonard, "South Asian Leadership of American Muslims," in *Muslims in the West: From Sojourners to Citizens*, ed. Yvonne Yazbeck Haddad (Oxford: Oxford University Press, 2001), 234.

8. Ilyas Ba-Yunus and Kassim Kone, *Muslims in the United States* (Westport, Conn.: Greenwood Press, 2006), 49.

9. Steve A. Johnson, "The Muslims of Indianapolis," in *Muslim Communities in North America*, ed. Yvonne Yazbeck Haddad and Jane Idleman Smith (Albany: State University of New York Press, 1994), 270–71.

10. Noreen S. Ahmed-Ullah, Sam Roe, and Laurie Cohen, "A Rare Look at Secretive Brotherhood in America," *Chicago Tribune*, September 19, 2004; "A Little Taste of History," MSA-National Website (Archive), http://web.archive.org/web/20060118061004/http://www.msa-national.org/about/history.html, accessed October 29, 2018; Ikhwan in America, Government Exhibit 003-0089 in United States v. Holy Land Foundation.

11. Ikhwan in America, Government Exhibit 003-0089.

12. "Former Muslim Brotherhood Member Reveals Banned Group's Inner Workings," *National* (Abu Dhabi), April 10, 2014.

13. Saied's story has been told by Paul M. Barrett in *American Islam: The Struggle for the Soul of a Religion* (New York: Picador, 2007) and in his long article "Student Journeys Into Secret Circle of Extremism," *Wall Street Journal*,

December 23, 2003. Quotes from Saied also appear in Ahmed-Ullah, Roe, and Cohen, "A Rare Look."

14. Barrett, "Student Journeys Into Secret Circle of Extremism."

15. Investigative Project on Terrorism, Profile, Yousef al-Qaradawi, MAYA Conference, 1995, Toledo, Ohio, https://www.investigativeproject.org /profile/167/yusuf-al-qaradawi, accessed October 29, 2018.

16. U.S. Department of the Treasury, "Treasury Designates Benevolence International Foundation and Related Entities as Financiers of Terrorism," press release, November 19, 2002, https://www.treasury.gov/press-center/press -releases/Pages/po3632.aspx.

17. Alamoudi's resume, introduced as evidence in U.S. v. Abdurahman Muhammad Alamoudi, U.S.D.C. of Eastern Virginia, Case 03-1009M, September 30, 2003.

18. "Pangs and Process of Self-Discovery," *Impact International*, October 14–27, 1983; interview with ISNA official, Chicago, December 2002; Larry Poston, *Islamic Da'wah in the West* (New York: Oxford University Press, 1992), 104.

19. Gutbi Mahdi Ahmed, "Muslim Organizations in the United States," in *The Muslims of America*, ed. Yvonne Yazbeck Haddad (Oxford: Oxford University Press, 1991), 14–18.

20. Ikhwan in America, Government Exhibit 003-0089 in United States v. Holy Land Foundation.

21. An Explanatory Memorandum on the Strategic Goals for the Group in North America, Government Exhibit 003-0085 in United States v. Holy Land Foundation.

22. An example of interlocking board membership is that of Sayyed Syeed. Holding a Ph.D. degree in sociolinguistics from Indiana University, Syeed has been president of MSA, secretary-general of IIFSO, founder and secretary-general of ISNA, editor-in-chief of the American Journal of Islamic Social Sciences, member of the Board of Advisors of CAIR, and director of Academic Outreach at the IIIT.

23. Ahmed-Ullah, Roe, and Cohen, "A Rare Look."

24. Ikhwan in America, Government Exhibit 003-0089 in United States v. Holy Land Foundation.

25. I interviewed Hussien Elmeshad in London in October 2018.

26. Ahmed-Ullah, Roe, and Cohen, "A Rare Look."

27. Interview with Yussuf Nada, Campione d'Italia, July 14, 2008. One of the companies was Nada International, one of the many entities Nada set up in Liechtenstein. Both Barzinji and al Talib served on its board of trustees for years. The relationship was so close that not only did Nada purchase a home

in Indianapolis (and three of his four children were born in the United States), even decades later he still refers to the three Kurds affectionately as "my boys."

28. Ahmed-Ullah, Roe, and Cohen, "A Rare Look."

29. American Muslim Council, "American Muslim Council: Our First Five Years," 1996; and Alamoudi's resume, introduced as evidence in U.S. v. Abdurahman Muhammad Alamoudi, U.S.D.C. of Eastern Virginia, Case 03-1009M, September 30, 2003.

30. Harry Jaffe, "Unmasking the Mysterious Mohamed Hadid," Hadid Design & Development Group, March 1988, http://www.mohamedhadid.com /press.php?id=200403280001; Steven Merley, "The Muslim Brotherhood in the United States," research monograph for the Hudson Institute, April 2009, 28.

31. Douglas Farah and John Mintz, "U.S. Trails Va. Muslim Money, Ties," *Washington Post*, October 7, 2002.

32. As reported in the affidavit of U.S. Immigration and Customs Enforcement Special Agent Brett Gentrup in U.S. v. Abdurahman Muhammad Alamoudi, U.S.D.C. of Eastern Virginia, Case 03-1009M, September 30, 2003. In reality, 12 American citizens died on that day, even though the majority of the 224 victims were citizens of Kenya and Tanzania.

33. Translated from *al-Da'wa*, no. 23 Jummada I 1398/April 1978, 15.

34. Abdur Rahman Muhammad, "A Singular Voice" (website), https:// singularvoice.wordpress.com/.

10. Joining and Leaving: What the Evidence Suggests

1. Noreen S. Ahmed-Ullah, Sam Roe, and Laurie Cohen, "A Rare Look at Secretive Brotherhood in America," *Chicago Tribune*, September 19, 2004.

2. Hazem Kandil, *Inside the Brotherhood* (Maldin, Mass.: Polity, 2015), 12.

3. I interviewed this member in Switzerland in 2011.

4. Xavier Ternisien, *Les Frères Musulmans* (Paris: Fayard, 2005), 110–11.

5. Sylvain Besson, *La conquête de l'Occident* (Paris: Seuil, 2005), 100.

6. Mohamed Louizi, *Pourquoi j'ai quitté les Frères Musulmans* (Paris: Michalon, 2016), 175.

7. Hakim El Karoui, "La fabrique de l'islamisme," Institut Montaigne, September 2018, 316–17.

8. Privot is the director of the European Network Against Racism (ENAR). While not a Brotherhood (or even a Muslim) organization, ENAR has connections to various Brotherhood-linked organizations (FEMYSO, of which

Privot was vice president, and FIOE are member organizations).
Michaël Privot, *Quand j'étais Frère musulman* (Paris: La Boîte à Pandore,
2017), 128.

. Privot, *Quand j'étais Frère musulman*, 108, 111.

10. Farid Abdelkrim, *Pourquoi j'ai cessé d'être islamiste: Itinéraire au coeur de l'islam en France* (Paris: Les Points sur les i, 2015), 228.

11. Privot, *Quand j'étais Frère musulman*, 108.

12. Samir Amghar and Fall Khadiyatoulah, "Disillusioned Militancy: The Crisis of Militancy and Variables of Disengagement of the European Muslim Brotherhood," *Mediterranean Politics* 22, no. 1 (2017): 54–70.

13. Amghar and Khadiyatoulah, "Disillusioned Militancy."

14. Interview with Kamal Helbawy, London, December 2008; interview with Yussuf Nada, Campione d'Italia, July 14, 2008; interview with German security authorities, Cologne, April 2005; filing of the Islamische Gemeinschaft Marburg/Omar Ibn al-Khattab Moschee at the Frankfurt Ausländeramt, January 25, 1990.

15. Interview with Helbawy, December 2008; interview with German security authorities, April 2005.

16. Lorenzo Vidino, "The Muslim Brotherhood in Austria," report by George Washington University Program on Extremism and University of Vienna, September 2017.

17. FEMYSO annual report, 2014.

18. Hajar al Kaddo, LinkedIn profile, https://www.linkedin.com/in/hajar-al-kaddo-24311541/, accessed October 29, 2018.

19. Adil Hussain Khan, "Political Islam in Ireland and the Role of Muslim Brotherhood networks," in *Muslims in Ireland: Past and Present*, ed. Oliver Scharbrodt et al. (Edinburgh: Edinburgh University Press, 2015); Shane Phelan, "'Fatwa' Sheikh with Links to Irish Muslims Is Refused Visa," *Independent*, August 8, 2011.

20. Interview with Khalid Chaouki, Rome, June 2018; Khalid Chaouki, *Salaam, Italia!* (Reggio Emilia: Aliberti, 2005), 83–87.

21. Chaouki, *Salaam, Italia!*.

22. Chaouki, *Salaam, Italia!*.

23. It should be noted that in the 1980s and 1990s some Brotherhood members living in Europe were targeted by the intelligence agencies of their countries of origin. A well-known example of this dynamic is the 1981 attempt on the life of Syrian Brotherhood leader Issam al Attar in the German city of Aachen. While al Attar survived, his wife died in the attack, widely believed to have been carried out by Syrian intelligence.

24. Privot, *Quand j'étais Frère musulman*, 152.

25. Abdelkrim, *Pourquoi j'ai cessé d'être islamiste*, 135.

11. The Western Brotherhood's Future: From the Arab Spring and Beyond

1. Samir Amghar and Fall Khadiyatoulah, "Disillusioned Militancy: The Crisis of Militancy and Variables of Disengagement of the European Muslim Brotherhood." *Mediterranean Politics* 22, no. 1 (2017): 54–70.

2. Neil Ketchley, *Egypt in a Time of Revolution: Contentious Politics and the Arab Spring* (Cambridge: Cambridge University Press, 2017); David D. Kirkpatrick, *Into the Hands of the Soldiers: Freedom and Chaos in Egypt and the Middle East* (New York: Penguin Books, 2018); Eric Trager, *Arab Fall: How the Muslim Brotherhood Won and Lost Egypt in 891 Days* (Washington, D.C.: Georgetown University Press, 2016).

3. Alison Pargeter, *Return to the Shadows: The Muslim Brotherhood and An-Nahda Since the Arab Spring* (London: Saqi Books, 2016).

4. Nathan J. Brown, "A Muslim Brotherhood Win Would Resonate Far Beyond Egypt," *Guardian*, May 27, 2012.

5. U.S. Treasury Department, "Treasury Designates Bosnian Charities Funneling Dollars to Al Qaida," press release, June 5, 2004, https://www.treasury .gov/press-center/press-releases/Pages/js1527.aspx. Aly was investigated but never charged. A German police report related to the investigation stated that "the constellation of accounts, money flows and persons indicate that the accounts in Germany of [German Brotherhood milieu's leader] Ibrahim El-Zayat and Ayman Sayed Ahmed Aly were used for carrying out fundamentalist Islamic activities in Europe." See Ian Johnson, "How Islamic Group's Ties Reveal Europe's Challenge a Conduit to Mainstream, Muslim Lobbyist Also Has Some Fundamentalist Links," *Wall Street Journal*, December 29, 2005.

6. Lorenzo Vidino, "The Muslim Brotherhood in Austria," report by the George Washington University Program on Extremism and the University of Vienna, September 2017.

7. "Egypt: Morsy Aides Moved from Secret Detention," *Human Rights Watch*, December 25, 2013.

8. Islamic Relief letter to Congress, July 19, 2018, http://irusa.org/wp-content /uploads/2018/07/2018.7.19-IRUSA-Congressional-Response-to-MEF -Cover-Letter-FINAL.docx.pdf.

9. "Brotherhood Spokesman Gehad al-Haddad Held in Egypt," BBC News, September 17, 2013.

10. Richard Spencer, Magdy Samaan, and Philip Sherwell, "Mohamed Morsi: from Cairo to California and Back," *Telegraph*, June 30, 2012.

11. Sarah Childress, "Wael Haddara: 'We Lost Our Country' on July 3," *Frontline*, September 17, 2013.

12. See Pargeter, *Return to the Shadows*.
13. Khalil al-Anani, "Upended Path: The Rise and Fall of Egypt's Muslim Brotherhood," *Middle East Journal* 69, no. 4 (Autumn 2015).
14. Pargeter, *Return to the Shadows*, 6.
15. Khaled el Qazzaz is an Egyptian graduate of the University of Toronto who served as Morsi's secretary of foreign affairs before being imprisoned in July 2013. Thanks also to the activism of his wife Sara, the daughter of El Tantawy Attia, a prominent leader of the Canadian Brotherhood milieu, and herself a former vice president of Canada of the Muslim Student Association, el Qazzaz's case caught the attention of the Canadian government and various international organizations. He was released in 2016.
16. Born in Egypt, Mohammed Sultan grew up in the United States and is an American citizen. His father is the well-known Islamic scholar Salah Sultan, who serves on the two most prominent Western Brotherhood jurisprudential bodies in the West: the European Council for Fatwa and Research and the Fiqh Council of North America. Mohammed was imprisoned in Egypt in the summer of 2013 and was released in May 2015.
17. Ibrahim Halawa grew up in Ireland. His father is Hussein Halawa, the imam of the Islamic Cultural Center of Ireland, which is the headquarters of the ECFR, and a close associate of Qaradawi. Ibrahim was arrested in Cairo in August 2013 and spent more than four years in prison.
18. Shaimaa Magued, "The Egyptian Muslim Brotherhood's Transnational Advocacy in Turkey: A New Means of Political Participation," *British Journal of Middle Eastern Studies* 45, no. 3 (2018): 480–97.
19. Interview with Mohammed Soudan, London, May 2014.
20. Interview with Abdullah el Haddad, London, May 2014.
21. Jonathan Wynne-Jones, "Egypt's Muslim Brotherhood Open London Office . . . Above a Disused Kebab Shop in Cricklewood," *Daily Mail* (London), January 13, 2014.
22. From 2014 to 2018 I attended some fifteen events organized by various "post-Rabaa" organizations in the United Kingdom, the United States, Italy, Switzerland, Holland, and Germany.
23. The name al Nahda was adopted in 1989. See Anne Wolf, *Political Islam in Tunisia: The History of Ennahda* (Oxford: Oxford University Press, 2017).
24. Azzam S. Tamimi, *Rachid Ghannouchi: A Democrat Within Islamism* (Oxford: Oxford University Press, 2001).
25. Yusra Ghannouchi, "The Media and Its Role in Spreading a Dichotomous Narrative in Tunisia," Al Jazeera, August 24, 2013.
26. Soumaya Ghannousi personal website, http://soumayaghannoushi.com/bio/, accessed October 29, 2018; James Brandon and Raffaello Pantucci, "UK

Islamists and the Arab Uprisings," *Current Trends in Islamist Ideology,* June 22, 2012.

27. "Interview with Intissar Kherigi on ENAR's Forgotten Women Project," *European Network Against Racism,* March 11, 2016.

28. Brandon and Pantucci, "UK Islamists and the Arab Uprisings."

29. Oral evidence taken before the Foreign Affairs Committee, November 29, 2011.

30. Brandon and Raffaello Pantucci, "UK Islamists and the Arab Uprisings."

31. "Retour sur le parcours politique de Hamadi Jebali," *Leaders,* December 14, 2011.

32. Rory McCarthy, "When Islamists Lose: The Politicization of Tunisia's Ennahda Movement," *Middle East Journal* 72, no. 3 (Summer 2018): 365–84.

33. Omar Ashour, "Between ISIS and a Failed State: The Saga of Libyan Islamists," Rethinking Political Islam Series, Brookings Institution, 2015.

34. Pargeter, *Return to the Shadows.*

35. Ashour, "Between ISIS and a Failed State."

36. Pargeter, *Return to the Shadows,* 127.

37. Pargeter, *Return to the Shadows,* 8, 132.

38. Andrew Engel, "Challenges Facing the Libyan Government," Policy Watch 1883, Washington Institute, December 19, 2011, https://www.washington institute.org/policy-analysis/view/challenges-facing-the-libyan-government.

39. Mary Fitzgerald, "Introducing the Libyan Muslim Brotherhood," *Foreign Policy,* 2012.

40. Members of the Ireland-based Libyan Brotherhood milieu include Adam Argiag, Sheikh Salem Faituri Muftah, Sheikh Khalid Shallabi, and Majda Fallah. For more on the Brotherhood in Ireland, see Adil Hussain Khan, "Political Islam in Ireland and the Role of Muslim Brotherhood Networks," in *Muslims in Ireland,* ed. Adil Hussain Khan et al. (Edinburgh: Edinburgh University Press, 2016).

41. Innes Bowen, *Medina in Birmingham, Najaf in Brent: Inside British Islam* (London: Hurst, 2014), 103.

42. Benjamin Barthe and Helene Sallon, "Why the Muslim Brotherhood Lags in Libya," SBS.com, February 24, 2015.

43. "Manchester Attacks: Libyan Community 'Ashamed and Devastated,'" BBC, May 26, 2017.

44. Valentina Colombo, Giuseppe Dentice, and Arturo Varvelli, "Political Party or Armed Faction? The Future of the Libyan Muslim Brotherhood," Libya's Fight for Survival: Defeating Jihadist Networks, Counter Extremism Project, European Foundation for Democracy, 2015.

45. Paul Cruickshank and Tim Lister, "Energized Muslim Brotherhood in Libya Eyes a Prize," CNN, March 25, 2011.

46. "Arab and Muslim National Security: Debating the Iranian Dimension," Cordoba Foundation, Series Briefing Paper No. 2, January 11, 2013.

47. Interview with Omar el Hamdoun, MAB president, London, May 2014; interviews with various young Muslim activists, London, June 2014 and September 2017; interviews with various Italian Muslim activists, Milan, August 2014.

48. "Ho 28 anni, sono italiano, e guido la lista degli islamici in Tunisia," *Linkiesta*, October 23, 2011.

49. Cristina Giudici, "Chi è il portavoce del Partito islamico tunisino Ennahda che parla italiano," *Il Foglio* (Rome), July 5, 2015.

50. "Voto in Tunisia, grande affluenza alle urne. In vantaggio partito filo islamico," *Adnkronos* (Rome), October 24, 2011.

51. Cristina Giudici, "Chi è il portavoce del Partito islamico tunisino Ennahda che parla italiano," *Il Foglio* (Rome), July 5, 2015; interview with various young Italian Muslims, Milan, June 2018.

52. For some of the post–Arab Spring debates within the Islamist movement, see Shadi Hamid, *Temptations of Power: Islamists and Illiberal Democracy in a New Middle East* (Oxford: Oxford University Press, 2014).

53. Frédéric Bobin, "Rached Ghannouchi: 'Il n'y a plus de justification à l'islam politique en Tunisie,'" *Le Monde*, May 19, 2016.

54. Brandon and Pantucci, "UK Islamists and the Arab Uprisings."

55. Amghar and Khadiyatoulah, "Disillusioned Militancy."

56. Brandon and Pantucci, "UK Islamists and the Arab Uprisings."

57. Matthew Hedges and Giorgio Cafiero, "The GCC and the Muslim Brotherhood: What Does the Future Hold?" *Middle East Policy Council* 24, no. 1 (Spring 2017).

58. "Saudi and the Brotherhood: From Friends to Foes," Al Jazeera, June 23, 2017.

59. William McCants, "Islamist Outlaws: Saudi Arabia Takes on the Muslim Brotherhood," *Foreign Affairs*, March 17, 2014.

60. Guido Steinberg, "The Gulf States and the Muslim Brotherhood," Project on Middle East Political Science, 2014.

61. Stéphane Lacroix, "Saudi Arabia's Muslim Brotherhood Predicament," *Washington Post*, March 20, 2014.

62. Habib Toumi, "Muslim Brotherhood Books Pulled Out of Saudi Schools," *Gulf News* (Abu Dhabi), December 1, 2015.

63. Hedges and Cafiero, "The GCC and the Muslim Brotherhood."

64. Samir Salama, "Rise and Fall of Muslim Brotherhood in UAE," *Gulf News* (Abu Dhabi), April 13, 2013.

65. "Gargash: Terrorism and Extremism Are Interdependent; UAE Believes in Need to Dismantle Relationship," WAM Emirates News Agency, November 30, 2015.

66. "List of Groups Designated Terrorist Organisations by the UAE," *National* (Abu Dhabi), November 16, 2014.

67. Interview with UAE officials, Abu Dhabi, March 2018.

68. David B. Roberts, "Qatar, the Ikhwan, and Transnational Relations in the Gulf," Project on Middle East Political Science, March 9, 2014.

69. Courtney Freer, "From Co-optation to Crackdown: Gulf States' Reactions to the Rise of the Muslim Brotherhood During the Arab Spring," Project on Middle East Political Science, May 3–4, 2016.

70. Marc Lynch, "How Trump's Alignment with Saudi Arabia and the UAE Is Inflaming the Middle East," *Washington Post*, June 7, 2017.

71. Lynch, "Trump's Alignment with Saudi Arabia."

72. Michael Stephens, "Why Key Arab Countries Have Cut Ties with Qatar— and What Trump Had to Do with It," *Washington Post*, June 7, 2017.

73. Roberts, "Qater, the Ikhwan, and Transnational Relations in the Gulf."

74. Eric Trager, "The Muslim Brotherhood Is the Root of the Qatar Crisis," *Atlantic*, July 2, 2017.

75. For more on the activities of the Qatar Charity in Europe, and particularly its funding of organizations linked to the Muslim Brotherhood network, see Christian Chesnot and Georges Malbrunot, *Qatar Papers: Comment l'émirat finance l'islam de France et d'Europe* (Paris: Lafron, 2019). The book is based on thousands of internal QC documents in possession of the authors.

76. "Qatar Commits USD 40 Million for UN Operations in Gaza," Wikileaks, May 12, 2009.

77. U.S. Treasury Department, "Union of Good," https://www.treasury.gov /resource-center/terrorist-illicit-finance/Pages/protecting-union-of-good .aspx (accessed October 29, 2018).

78. Qatar Charity, "QC Opens First Islamic Center in Luxembourg," November 6, 2015, https://www.qcharity.org/en/qa/news/details/2316-qc-opens -first-islamic-center-.

79. Qatar Charity, "Qatar Charity Launches 'Ghaith' Initiative for Islamic Projects Around the World," August 9, 2015, https://www.qcharity.org/ar/qa /news/details/2399; "Qatar Charity Opens First Islamic Centre in Luxembourg," *Gulf Times* (Doha), June 2, 2015; Qatar Ministry of Foreign Affairs, "Financed by Qatar, the First Mosque 'Masjid' Opened in Slovenia," Qatar Fund for Development, January 7, 2018.

80. Nectar Trust, Trustees' report for the year ended March 31, 2017, http://beta .charitycommission.gov.uk/charity-details/?subid=0&regid=1146597.

81. Nectar Trust, Trustees' report for the year ended March 31, 2017.

82. "Rapport d'Activite du Fonds de Dotation al Wakf France, 2014," http:// www.journal-officiel.gouv.fr/publications/assoccpt/pdf/2014/3112 /794458620_31122014.pdf (accessed October 29, 2018).

83. "Qatar Charity Building QR110m Islamic Centre in France," *Peninsula* (Doha), June 16, 2016.

84. Frédérique Meichler, "Mosquée An-Nour: Reprise du chantier," *L'Alsace*, April 30, 2015.

85. Marie Vandekerkhove, "La mosquée veut s'agrandir, la ville la somme de se mettre aux norms," *La Voix du Nord* (Lille), October 30, 2016; "Le Qatar contribue à financer la mosquée UOIF de Villeneuve d'Ascq," *Observatoire de L'Islamisation,* October 31, 2016; Willy Le Devin, "Les musulmans dans la mire du Qatar," *Libération*, April 26, 2013.

86. Documents in my possession.

87. Business card of Mr. Ibrahim in my possession.

88. Vladimiro Polchi, "Chi finanzia le moschee. Dal Qatar alla Turchia: fondazioni e (tanti) soldi per l'Islam italiano," *La Repubblica* (Rome), August 4, 2016.

89. David Vielhaber, "The Milli Görüs of Germany," Hudson Institute, June 13, 2012.

90. Ihsan Yilmaz and James Barry, "Instrumentalizing Islam in a 'Secular' State: Turkey's Diyanet and Interfaith Dialogue," *Journal of Balkan and Near Eastern Studies*, 2018.

91. For some historical links, see also Gerald MacLean, *Abdullah Gul and the Making of New Turkey* (London: Oneworld, 2014).

92. Vielhaber, "The Milli Görüs of Germany."

93. See Lorenzo Vidino, *The New Muslim Brotherhood in the West* (New York: Columbia University Press, 2010).

94. For an excellent overview of some of the most relevant Brotherhood-related policy issues in the West (albeit with an emphasis on the United Kingdom and the United States), see Martyn Frampton, *The Muslim Brotherhood and the West: A History of Enmity and Engagement* (Cambridge, Mass.: Harvard University Press, 2018), 377–451.

95. Kamran Bokhari, "Countering Violent Extremism and American Muslims," Program on Extremism at George Washington University, October 2015.

96. Federal Republic of Germany, Office for the Protection of the Constitution, Annual Report, 2005, 190.

97. Comité Permanent de Contrôle des Services de Renseignements et de Sécurité (Comité R), Report to the Belgian Parliament, July 19, 2002, Brussels.

98. Netherlands, Algemene Inlichtingen-en Veiligheidsdienst (AIVD), "The Radical Dawa in Transition: The Rise of Islamic Neoradicalism in the Netherlands," February 2008, 51.

99. Landesverwaltungsgericht Steiermark, cases LVwG 70.8-3597/2015-34, LVwG 41.8-37/2016-34 and LVwG 41.8-39/2016-34, Graz, September 9, 2016.

100. Sentence of Hesse's Verwaltungsgerichtshof, number Az.: 5 A 2126/16, November 21, 2017.

101. U.K. Prime Minister's Office, "Government Review of the Muslim Brotherhood," April 17, 2014, https://www.gov.uk/government/news/government-review-of-the-muslim-brotherhood.

102. I was retained by the U.K. Cabinet Office as an external consultant.

103. Interview with Sir John Jenkins, London, April 2018.

104. U.K. Prime Minister's Office, "Muslim Brotherhood Review: Main Findings," December 17, 2015, https://www.gov.uk/government/publications/muslim-brotherhood-review-main-findings.

105. U. K. House of Commons, Foreign Affairs Committee, 'Political Islam,' and the Muslim Brotherhood Review," House of Commons Paper HC 118, November 7, 2016, https://publications.parliament.uk/pa/cm201617/cmselect/cmfaff/118/118.pdf.

106. They include H.R. 5194, The Muslim Brotherhood Designation Act of 2014, introduced by Representative Michele Bachmann (R-MN) on July 24, 2014; S. 2230, the Muslim Brotherhood Terrorist Designation Act of 2015, introduced by Senator Ted Cruz (R-TX) on November 3, 2015, ; H.R. 3892, also titled the Muslim Brotherhood Designation Act of 2015, introduced by Representative Mario Diaz-Balart (R-FL) on November 3, 2015; S. 68, the Muslim Brotherhood Terrorist Designation Act of 2017, introduced by Senator Cruz (R-TX) on January 9, 2017; and H.R. 377, an identical bill to S. 68, introduced by Representative Diaz-Balart (R-FL) on January 9, 2017.

107. Amghar and Khadiyatoulah, "Disillusioned Militancy."

108. Amghar and Khadiyatoulah, "Disillusioned Militancy."

109. Interview with Ahmed Akkari, Qaqortoq, Greenland, June 2018.

Bibliography

Books and Articles

Abdelkrim, Farid. *Pourquoi j'ai cessé d'être islamiste: Itinéraire au coeur de l'islam en France.* Paris: Les Points sur les i, 2015.

Abdel-Latif, Omaima. "In the Shadow of the Brothers: The Women of the Egyptian Muslim Brotherhood." Occasional paper, Carnegie Endowment for International Peace, October 31, 2008. http://carnegieendowment.org/2008/10/31/in-shadow-of-brothers-women-of-egyptian-muslim-brotherhood/ifm.

Abdullah, Aslam, and Gasser Hathout. *The American Muslim Identity: Speaking for Ourselves.* Los Angeles: Multimedia Vera International, 2003.

Akkari, Ahmed. *Min afsked med islamismen: Muhammedkrisen, dobbeltspillet og kampen mod Danmark.* Np: ArtPeople, 2014.

———. *Mod til at Tilve.* Oslo: Gyldendal, 2018.

American Muslim Council. "American Muslim Council: Our First Five Years." 1996.

Amghar, Samir, and Fall Khadiyatoulah, "Disillusioned Militancy: The Crisis of Militancy and Variables of Disengagement of the European Muslim Brotherhood." *Mediterranean Politics* 22, no. 1 (2017): 54–70.

Anani, Khalil al-. *Inside the Muslim Brotherhood: Religion, Identity, and Politics.* Oxford: Oxford University Press, 2016.

———. "Upended Path: The Rise and Fall of Egypt's Muslim Brotherhood." *Middle East Journal* 69, no. 4 (Autumn 2015): 527–43.

Ashour, Omar. "Between ISIS and a Failed State: The Saga of Libyan Islamists." Rethinking Political Islam Series, Brookings Institution, 2015.

———. *The De-Radicalization of Jihadists: Transforming Armed Islamist Movements.* New York: Routledge, 2009.

Awad, Mokhtar. "The Rise of the Violent Muslim Brotherhood." *Current Trends in Islamist Ideology.* November 6, 2017.

Awadi, Hesham Al-. *The Muslim Brothers in Pursuit of Legitimacy.* London: I. B. Tauris, 2014.

Bakker, Edwin, and Roel Meijer, eds. *The Muslim Brotherhood in Europe.* New York: Oxford University Press, 2013.

Barrelle, Kate. "Pro-integration: Disengagement from and Life After Extremism." *Behavioral Sciences of Terrorism and Political Aggression* 7, no. 2 (2015): 129–42.

Barrett, Paul M. *American Islam: The Struggle for the Soul of a Religion.* New York: Picador, 2007.

Ba-Yunus, Ilyas, and Kassim Kone. *Muslims in the United States.* Westport, Conn.: Greenwood Press, 2006

Bergeaud-Blackler, Florence. *Le marché halal ou l'invention d'une tradition.* Paris: Seuil, 2017.

Besson, Sylvain. *La conquête de l'Occident. Le projet secret des islamistes.* Paris: Seuil, 2005.

Bjørgo, Tore, and John G. Horgan, eds. *Leaving Terrorism Behind: Individual and Collective Disengagement.* London: Routledge, 2008.

Bokhari, Kamran. "Countering Violent Extremism and American Muslims." Program on Extremism at George Washington University, October 2015.

Bowen, Innes. *Medina in Birmingham, Najaf in Brent: Inside British Islam.* London: Hurst, 2014.

Brandon, James, and Raffaello Pantucci. "UK Islamists and the Arab Uprisings." *Current Trends in Islamist Ideology.* June 22, 2012.

Caeiro, Alexandre, and Mahmoud al-Saify. "Qaradawi in Europe, Europe in Qaradawi? The Global Mufti's European Politics." In *The Global Mufti: The Phenomenon of Yusuf Al-Qaradawi,* edited by Bettina Gräf and Jakob Skovgaard-Petersen. New York: Columbia University Press, 2009.

Carlbom, Aje. "Islamic Activism in a Multicultural Context—Ideological Continuity or Change?" Report by the Swedish Civil Contingency Agency and Malmö University, 2017.

———. "Mångkulturalismen och den politiska mobiliseringen av islam." In *Centrum för Danmarksstudier,* edited by Ulf Hedetoft, Bo Betersson, and Lina Sturfelt, 26–65. Stockholm: Makadam förlag, 2006.

Chaouki, Khalid. *Salaam Italia!* Reggio Emilia: Aliberti, 2005.

Chesnot, Christian, and Georges Malbrunot. *Qatar Papers: Comment l'émirat finance l'islam de France et d'Europe.* Paris: Lafron, 2019.

Colombo, Valentina, Giuseppe Dentice, and Arturo Varvelli. "Political Party or Armed Faction? The Future of the Libyan Muslim Brotherhood." Libya's Fight for Survival: Defeating Jihadist Networks. Counter Extremism Project, European Foundation for Democracy, 2015.

Crouch, Mira, and Heather McKenzie. "The Logic of Small Samples in Interview-Based Qualitative Research." *Social Science Information* 45, no 4 (2006): 483–99.

Curtis, Edward E. *Islam in Black America: Identity, Liberation, and Difference in African-American Islamic Thought.* Albany, N.Y.: SUNY Press, 2002.

Dalgaard-Nielsen, Anja. "Promoting Exit from Violent Extremism: Themes and Approaches." *Studies in Conflict and Terrorism* 36, no. 2 (2013): 99–115.

Dannin, Robert. *Black Pilgrimage to Islam.* New York: Oxford University Press, 2002.

Davenport, Christian. *How Social Movements Die: Repression and Demobilization of the Republic of New Africa.* Cambridge: Cambridge University Press, 2014.

Davis, Joyce M. *Between Jihad and Salaam: Profiles in Islam.* New York: St. Martin's, 1997.

Dawson, Lorne L., and Amarnath Amarasingam. "Talking to Foreign Fighters: Insights Into the Motivations for *Hijrah* to Syria and Iraq." *Studies in Conflict and Terrorism* 40, no. 3 (2017): 191–210.

Della Porta, Donatella. "Leaving Underground Organizations: A Sociological Analysis of the Italian Case." In *Leaving Terrorism Behind: Individual and Collective Disengagement,* edited by Tore Bjorgo and John Horgan, 49–65. London: Routledge, 2008.

Demant, Froujke, Marieke Slootman, Frank Buijs, and Jean Tillie. *Decline and Disengagement: An Analysis of Processes of Deradicalisation.* Amsterdam: IMES, University of Amsterdam Press, 2008.

Disley, Emma, Kristin Weed, Anais Reding, Lindsay Clutterbuck, and Richard Warnes. "Individual Disengagement from Al Qa'ida-Influenced Terrorist Groups. A Rapid Evidence Assessment to Inform Policy and Practice in Preventing Terrorism." London: RAND Europe, 2012.

Durrani, Peter. "Leaving the Religious Sandpit." In *Yalla! Let's Redecorate the Tree—Sweden and the Muslim Cultural Sphere,* edited by Gustav Adolphs, 120–22. Stockholm: Swedish Ministry for Foreign Affairs, 2002.

Edwards, Rosalind, and Janet Holland. *What Is Qualitative Interviewing?* Edited by Graham Crow. London: Bloomsbury Academic, 2013.

European Forum of Muslim Women. "Positively European." Accessed October 29, 2018. http://www.efomw.eu/www.efomw.eu/index9fco.html?p=475&lang=en.

Fadl, Khaled Abou El. "Striking a Balance: Islamic Legal Discourse on Muslim Minorities." In *Muslims on the Americanization Path?,* edited by Yvonne Yazbeck Haddad and John L. Esposito. New York: Oxford University Press, 2000.

Farag, Mona Kamal. "Evolving Female Participation in Egypt's Muslim Brotherhood." Doctoral dissertation, University of Exeter, April 2013. https://ore.exeter.ac.uk/repository/bitstream/handle/10871/14681/FaragM.pdf;sequence=1.

Fitzgerald, Mary. "Introducing the Libyan Muslim Brotherhood." *Foreign Policy.* 2012.

Forum for Muslim Youth and Student Organisations. "FEMYSO-Annual Report 2014." https://femyso.org/check-out-our-annual-reports/.

Fourest, Caroline. *Frère Tariq: Discours, stratégie et méthode de Tariq Ramadan.* Paris: Grasset & Fasquelle, 2004.

Fradkin, Hillel. "The History and Unwritten Future of Salafism." *Current Trends in Islamist Ideology.* November 25, 2007. https://www.hudson.org/content /researchattachments/attachment/1338/fradkin_vol6.pdf.

Frampton, Martyn. *The Muslim Brotherhood and the West: A History of Enmity and Engagement.* Cambridge, Mass.: Harvard University Press, 2018.

Freer, Courtney. "From Co-optation to Crackdown: Gulf States' Reactions to the Rise of the Muslim Brotherhood During the Arab Spring." Project on Middle East Political Science. May 3–4, 2016.

Galanter, Marc. "Unification Church ('Moonie') Dropouts: Psychological Readjustment After Leaving a Charismatic Religious Group." *American Journal of Psychiatry* 140, no. 8 (August 1983): 984–89.

Gambetta, Diego, and Steffen Hertog. *Engineers of Jihad: The Curious Connection Between Violent Extremism and Education.* Princeton, N.J.: Princeton University Press, 2016.

Godard, Bernard, and Sylvie Taussig. *Les Musulmans en France: Courants, institutions, communautés: Un état des lieux.* Paris: Laffont, 2007.

Gove, Michael. *Celsius 7/7.* London: Phoenix, 2006.

Haines, Herbert H. "Black Radicalization and the Funding of Civil Rights: 1957–1970." In *Social Movements,* edited by Doug McAdam and David A. Snow, 440–49. Los Angeles: Roxbury, 1997.

Hamid, Shadi. *Temptations of Power: Islamists and Illiberal Democracy in a New Middle East.* Oxford: Oxford University Press, 2014.

Hatina, Meir. "Redeeming Sunni Islam: Al-Qa'ida's Polemic Against the Muslim Brethren." *British Journal of Middle Eastern Studies* 39, no. 1 (2012): 101–13.

Hedges, Matthew, and Giorgio Cafiero. "The GCC and the Muslim Brotherhood: What Does the Future Hold?" *Middle East Policy Council* 24, no. 1 (Spring 2017).

Hegghammer, Thomas. "Abdallah Azzam, Imam of Jihad." In *Al Qaeda in Its Own Words,* edited by Gilles Kepel and Jean-Pierre Milelli, translated by Pascale Ghazaleh. Cambridge, Mass.: Belknap Press of Harvard University Press, 2008.

Horgan, John. *Walking Away from Terrorism: Accounts of Disengagement from Radical and Extremist Movements.* London: Routledge, 2009.

Horgan, John, Mary Beth Altier, Neil Shortland, and Max Taylor. 2017. "Walking Away: The Disengagement and de-Radicalization of a Violent Right-Wing Extremist." *Behavioral Sciences of Terrorism and Political Aggression* 9, no. 2 (2017): 63–77. https://doi.org/10.1080/19434472.2016.1156722.

Hussain Khan, Adil. "Political Islam in Ireland and the Role of Muslim Brotherhood Networks." In *Muslims in Ireland: Past and Present*, edited by Oliver Scharbrodt, Tuula Sakaranaho, Adil Hussain Khan, Yafa Shanneik, and Vivian Ibrahim. Edinburgh: Edinburgh University Press, 2015.

Investigative Project on Terrorism. Profile, Yousef al-Qaradawi. MAYA Conference, 1995, Toledo, Ohio. https://www.investigativeproject.org/profile/167/yusuf-al-qaradawi.

Islamic Society of North America. *History of ISNA*. Documentary. Accessed October 29, 2018. http://www.isna.net/ISNAHQ/pages/Documentary.aspx.

Jacobson, Michael. "Terrorist Dropouts: Learning from Those Who Have Left." Washington Institute for Near East Policy. January 2010.

Johnson, Ian. *A Mosque in Munich: Nazis, the CIA, and the Rise of the Muslim Brotherhood in the West*. Boston: Houghton Mifflin Harcourt, 2010.

Johnson, Steve A. "The Muslims of Indianapolis." In *Muslim Communities in North America*, edited by Yvonne Yazbeck Haddad and Jane Idleman Smith. Albany: State University of New York Press, 1994.

Kandil, Hazem. *Inside the Brotherhood*. Malden, Mass.: Polity, 2014.

Karnieli-Miller, Orit, Roni Strier, and Liat Pessach. "Power Relations in Qualitative Research." *Qualitative Health Research* 19, no. 2 (2009): 280–81.

Karoui, Hakim El. "La fabrique de l'islamisme." Institut Montaigne. September 2018.

Kepel, Gilles. *Allah in the West: Islamic Movements in America and Europe*. Stanford, Calif.: Stanford University Press, 1997.

Ketchley, Neil. *Egypt in a Time of Revolution: Contentious Politics and the Arab Spring*. Cambridge: Cambridge University Press, 2017.

Khalil, James. "A Guide to Interviewing Terrorists and Violent Extremists." *Studies in Conflict and Terrorism* 42, no. 4 (2019): 429–43.

Kirkpatrick, David D. *Into the Hands of the Soldiers: Freedom and Chaos in Egypt and the Middle East*. New York: Penguin Books, 2018.

Leonard, Karen. "South Asian Leadership of American Muslims." In *Muslims in the West: From Sojourners to Citizens*, edited by Yvonne Yazbeck Haddad. Oxford: Oxford University Press, 2001.

Lia, Brynjar. *The Society of the Muslim Brothers in Egypt: The Rise of an Islamic Mass Movement 1928–1942*. Reading, U.K.: Ithaca Press, 1999.

Louizi, Mohamad. *Liberer l'Islam de l'Islamisme*. Paris: Fondation pour l'Innovation Politique, 2018.

———. *Pourquoi j'ai quitté les Frères Musulmans*. Paris: Michalon, 2016.

Lynch, Marc. "Islam Divided Between Salafi-jihad and the Ikhwan." *Studies in Conflict and Terrorism* 33, no. 6 (2010): 467–87.

MacLean, Gerald. *Abdullah Gul and the Making of New Turkey*. London: Oneworld, 2014.

Maghraoui, Abdeslam. "Morocco: The King's Islamists." Wilson Center Report. August 27, 2015.

Magued, Shaimaa. "The Egyptian Muslim Brotherhood's Transnational Advocacy in Turkey: A New Means of Political Participation." *British Journal of Middle Eastern Studies* 45, no. 3 (2018): 480–97.

Mahdi Ahmed, Gutbi. "Muslim Organizations in the United States." In *The Muslims of America*, edited by Yvonne Yazbeck Haddad. Oxford: Oxford University Press, 1991.

Maréchal, Brigitte. "The European Muslim Brothers' Quest to Become a Social (Cultural) Movement." In *The Muslim Brotherhood in Europe*, edited by Edwin Bakker and Roel Meijer. New York: Oxford University Press, 2013.

———. *The Muslim Brothers in Europe: Roots and Discourse.* Leiden: Brill, 2008.

Marongiu-Perria, Omero. "La stratégie suicidaire des ramadanien.ne.s." Oumma .com. February 17, 2018.

———. "Omero Marongiu-Perria: Ab esse ad posse valet, a posse ad esse non valet consenquentia." Accessed October 29, 2018. http://omeromarongiu.unblog.fr/.

Matteson, Shirley M., and Yvonna S. Lincoln. "Using Multiple Interviewers in Qualitative Research Studies: The Influence of Ethic of Care Behaviors in Research Interview Settings." *Qualitative Inquiry* 15, no. 4 (2009): 659–74.

McAdam, Doug. "Studying Social Movements: A Conceptual Tour of the Field." Program on Nonviolent Sanctions and Cultural Survival, Weatherhead Center for International Affairs, Harvard University, 1992.

McCants, William. "The Believer: How an Introvert with a Passion for Religion and Soccer Became Abu Bakr Al-Baghdadi, Leader of the Islamic State." *Brookings Essay.* September 1, 2015.

———. "Islamist Outlaws: Saudi Arabia Takes on the Muslim Brotherhood." *Foreign Affairs.* March 17, 2014.

McCarthy, Rory. "When Islamists Lose: The Politicization of Tunisia's Ennahda Movement." *Middle East Journal* 72, no. 3 (Summer 2018): 365–84.

McCloud, Aminah Beverly. *African American Islam.* New York: Routledge, 1994.

Meining, Stefan. *Eine Moschee in Deutschland: Nazis, Geheimdienste und der Aufstieg des politischen Islam im Westen.* Munich: Beck Verlag, 2011.

Merley, Steven. "The Muslim Brotherhood in the United States." Research monograph for the Hudson Institute, April 2009.

Middle East Media and Research Institute (MEMRI). "Leading Sunni Sheikh Yousef al-Qaradhawi and Other Sheikhs Herald the Coming Conquest of Rome." Special Dispatch No. 447, December 6, 2002.

———. "New Muslim Brotherhood Leader: Resistance in Iraq and Palestine is Legitimate; America is Satan, Islam Will Invade America and Europe." Special Dispatch No. 655, February 4, 2004.

Mitchell, Richard. *The Society of the Muslim Brothers*. New York: Oxford University Press, 1969.

Moghadam, Assaf, and Brian Fishman, eds. *Fault Lines in Global Jihad: Organizational, Strategic, and Ideological Fissures*. New York: Routledge, 2011.

Mubaraz, Ahmed, Milo Comerford, and Emman El-Badawy. "Milestones to Militancy: What the Lives of 100 Jihadis Tell Us About a Global Movement." Tony Blair Institute for Global Change. April 2016.

Muslim World League and World Assembly of Muslim Youth. Muslim Networks and Movements in Western Europe Project. September 15, 2010. http://www.pewforum.org/2010/09/15/muslim-networks-and-movements-in-western-europe-muslim-world-league-and-world-assembly-of-muslim-youth/.

Nectar Trust. "Trustees' Report for the Year Ended March 31, 2017." http://beta.charitycommission.gov.uk/charity-details/?subid=0&regid=1146597.

Norell, Magnus, Aje Carlbom, and Pierre Durrani. "The Muslim Brotherhood in Sweden." Report commissioned by MSB (Swedish Civil Contingencies Agency). November–December 2016.

Nunkoosing, Karl. "The Problems with Interviews." *Qualitative Health Research* 15, no. 5 (2005): 698–706. https://doi.org/10.1177/1049732304273903.

Ouis, Pernilla, and Anne Sofie Roald. *Muslim i Sverige*. Stockholm: Wahlström & Widstrand, 2003.

Otterback, Jonas. *Islam på svenska: tidskriften Salaam och islams globalisering*. Lund Studies in the History of Religion. Stockholm: Almqvist & Wiksell, 2000. https://lup.lub.lu.se/search/ws/files/8593272/Islam_pa_svenska.pdf.

Pargeter, Alison. *Return to the Shadows: The Muslim Brotherhood and An-Nahda Since the Arab Spring*. London: Saqi Books, 2016.

——. *The Muslim Brotherhood: From Opposition to Power*. London: Saqi Books, 2013.

——. *The Muslim Brotherhood: The Burden of Tradition*. London: Saqi Books, 2010.

Petersen, Marie Juul. "For Humanity or for the Umma? Ideologies of Aid in Four Transnational Muslim NGOs." Thesis, University of Copenhagen, 2011.

Poston, Larry. *Islamic Da'wah in the West*. New York: Oxford University Press, 1992.

Privot, Michaël. *Quand j'étais Frère musulman*. Paris: La Boîte à Pandore, 2017.

Qaradawi, Yusuf al-. *Islamic Awakening Between Rejection and Extremism*. Herndon, Va.: International Institute of Islamic Thought, 1991.

——. *Priorities of the Islamic Movement in the Coming Phase*. Swansea, U.K.: Awakening Publications, 2000.

Roberts, David. "Qater, the Ikhwan, and Transnational Relations in the Gulf." Project on Middle East Political Science. March 9, 2014.

Rostbøll, Christian F. "Autonomy, Respect, and Arrogance in the Danish Cartoon Controversy." *Political Theory* 37, no. 5 (October 2009): 623–48.

Roy, Olivier. *Secularism Confronts Islam*. New York: Columbia University Press, 2007.

Rusbult, Caryl E., Christopher Agnew, and Ximena Arriaga. "The Investment Model of Commitment Processes." Department of Psychological Sciences Faculty Publications. Purdue University, Paper 26. 2011.

Shadid, Wasif, and Pieter Sjoerd van Koningsveld. "Loyalty to a Non-Muslim Government." In *Political Participation and Identities of Muslims in Non-Muslim States*, edited by Wasif Shadid and P. S. van Konignsveld, 84–115. Kampen: Kok Pharos, 1996.

Steinberg, Guido. "The Gulf States and the Muslim Brotherhood." Project on Middle East Political Science. 2014.

Tamimi, Azzam S. *Rachid Ghannouchi: A Democrat Within Islamism*. Oxford: Oxford University Press, 2001.

Tammam, Husan. "Yusuf Qaradawi and the Muslim Brothers: The Nature of a Special Relationship." In *The Global Mufti: The Phenomenon of Yusuf Al-Qaradawi*, edited by Bettina Gräf and Jakob Skovgaard-Petersen. New York: Columbia University Press, 2009.

Ternisien, Xavier. *Les Frères Musulmans*. Paris: Fayard, 2005.

Trager, Eric. *Arab Fall: How the Muslim Brotherhood Won and Lost Egypt in 891 Days*. Washington, D.C.: Georgetown University Press, 2016.

——. "The Muslim Brotherhood Is the Root of the Qatar Crisis." *Atlantic*. July 2, 2017.

"The Unbreakable Muslim Brotherhood: Grim Prospects for a Liberal Egypt." *Foreign Affairs* 90, no. 5 (September–October 2011): 114–26.

Union des Organisations Islamiques de France. "UOIF Actualites." Accessed October 29, 2018. http://www.uoif-online.com/equipe-de-direction/.

van Stekelenburg, Jacquelien, and Bert Klandermans. "Individuals in Movements: A Social Psychology of Contention." In *Handbook of Social Movements Across Disciplines*, edited by Bert Klandermans and Conny Roggeband, 103–39. New York: Springer US, 2010.

Vidino, Lorenzo. "The Muslim Brotherhood in Austria." Report by the George Washington University Program on Extremism and the University of Vienna. September 2017.

——. *The New Muslim Brotherhood in the West*. New York: Columbia University Press, 2010.

Vielhaber, David. "The Milli Görüs of Germany." Hudson Institute, June 13, 2012.

Wickham, Carrie Rosefsky. *Mobilizing Islam: Religion, Activism and Political Change in Egypt*. New York: Columbia University Press, 2002.

——. *The Muslim Brotherhood: Evolution of an Islamist Movement*. Princeton, N.J.: Princeton University Press, 2012.

Windisch, Steven, Pete Simi, Gina Sott Ligon, and Hillary McNeel. "Disengagement from Ideologically-Based and Violent Organizations: A Systematic Review of the Literature." *Journal for Deradicalization* 9 (Winter 2016/17): 1–38.

Wolf, Anne. *Political Islam in Tunisia: The History of Ennahda.* Oxford: Oxford University Press, 2017.

Wright, Stuart A. "Reconceptualizing Cult Coercion and Withdrawal: A Comparative Analysis of Divorce and Apostasy." *Social Forces* 70, no. 1 (September 1991): 125–45.

Yilmaz, Ihsan, and James Barry. "Instrumentalizing Islam in a 'Secular' State: Turkey's Diyanet and Interfaith Dialogue." *Journal of Balkan and Near Eastern Studies* (2018).

Government Reports and Documents

Abdurahman Alamoudi resume. Introduced as evidence in U.S. v. Abdurahman Muhammad Alamoudi, U.S.D.C. of Eastern Virginia, Case 03-1009M, September 30, 2003.

Affidavit of U.S. Immigration and Customs Enforcement Special Agent Brett Gentrup in U.S. v. Abdurahman Muhammad Alamoudi. U.S.D.C. of Eastern Virginia, Case 03-1009M, September 30, 2003.

Akram, Mohammed. "An Explanatory Memorandum on the Strategic Goals for the Group in North America." Government Exhibit 003-0085 in United States v. Holy Land Foundation et al., 3:04-cr-240 (ND, Tex.).

Comité Permanent de Contrôle des Services de Renseignements et de Sécurité (Comité R). Report to the Belgian Parliament, July 19, 2002, Brussels.

Erhvervs- og Selskabsstyrelsen (Danish Commerce and Companies Agency). Filings, April 7, 1983, Denmark.

Federal Republic of Germany, Office for the Protection of the Constitution. Annual Report, 2005.

"Ikhwan in America." Government Exhibit 003-0089 in United States v. Holy Land Foundation et al., 3:04-cr-240 (ND, Tex.).

International Islamic Bank. Annual reports, 1982–1996. Erhvervs- og Selskabsstyrelsen, Denmark.

Islamic Relief USA. Letter to Congress, July 19, 2018. http://irusa.org/wp-content/uploads/2018/07/2018.7.19-IRUSA-Congressional-Response-to-MEF-Cover-Letter-FINAL.docx.pdf.

Islamische Gemeinschaft Marburg/Omar Ibn al-Khattab Moschee. Filing at the Frankfurt Ausländeramt, January 25, 1990.

Morocco, Head of Government. "Biographie du Dr Saad Dine El Otmani."
    Accessed October 29, 2018. http://www.pm.gov.ma/fr/fichier.29.34.Biographie.
Netherlands. Algemene Inlichtingen-en Veiligheidsdienst (AIVD). "The Rad-
    ical Dawa in Transition: The Rise of Islamic Neoradicalism in the Nether-
    lands." General Intelligence and Security Service of the Netherlands, February
    2008.
Qatar Ministry of Foreign Affairs. "Financed by Qatar, the First Mosque 'Mas-
    jid' Opened in Slovenia." Qatar Fund for Development, January 7, 2018.
"Rapport d'Activite du Fonds de Dotation al Wakf France, 2014." http://www
    .journal-officiel.gouv.fr/publications/assoccpt/pdf/2014/3112/794458620_311
    22014.pdf.
U.K. House of Commons. "Muslim Brotherhood Review: Main Findings." Pol-
    icy paper, House of Commons, U.K., December 17, 2015. https://www.gov.uk
    /government/publications/muslim-brotherhood-review-main-findings.
——. Foreign Affairs Committee. Oral evidence, November 29, 2011.
——. "'Political Islam,' and the Muslim Brotherhood Review." House of Com-
    mons Paper HC 118, November 7, 2016. https://publications.parliament.uk/pa
    /cm201617/cmselect/cmfaff/118/118.pdf.
U.K. Prime Minister's Office. "Government Review of the Muslim Brotherhood,"
    2014. https://www.gov.uk/government/news/government-review-of-the
    -muslim-brotherhood.
U.S. Department of the Treasury. "Treasury Designates Benevolence International
    Foundation and Related Entities as Financiers of Terrorism," November 19,
    2002. https://www.treasury.gov/press-center/press-releases/Pages/po3632.aspx.
——. "Treasury Designates Bosnian Charities Funneling Dollars to Al Qaida,"
    June 5, 2004. https://www.treasury.gov/press-center/press-releases/Pages/js1527
    .aspx.
——. "Union of Good." Accessed October 29, 2018. https://www.treasury.gov
    /resource-center/terrorist-illicit-finance/Pages/protecting-union-of-good.aspx.

Interviews

Abu Hajar, Adly. Interview by author, April 2018, Malmoe, Sweden.
Akaf, Mohammed. "Interview with Mohammed Akef." *Asharq Al-Awsat*, Decem-
    ber 11, 2005.
Akkari, Ahmed. Interview by author, June 2018, Qaqortoq, Greenland.
Benmakhlouf, Chakib. "Interview with Chakib Benmakhlouf." *Asharq Al-Awsat*,
    May 20, 2008, http://archive.aawsat.com/details.asp?section=17&article=4714
    38&issueno=10766#.W3bdG-hKg2x. "Interview with MB Deputy Chairman

in *al Ahrar Daily.*" Ikhwanweb, June 16, 2008. http://www.ikhwanweb.com /Article.asp?ID=17267&LevelID=1&SectionID=0.

Breze, Lhaj Thami. Interview by author, May 2009, La Courneuve, France.

Chaouki, Khalid. Interview by author, June 2018, Rome.

Durrani, Pierre. Interviews by author, 2017 and 2018, Stockholm and Malmoe, Sweden.

Elmeshad, Hussien. Interview by author, October 2018, London.

Fotouh, Abd El Monem Abou El. Interview by author, December 2008, Cairo.

Haddad, Abdullah el. Interview by author, May 2014, London.

Hamdoun, Omar el. Interview by author, May 2014, London.

Helbawy, Kamal. Interviews by author, December 2008 and May and December 2017, London.

Jenkins, Sir John. Inteview by author, April 2018, London.

Kherbawy, Tharwat El-. "Interview with Tharwat El-Kherbawy: An Insider's Look at the Muslim Brotherhood." By Sara Abou Barker. *Egypt Daily News*, November 20, 2012.

Kherigi, Intissar. "Interview with Intissar Kherigi on ENAR's Forgotten Women Project." European Network Against Racism, March 11, 2016.

Louizi, Mohamed. Interview by author, April 2018, Lille, France.

Madi, Abul Ila Al. "Interview with Abul Ila Al Madi." *Arab Reform Bulletin*, December 2005. https://carnegieendowment.org/2005/12/15/arab-reform-bull etin-december-2005-pub-17786.

Marongiu, Omero. Interview by author, April 2018, Lille, France.

Muhammad, Abdur-Rahman. Interview by author, January 2018, Washington, D.C.

Nada, Yussuf. Interview by author, July 2008, Campione d'Italia, Italy.

Ouis, Pernilla. Interview by author, April 2018, Malmoe, Sweden.

Soudan, Mohammed. Interview by author, May 2014, London.

Zafarani, Ibrahim El. "A Talk with EX-MB Leader Ibrahim El Zafarani." *Asharq Al-Awsat*, July 29, 2012, https://eng-archive.aawsat.com/theaawsat/features/a -talk-with-ex-mb-leader-ibrahim-el-zafarani.

Index

anti-Semitism, 104
anti-Swedish racism, 147
Arabization, 86
Arab Spring: antiregime protests in
   Tahrir Square, 69; impact of, x, 25,
   48, 189–91, 216–17, 223–24; leaving
   Muslim Brotherhood after, 29, 56;
   Muslim Brotherhood involvement
   in, 197–200, 202–6; Saudi Arabia
   and, 208–10
arrabt al-'am (general connectivity), 15
Asharq al Awsat newspaper, 121
Association of Imams of France, 118–19
Association of Muslim Young and
   Students in Italy (Associazione
   Giovani e Studenti Musulmani in
   Italia, AGESMI), 185
Attar, Issam al, 144
Attia, Gamal, 62
Attia, Mona Omar, 68
Austrian Muslim Brotherhood, 219–20
Awlani, Taha, 61
Azzam, Abdullah, 26, 39–40

Badawi, Jamal, 43
Badie, Mohammed, 52
Baghdadi, Abu Bakr al, 27
Banna, Hassan al: commitments to, 29,
   55; impact of, 17, 50–51, 65, 74,
   127–28, 163, 165; Muslim activism
   and, 89; Muslim Brotherhood's
   organizational structure by, 2–3, 5, 8;
   program of gradual Islamization,
   22–23; the Sisterhood and, 147;
   translation of works by, 61
Barazi, Mohammad Fouad al, 60, 65
Barzinji, Jamal, 38, 42, 166, 233n4
Bashar, Abu (Mohamad Al Khaled
   Samha), 60
Battle of the Trench, 121
baya (oath of allegiance), 16

Belgian Muslim Brotherhood, 174,
   180–81, 218–19, 224
Benaouda, Mohammed, 142
Benevolence International Foundation
   (BIF), 159
Benkirane, Abdelilah, 109
Benmakhlouf, Chakib, 121
Bialy, Ahmed al, 19
Bill and Melinda Gates Foundation, 211
bin Laden, Osama, 26–27, 51–52
Bitter Harvest, The (al Zawahiri), 27
Black Panthers, 151
Bouchlaka, Rafik Abdesselem, 197
Bouti, Mohammed Said Ramadan Al,
   59
Brotherhood families, 16, 22
Brown, H. Rap, 151
Buddhism, 140
Bush, George W., 168

Cameron, David, 221, 223
Canadian Muslim Brotherhood, 246n15
Carlbom, Aje, 103–4
cathedral mosques, 122–23
Central Training Organization, 36
Centre for the Study of Terrorism, 48
Chaouki, Khalid, 185–86, 203
charismatic leaders: Arab Spring and,
   202; attraction of recruits by, 64, 143,
   161; goals of, 104; influence of, 42,
   74, 85, 149, 154; Tunisian Muslim
   Brotherhood and, 196–97
Charity Commission to the Department
   of Education, 221
Charlie Hebdo attacks (2015), 119
Chicago Tribune, 173
Chomsky, Noam, 115
Chouet, Alain, 81
Christian Democrats, 191
Christianity, 58, 78, 117, 127, 152
civil society, 100, 103–5, 150, 225

closed *dawa*, 60, 64
colonialism, 147
Commission for Government Support
  for Faith Communities, 103
Constituent Assembly, 54
conversion to Islam: Christians and, 117;
  family disapproval, 125–26, 153;
  family support, 92, 97–98; of peers,
  181; reluctance over, 86
Cordoba Foundation, 202
countering violent extremism (CVE),
  217
counterradicalization strategy, 13, 217
criminal gangs, 20
cults, 20, 75
cultural impermeability, 9

Danish Islamic Council (Dansk Islamisk
  Råd), 65–66
Danish Muslim Brotherhood,
  57–83, 94
Danmarksgade mosque, 58
dar al dawa (land of preaching), 5
dar al harb (land of war), 5
Dar Al Hijrah Islamic Center, 161,
  167–68
dar al Islam (land of Islam), 5
dawa (proselytizing), 2, 50–52, 55, 64,
  159
Dawoud, Khaled, 29
democracy, 27, 102, 187, 190–91
Desouqi, Sayed Hassan, 43
destabilization fears, 208
discrimination within Muslim
  Brotherhood, 133–34, 147–49
disenchantment with Muslim
  Brotherhood, 21–28
divisive ideology, 123
*Doctrine of the First Son of Adam, or The
  Problem of Violence in the Islamic
  Action, The* (Said), 117

Durrani, Pierre: joining Muslim
  Brotherhood, 84–96, 173; leaving
  Muslim Brotherhood, 96–107; racism
  concerns by, 97–98, 106, 147

Egypt, 13, 25, 27, 120, 192–96
Egyptian Muslim Brotherhood: *dawa*
  and, 55; disenchantment with, 21;
  family meetings, 175; introduction
  to, 2, 14; main refuges for, 36; as
  mother branch, 172; overview of,
  192–96
Egyptian Revolution (2011), 35, 49
Elkadi, Ahmed, 166
Elmeshad, Hussien, 164–66, 176
Elsayed, Shaker, 163
Erbakan, Mehmet Sabri, 184
Erbakan, Necmettin, 37, 184
Erbakan, Sabiha, 184
Erdogan, Recep Tayyip, 38, 214
ethnic biases, 186–87
European Commission's Humanitarian
  Aid and Civil Protection
  Department, 47
European Council for Fatwa and
  Research, 185, 201
European Forum of Muslim Women
  (EFOMW), 112
European Institute for Human Sciences
  (IESH), 87–90
European Muslim Brotherhood, 4–5, 11,
  184
evangelical churches, 20
ever-shifting alliances, 122
excommunication, 19, 118
External Relations Committee, 197
Extremism Analysis Unit (EAU), 222
extremist youth, 75–76

family meetings, 175
Farra, Jehad al (Abu Abdel-Alim), 65

Farrakhan, Louis, 152
fatwa, 78, 145
Fayez, Sameh, 30
Federation of Islamic Organizations in
    Europe (FIOE), 42, 66, 94–95, 112,
    121, 148
fee-paying membership, 7
Ferjani, Said, 198–99
fiqh (jurisprudence), 61
foreign policy influencers, 11
formal induction recruitment, 7
Forum of European Muslim Youth and
    Student Organizations (FEMYSO),
    94–95, 112, 144, 148, 184
Freedom and Justice Party (FJP), 195
Freeing Islam from Islamism (Louizi),
    119–20
Freer, Courtney, 209
French Council of the Muslim Faith
    (Conseil français du culte musulman,
    CFCM), 123
French League of the Muslim Woman
    (Ligue Française de la Femme
    Musulmane, LFFM), 112
French Muslim Brotherhood, 111–12,
    123–24, 130–35, 177, 183
Futuh, Abdel Moneim al, 49

Gaair, Mohamed, 201
Gaith Initiative, 211
gender conservatism, 133–34, 148
gender discrimination, 147–49
General Directorate for External
    Security (Direction générale de la
    sécurité extérieure, DGSE), 81
geopolitical influence, 36
German Muslim Brotherhood, 144, 184
Ghanem, Ahmed, 91–92, 142
Ghanem, Mohammed, 195
Ghannouchi, Rachid, 148, 184, 190, 197,
    199, 204

Ghannouchi, Soumaya, 197
Ghannouchi, Yusra, 197
Gharbiya governorate, 19
Ghazali, Mohammed el, 109
Ghazali, Zaynab al, 148
goodwill ambassador, 153
grassroots Islamic traditions, 22–23
Green Party, 105
Grey Wolves, 106
Guardian, 197
Guidance Bureau, 193
Guidance Office (Makhtab al Irshad),
    47, 49, 52
Gulf Cooperation Council (GCC)
    country, 205–6, 210

Habib, Mohamed, 3
Haddad, Abdullah el, 195
Haddad, Essam el, 47, 193
Hakim, Nazir, 135
Halabi, Khaled, 117–18
Halawa, Ibrahim, 246n17
Hamza, Khaled, 15
Haq, Inamul, 166
Harakat Muslimiya (Islamic Movement),
    88
Hawwa, Said, 59, 109, 128
Helbawy, Kamal: assessment of Muslim
    Brotherhood, 1–2; joining Muslim
    Brotherhood, 33–35, 172–73; leaving
    Muslim Brotherhood, 47–56, 187;
    life inside Muslim Brotherhood,
    35–47, 178
Himmat, Ghaleb, vii–viii, 38, 185
Himmat, Youssef, 185
HIV awareness, 133
Hlayhel, Raed, 67
Hossani, Jamal al, 157
Howard University, 151–52, 154
Howard University Muslim Student
    Association, 154, 161

Huffington Post, 197
Human Appeal, 185
human rights: AKP government and,
   215; Islamic basic values and, 55;
   support of, 27, 137, 191; Swedish
   Muslim Brotherhood and,
   102, 104–5; Tunisian Muslim
   Brotherhood and, 198; violation of,
   194, 196; Western interlocutors and,
   202
Hummasten, Helena, 142
Hussain, Dilwar, 205
Hussein, Mahmoud, 231n44
Hussein, Saddam, 206

Ibn Rushd Educational Association, 92
Ibrahim, Mohammed, 213
ideology of Muslim Brotherhood in the
   West, 8–11, 24–28, 61
Ikhwanism, 3, 225
Indian American, 174
inner workings, disenchantment with,
   21–24
Interagency Intelligence Committee on
   Terrorism, 211
interfaith dialogue, 117, 130, 211,
   224
intermediary-free relationship, 125
International Institute of Islamic
   Thought (IIIT), 75, 233n4
International Islamic Federation of
   Student Organizations (IIFSO), 144,
   166, 233n4
International Organization of the
   Muslim Brotherhood, 3
International Union for Muslim
   Scholars (IUMS), 70
Iquioussen, Hassan, 126–29
Iraqi Muslim Brotherhood, 43
Iraq invasion (U.S.), 48
Irish Muslim community, 201

Islam: activism by, 3, 126; conversion to,
   86, 97–98, 117, 126, 140–48, 152–53;
   difference between, 124; grassroots
   traditions, 22–23; interpretation of,
   28; rejection of, 188; teaching in
   public schools, 13
Islamic Action Front, 42
Islamic Awakening Between Rejection and
   Extremism (al Qaradawi), 75–76
Islamic Bank International of Denmark,
   62
Islamic Center of Stuttgart, 62
Islamic centers, 46, 126
Islamic Community of Germany
   (Islamische Gemeinschaft
   Deutschland IGD), 144
Islamic Cultural Centre of Ireland
   (ICCI), 185
Islamic Federation in Stockholm, 91
Islamic Federation in Sweden
   (Islamiska Förbundet i Sverige,
   IFiS), 91–93
Islamic identity, 9, 12, 77–79, 143.
   See also Muslim identity
Islamic Information Society (Islamiska
   Informationsföreningen), 91
Islamic law, 52, 74–75, 119, 221
Islamic organizations, 58, 131, 184
Islamic Relief Worldwide (IRW), 47,
   92, 104, 193
Islamic Society in Denmark (Islamisk
   Trossamfund), 60
Islamic Society of Germany, 62, 126
Islamic Society of North America
   (ISNA), 42, 43, 162, 165
Islamic State in Levant (ISIL), 216
Islamic State in Syria (ISIS, Daesh), 27,
   216
Islamisches Religion pädagogisches
   Akademie (IRPA), 184
Islamophobia, 223

observation stage of recruitment, 35–36
Office for the Protection of the
    Constitution, 218
open circle groups, 58–59, 61, 173
open *dawa*, 64
Open Society, 81–82
Organization of Islamic Cooperation
    (OIC), 68
ostracism by Muslim Brotherhood,
    29–30, 135–36
Otmani, Saad Dine El, 109
Oubrou, Tareq, 135
Ouis, Pernilla, 140–49, 178

Palestine, 11, 26, 51–52, 58, 122, 181,
    209
Pargeter, Alison, 194
Pitts, Kwame, 152
pluralism, 27
political asylum, 57, 195
political movements, 28, 80, 82, 152
*Priorities of the Islamic Movement in the
    Coming Phase* (Qaradawi), 9, 76, 190
Private Apparatus, 51
Privot, Michaël, 174, 182–83
Public Inheritance Fund, 103
pure Muslim Brotherhood, 6–7, 44, 46,
    156
pyramidal structure of Muslim
    Brotherhood, 7

Qaddafi, Muammar al, 200, 201
Qader, Sumaya Abdel, 148
Qaradaghi, Ali al, 61
Qaradawi, Yusuf al: Danish cartoons
    and, 70, 71; European Council for
    Fatwa and Research, 185; European
    Institute for Human Sciences, 87–88;
    influence of, 59; jurisprudence of, 61;
    Muslim ghetto and, 103; status of,
    209–11; Western activism by, 5, 9–11;

writings of, 75–78, 109, 128, 158–59,
    190
Qassas, Mohamed al, 29
Qatar, 13, 109–212, 195, 201, 209–13
Qatar Charity (QC), 211–13
Qazzaz, Khaled el, 246n15
Qazzaz, Mona el, 195
Quand j'étais Frère musulman (When I
    was a Muslim Brother) (Privot), 174
Quran, 89, 127, 152
Qutb, Mohammed, 59, 109
Qutb, Sayyid, 25–26, 39, 50–52, 61, 76,
    109, 115, 117

racism by Muslim Brotherhood:
    anti-Swedish racism, 147; criticism
    of, 169; toward members, 170, 187;
    toward recruits, 97–98, 106, 147, 149,
    170
radicalization process, 106, 141–42, 204
Ramadan, Hani, 126–27
Ramadan, Said, 4, 43, 126
Rasmussen, Anders Fogh, 68
Rawi, Ahmed al, 43–44
recruitment systems, 7, 14, 34
religious extremism, 76
religious moral values, 35
religious movements, 20, 28
repression of Muslim Brotherhood, 36
right-wing extremism, 83, 106–7, 122,
    155
Risalat al Ikhwan magazine, 195
Roald, Anne Sofie, 143, 146, 149
Rose, Flemming, 67

Saadawi, Nawal, 119
SAAR Foundation, 161, 166–67
Sabiq, Said, 61
Sadat, Anwar, 39, 50
Saghir, Osama al, 203
Saghrouni, Anas, 112

COLUMBIA STUDIES IN TERRORISM AND IRREGULAR WARFARE
Bruce Hoffman, Series Editor

This series seeks to fill a conspicuous gap in the burgeoning literature on terrorism, guerrilla warfare, and insurgency. The series adheres to the highest standards of scholarship and discourse and publishes books that elucidate the strategy, operations, means, motivations, and effects posed by terrorist, guerrilla, and insurgent organizations and movements. It thereby provides a solid and increasingly expanding foundation of knowledge on these subjects for students, established scholars, and informed reading audiences alike.

Ami Pedahzur, *The Israeli Secret Services and the Struggle Against Terrorism*
Ami Pedahzur and Arie Perliger, *Jewish Terrorism in Israel*
Lorenzo Vidino, *The New Muslim Brotherhood in the West*
Erica Chenoweth and Maria J. Stephan, *Why Civil Resistance Works: The Strategic Logic of Nonviolent Conflict*
William C. Banks, editor, *New Battlefields/Old Laws: Critical Debates on Asymmetric Warfare*
Blake W. Mobley, *Terrorism and Counterintelligence: How Terrorist Groups Elude Detection*
Jennifer Morrison Taw, *Mission Revolution: The U.S. Military and Stability Operations*
Guido W. Steinberg, *German Jihad: On the Internationalization of Islamist Terrorism*
Michael W. S. Ryan, *Decoding Al-Qaeda's Strategy: The Deep Battle Against America*
David H. Ucko and Robert Egnell, *Counterinsurgency in Crisis: Britain and the Challenges of Modern Warfare*
Bruce Hoffman and Fernando Reinares, editors, *The Evolution of the Global Terrorist Threat: From 9/11 to Osama bin Laden's Death*
Boaz Ganor, *Global Alert: The Rationality of Modern Islamist Terrorism and the Challenge to the Liberal Democratic World*
M. L. R. Smith and David Martin Jones, *The Political Impossibility of Modern Counterinsurgency: Strategic Problems, Puzzles, and Paradoxes*
Elizabeth Grimm Arsenault, *How the Gloves Came Off: Lawyers, Policy Makers, and Norms in the Debate on Torture*
Assaf Moghadam, *Nexus of Global Jihad: Understanding Cooperation Among Terrorist Actors*
Bruce Hoffman, *Inside Terrorism*, 3rd edition
Stephen Tankel, *With Us and Against Us: How America's Partners Help and Hinder the War on Terror*
Wendy Pearlman and Boaz Atzili, *Triadic Coercion: Israel's Targeting of States That Host Nonstate Actors*
Bryan C. Price, *Targeting Top Terrorists: Understanding Leadership Removal in Counterterrorism Strategy*
Mariya Y. Omelicheva and Lawrence P. Markowitz, *Webs of Corruption: Trafficking and Terrorism in Central Asia*
Aaron Y. Zelin, *Your Sons Are at Your Service: Tunisia's Missionaries of Jihad*